# Napoleon's Dragoons
# and Lancers

*To Bertrand Malvaux*

*Thank you for your friendship, encouragement and support of my research.*

# Napoleon's Dragoons and Lancers

## Uniforms and Equipment

Paul L. Dawson

Frontline Books

First published in Great Britain in 2025 by
Frontline Books
An imprint of Pen & Sword Books Limited
Yorkshire – Philadelphia

Copyright © Paul L. Dawson 2025

ISBN 978 1 39907 855 9

The right of Paul L. Dawson to be identified as
Author of this Work has been asserted by him in accordance
with the Copyright, Designs and Patents Act 1988.

A CIP catalogue record for this book is
available from the British Library

All rights reserved. No part of this book may be reproduced or
transmitted in any form or by any means, electronic or mechanical
including photocopying, recording or by any information storage and
retrieval system, without permission from the Publisher in writing.

Typeset by Mac Style
Printed and bound in India by Replika Press Pvt. Ltd.

Pen & Sword Books Limited incorporates the imprints of After the Battle,
Atlas, Archaeology, Aviation, Discovery, Family History, Fiction, History,
Maritime, Military, Military Classics, Politics, Select, Transport, True Crime,
Air World, Frontline Publishing, Leo Cooper, Remember When, Seaforth
Publishing, The Praetorian Press, Wharncliffe Local History, Wharncliffe
Transport, Wharncliffe True Crime and White Owl.

For a complete list of Pen & Sword titles please contact:

PEN & SWORD BOOKS LIMITED
47 Church Street, Barnsley, South Yorkshire, S70 2AS, England
E-mail: enquiries@pen-and-sword.co.uk
Website: www.pen-and-sword.co.uk
or
PEN AND SWORD BOOKS
1950 Lawrence Road, Havertown, PA 19083, USA
E-mail: uspen-and-sword@casematepublishers.com
Website: www.penandswordbooks.com

# Contents

*Acknowledgements* vi
*Glossary of Uniform Terms* vii
*Introduction* xi

**Chapter 1**  Dragoon Uniforms  1

**Chapter 2**  Change and Change Again  12

**Chapter 3**  Bardin Regulation  29

**Chapter 4**  Regulations in Practice  38

**Chapter 5**  Dragoon Concluding Remarks  151

**Chapter 6**  The Lancers  164

**Chapter 7**  Regulations in Practice  173

**Chapter 8**  Polish Lancers  200

*Notes* 210
*Bibliography* 221

# Acknowledgements

This book marks the culmination of more than a decade of research, and a combined period of almost six months' daily study in the French Army Archives in Paris, accessing, perhaps, 500 archive boxes. Such an extensive degree of research was only possible through collaboration with a core team of friends who supported me in my endeavour:

I am indebted to Jean-Charles Lair, Sally Fairweather and Yves Martin for their most generous and gracious assistance with, and photographing of, archival material at the Archives Nationales and Service Historique de la Défence Armée de Terre, in Paris. Without their help, this book could not have been written. It has taken seven years of hard work to get to this point, and many thousands of pounds spent on flights, hotels and excellent food accompanied by dozens of bottles of wine than one cares to remember. Yves is also to be thanked for his friendship, advice and most generous provision of research notes. My esteemed friend and research colleague Robert Cooper is to be thanked for his steadfast friendship and comments on my essay and critical comments on my thought processes in understanding the archive sources and supply issues for the army.

Jerome Croyet must be thanked for his permission to reproduce the photographs I have taken of the former Brunon collection. He is also to be thanked for providing research notes.

Also to be thanked is Bertrand Malvaux for permission to use images of items in his collection. An expert of world renown, it is always a pleasure to be in his company. I must also thank Jean-Pascal Tranie for his friendship, and allowing me access to his collection of $1^e$ Empire items. It is an honour and privilege to know both these men, and call them friends.

Lastly, the long-suffering staff at Service Historique de la Défence Armée de Terre, in Paris need to be thanked for answering questions and locating items of research that have made this book possible.

Paul L. Dawson, Paris, 5 May 2024

# Glossary of Uniform Terms

**Aigrette:** A plume made from horse hair, measuring either 26cm (10.23 inches) tall in January 1812 or 17cm (6.69 inches) tall in October/November 1812. Grenadiers used scarlet examples and voltigeurs yellow.

**Aiguillettes:** Ornamental braided shoulder cords secured at the shoulder.

**Banderole:** Shoulder belt from which the carbine was carried.

**Baudrier:** A broad belt worn over the shoulder that would support a sword or other item.

**Bearskin:** A tall headdress originally made from bearskin but usually from goat skins. A status symbol of elite units such as grenadiers, sappers, and Old Guard infantry.

**Bicorne:** A two-corner or cocked hat, usually worn "en colonne" perpendicular to the shoulders while Napoleon wore his "en bataille" or parallel to the shoulders.

**Bombe:** The skull portion of a metal helmet.

**Bonnet de Police:** Garrison or fatigue cap.

**Capote:** Double or single-breasted overcoat, worn over the *gilet manche* (jacket) in lieu of the habit when on the march.

**Chaperons:** Decorated cloth covers on the pistol holsters.

**Chasseurs:** Literally means "hunters" and was used for mounted men—*chasseurs à cheval*—as well as foot soldiers in light infantry units and the Imperial Guard.

**Chenille:** A horsehair crest in the form of a caterpillar.

**Cimier:** metal crest on a helmet.

**Colpack:** A round bearskin hat usually with a bag or flap on top, worn by elite companies and often officers. Also called a busby.

**Contre-epaulette:** An epaulette without fringe.

**Criniere:** Horsehair helmet tail as worn by cuirassiers and dragoons.

**Culottes de peau:** Knee breeches or leather riding breeches made from doe hide or sheepskin.

**Culottes Hongroise:** Tight fitting, ankle length riding breeches, frequently decorated with cloth tape on the side seam and fall-front opening.

**Czapka:** Russian and Polish word for a four-cornered cap but most well-known for the unique headgear worn by Polish lancers.

**Dolman:** A short shell jacket with rows of buttons connected by braid loops that fasten along its entire front.

**Epaulettes:** Ornamented shoulder boards with fringe worn by officers and elite troops. grenadiers.

**Gaiters:** A protective covering for the upper foot and lower leg, usually of cloth, with a strap passing under the shoe and numerous small buttons to close it along the outside of the leg.

**Giberne:** A cartridge box, usually carried on a shoulder belt called a *porte-giberne*.

**Gilet:** A sleeveless, straight cut-waistcoat without tails, closed in front with a row of 12 small uniform buttons sometimes referred to as a *gilet sans manche*.

**Gilet d'Ecurie:** See *Veste d'Ecurie* but cut round in front.

**Gilet Manche:** Single-breasted sleeved jacket. Front closed by a row of 12 small uniform buttons.

**Habit à la Kinksi:** Single-breasted sleeved jacket with short tails often referred to as simply a *kinski*.

**Habit or Habit-Longue:** Double-breasted coat with long tails and cutaway at the front to expose the vest worn underneath.

**Habit-veste:** Double-breasted, short-tailed coat closing the length of the front with a straight-cut waist.

# Glossary of Uniform Terms

**Haversack:** Cowhide backpack in which the soldier kept his personal belongings and spare items of clothing.

**Houpette:** Felted pompom with worsted tuft at the top.

**Housse:** A square, decorated saddle blanket. See *schabraque*.

**Imperial Livery:** A coat of dark green cloth with Imperial lace on the collar, cuffs, turnbacks, and pocket edges. On the arms seven bands of lace were worn from the front seam around to the rear seam. On the chest double rows of lace, ending in a point, were worn on the 1st, 3rd, 5th, 7th, and 9th buttons. The Imperial lace was usually yellow, edged with scarlet with alternating squares of "N" and a green Imperial eagle.

**Kurtka:** Short jacket worn by lancers. The rear seams to the sleeves and body were piped in the regiment's facing color. The center back had no seam.

**Manteau-capote:** A long greatcoat with a short shoulder cape attached, which allowed the wearer to place his crossbelts on the outside of the garment.

**Sous-officier:** Sergeant, fourrier (company clerk) or sergeant-major

**Pantalons de route**: Overalls made of canvas, linen, or wool that were worn on campaign. Various versions included *pantalons à cheval* with inner seat reinforced with black leather, and tight-fitting *pantalons de tricot* and *de toile* that fit over them.

**Pelisse:** A short jacket, trimmed with fur and 18 rows of buttons connected by braid loops, typically worn by hussars. When worn with the dolman the pelisse would be slung over the left shoulder and held by a loop over the right shoulder.

**Plume:** A decoration made of feathers, usually worn rising from the front or side of a shako, hat, or helmet. Often associated with elites such as *cuirassiers* (heavy cavalry with armor breastplates), grenadiers, and Old Guard infantry.

**Pompom:** A decorative tuft of wool, usually smaller than a plume, affixed to the front or side of a headdress. Various shapes and colors denoted the wearer's branch of service or unit.

**Portmanteau ( plural, Portmanteaux ) :** Valise or case carried behind the saddle.

**Porte-mousqueton:** A hook at the bottom of a shoulder strap, which the rider used to carry his musket.

**Sabretache**: A large, flat, leather pouch, commonly part of the hussar uniform, that was carried on three straps and hung from the cavalryman's waistbelt. The outer flap usually bore the regimental number and often an Imperial eagle. This outer flap could be elaborately decorated with embroidery or simply of leather with metal regimental number and eagle.

**Schabraque**: A term applied to both an animal-skin cover and decorative cloth saddle covers used to improve the rider's comfort and cut to be draped over the saddle upon which the rider sat.

**Surculotte**: Woolen broadcloth overalls with leather or broadcloth insert to the inner leg. The outside seam was closed by bone buttons and fastened below the knee with an iron buckle and tab.

**Surtout**: A single-breasted coat with the long tails, worn on campaign.

**Turnback**: The decorated portion of the tails of a coat.

**Veste**: Sleeveless waistcoat, with a low collar. Cut to have a V-notch at the center front. The *veste à manche* has sleeves.

**Veste d'Ecurie**: Single-breasted, sleeved jacket worn in stable duties, notable for having a "V" at the center front. The front was closed by a row of 12 small uniform buttons.

# Introduction

Why is this book important? Surely nothing new can be said on the dress of the French army? A single book from the Osprey stable, written nearly 50 years ago, and three plates by Rousselot are almost the entirety of published material on the dragoons and lancers: so YES somthing new can be said, which inpart overturns what is published.

This book seeks to describe the dress and equipment of each regiment of dragoons and lancers in the 1$^e$ Empire: the data I have presented is 'the tip of the iceberg' of what regimental records can tell us about fashion, regulations and their impact on the dress of the army. More records certainly await to be discovered in various archives in France.

This book seeks to answer two questions: what did the various regiments of dragoons and lancers actually wear and was the Bardin regulation real. I hope this book answers those questions and provides an invaluable reference for all those interested in the period. I hope the thousands spent on research is 'money well spent', and it becomes the de facto study of the subject.

For 200 years, the primary source of information has been iconography: this study in using all available sources will shed new light on the dress of the Grande Armée.

In creating my narrative, I have endeavoured to let the primary sources speak for themselves without having to fit what they say into a superficial construct, created by other authors. This approach has allowed a fresh and revisionary narrative to be produced on the uniform of the Grande Armée. However, I must also stress the roll of the interpreter, i.e., me the author, in the creation of the narrative. We all have pre-conceived ideas and personal biases towards historical events based on political, economic, sociological and ideological grounds, these will impact on the way that the interpreter interprets the source material. No historian is free from bias. Interpretation of source material to construct a narrative is thereby affected by the response, desire and needs of the interpreters. Someone else may well read different conclusions to the original sources to those I have made.

French dragoons *(dragon* in French) were the most ubiquitous cavalry of the epoch: of which Napoléon inherited 20 regiments in 1799, their number rising to 30 by 1808, and reducing to 24 in 1811. As well as regular regiments, provisional regiments of dragoons were raised. At the start of March 1807, Napoléon ordered Marshal Kellermann to form four provisional regiments of cavalry from the men at depots in France who were equipped, mounted and trained and had arrived at Potsdam. Each regiment was to have five companies. In each regiment the 1st company were to be hussars, the 2nd *chasseurs à cheval,* and the 3rd and 4th company were to be dragoons and finally a 5th company were to be either *carabiniers* or *cuirassiers*. Each company was to have 120 men, the regiment 600 men. The men were to be mounted at Potsdam on captured Prussian and Saxon horses. These four units were disbanded in October 1807.

Deployed in Spain from 1807 to 1814, these units operated equally as well as heavy cavalry, on scout and reconnaissance work, as well as infantry: service they performed adequately in 1805 and 1806 in Germany. More provisional regiments had been raised for service in Spain in autumn 1807. A brigade of dragoons was to be formed of two provisional regiments, the first formed from the 11$^e$, 14$^e$, 18$^e$, and 19$^e$ regiments, totalling 480 men, and the second from the 20$^e$, 21$^e$, 25$^e$ and 26$^e$ regiments, to consist of 500 men. By the end of 1808, eight provisional regiments had been created for service in Spain.[1]

Not quite heavy cavalry or light cavalry, they were in a league of their own, often described as 'medium cavalry'. Dragoons were the ideal troops for the war in Spain, as Joseph Naylies of the 19$^e$ *Dragons* noted: 'The Spanish were ignorant that our soldiers had the advantage of being trained to fight on horse and foot, and with the bayonet at gunpoint, they carried off positions inaccessible to cavalry.'[2]

In general terms, the dragoons were equipped with a long straight sword (for thrusting), pistols, a dragoon musket (which was shorter than the infantry models), and a bayonet. The trademark brass helmets and tall boots characterised the dragoon regiments.

Since the 1790s Poles had fought in the ranks of the French army, with distinctive *czapka* headdress and carrying a lance. They were codified as the Vistula Legion, providing two regiments of lancers.

The ranks of the medium cavalry were bolstered in 1811 with the introduction of lancers into the French cavalry. This was achieved by converting six regiments and drawing manpower from the remaining 24 regiments. For example, the 30$^e$ *Dragons* were based at Lyon. The squadrons withdrawn from Spain in May 1811 were to be remounted at Auxonne, replacement officers, *sous-officiers* and men were to be drawn from the pool of dismounted men at Saintes. The men of the regiment remaining at their depot in Lyon were to be sent to the new lancer regiments. Napoléon had a specific objective that the lancers were to fulfil. He ordered that: 'In order to preserve the combat effectiveness of the heavy cavalry in battle, the tasks of courier duty, screening, reconnaissance and pursuit' were to fall to light cavalry units so that 'the heavy cavalry could be employed with maximum effectiveness at the critical time in battle.' He further ordered that: 'Under no consideration shall cuirassiers be detailed as orderlies. This duty shall be done by lancers; even generals shall use lancers. The service of communications, escort, sharpshooters, shall be done by lancers.' To this end, lancers were issued a sabre, lance, a pair of pistols and the elite company were designated as *carabiniers*: they carried a light cavalry carbine rather than a lance. From 1813, only front-rank men were issued lances, rear-rank men carried carbines.

The lance was approximately 9ft long, 1in in diameter, made of a hard wood, such as ash and weighed approximately 4kg. With its extended length, the lance also afforded its owner three distinct advantages over the sabre. First, during cavalry-on-cavalry melees, the lance increased the shock effect on the opponent by being able to engage the enemy before he could use his sabre effectively. Second, the lance proved superior to the sabre when attacking the infantry squares. The infantry would typically form into squares to defend themselves against cavalry charges and relied on their bayonets once they had expended their rounds. Because of the lance's extended reach, lancer units were sometimes employed as the breach force unit to penetrate the infantry squares. Lastly, the extended reach of the lance proved far more effective than the sabre during pursuit missions when it was the cavalry's role to chase down and destroy enemy units attempting to retreat to safety: the best example perhaps being the 3$^e$ and 4$^e$ Lancers attacking the Union Brigade at Waterloo. Although the lance did provide a significant advantage over the sabre, it had one significant drawback during extremely close combat. Because of the extended length of the weapon, the lance often became too awkward and cumbersome for close-in fighting. The addition of the lancers to French cavalry organisations was one of the more significant contributions Napoléon made to the mounted combat arm of decision.

The dragoon regiments provided the nucleus for the new heavy cavalry formations in the campaign of 1813 as very few units had served in Russia, and provided a pool of experienced men. By the time of Waterloo, the dragoons were perhaps the best cavalry in the French army: battle-hardened by campaigns in Spain and Germany, and containing a far higher number of veterans than the *cuirassiers* and *carabiniers*.

In 1814 the number of dragoon regiments was reduced to 20 and the lancers to six with the disbandment of the 7$^e$, 8$^e$ and 9$^e$ regiments. A 7$^e$ lancer regiment appeared briefly in 1815. What follows is a comprehensive discussion of what these regiments wore.

# Chapter 1

# Dragoon Uniforms

When he rose to power in 1799 as First Consul, Napoléon inherited 85 regiments of cavalry, grouped into three different categories: 38 regiments of *hussards* and *chasseurs* considered light cavalry, 20 regiments of dragoons, and 27 heavy regiments of cavalry, each type being employed in various manners. Each arm of cavalry had its own traditions, its own uniforms and *esprit de corps*. The basic building block for the dress of the 20 regiments of dragoons was the An X regulation, which gave each trooper:

*Cavalerie*, *carabiniers* and *dragons*

| Objects | Duration (years) |
|---|---|
| Cloth *habits*: | 4 |
| Cloth *surtouts*: | 4 |
| *Manteaux*: | 10 |
| *Chapeaux*: | 2 |
| Helmets: | 8 |
| White buff leather waist belts: | 20 |
| *Gibernes*: | 20 |
| White buff leather *giberne* belts: | 20 |
| Musket slings: | 20 |
| *Porte-manteaux*: | 8 |
| Saddles: | 20 |
| *Housses*: | 8 |
| *Chaperons*: | 8 |
| Boots: | 2 |

For Year X, a sheepskin *culottes* (breeches) will be provided to each man of the cavalry and dragoons. As of the year XI, each *sous-officier*, cavalryman and *dragon* will have two pairs of hide *culotte*, one in sheepskin, and one of doeskin. They will supply these two *culottes* with a sum of six francs, which will be issued to them as part of the clothing mass. All in accordance with the provisions of the instruction to be drafted and addressed to the Minister of War.

Each *sous-officier*, cavalryman and dragoon will receive, each year, a *veste*, which will be worn with the old *surtout*.

The *sous-officier* and soldiers will provide, at their expense, the repair and maintenance of the boots.

An excellent example of a trooper's helmet from the middle years of the First Empire. (*Photograph and collection of Bertrand Malvaux*)

The above provisions prescribed for infantry, in Articles IV, VI, VIII, IX and X, will be common to cavalry and dragoons, Viz:.

IV. Non-commissioned officers and soldiers will be required to provide *bonnets de police* at their expense.[1]

As *bonnets de police* were non-army issue, so we are left to wonder as to their exact appearance. Seemingly the practice of wearing white linen legwear in summer was officially sanctioned; fatigue smocks were also introduced for the line. Smocks, however, seldom appear in inspection returns. As summer ended in 1802 another decree was issued on 23 September. Point 9 elaborated on the *bonnets de police*: 'Sous-officiers and soldiers will be provided with a *bonnet de police*, which will be made with off cuts from making the new clothing and the best pieces of the debris of the old clothing.' An early case of recycling! Point 13 introduced loose-fitting linen overalls for fatigue duties to be worn with the smock.[2] Nothing was 'written down' about trumpeters' clothing. The regulation lists *chapeaux*, but these have never been traced in archives as ever being issued for general use beyond exceptional circumstances for foot dragoons or adjutants.

## Clothing the Dragoons

The men's clothing was paid for by stoppages from their pay: the men of the Grande Armée were paid – in theory! – professionals. Upon joining the army, they were issued their first complete set of uniform (1$^e$ *Messe*) which came from stoppages in their pay. For soldiers serving over a year, the regimental Council of Administration drew its necessary funds to fund repairs to clothing and equipment, as well to produce replacement items. This enabled the purchase of raw materials to make equipment, headdress etc. and to pay the regimental workmen to make them. This was called the *Masse d'Habillement*. Each workman would take on at least two of the regiment's children as apprentices. The workmen included:

Master tailor. He ranked as a sergeant and was responsible for manufacturing uniforms for his regiment, as well as making repairs to the uniforms. Every man that joined the regiment would be measured and have a uniform altered to fit. Uniforms came in three sizes. In addition, from 1810 it seems each company had at least one tailor, and company funds were used to pay his wages.

Master armourer. He ranked as a corporal, and it was his duty to ensure weapons were kept in good repair and repaired as needed.

Master cordwainer. The master shoe maker ranked as a corporal and was responsible for manufacture and repair of shoes and boots.

Master gaiter-maker. The gaiters of a regiment had prior to 9 September 1799 been made by the master tailor, after that date the duties were passed to the gaiter-maker.

For clothing, in many cases the regiment bought cloth and paid for the items to be made in house by the regiment's tailors. Items such as shoes were often bought in bulk from

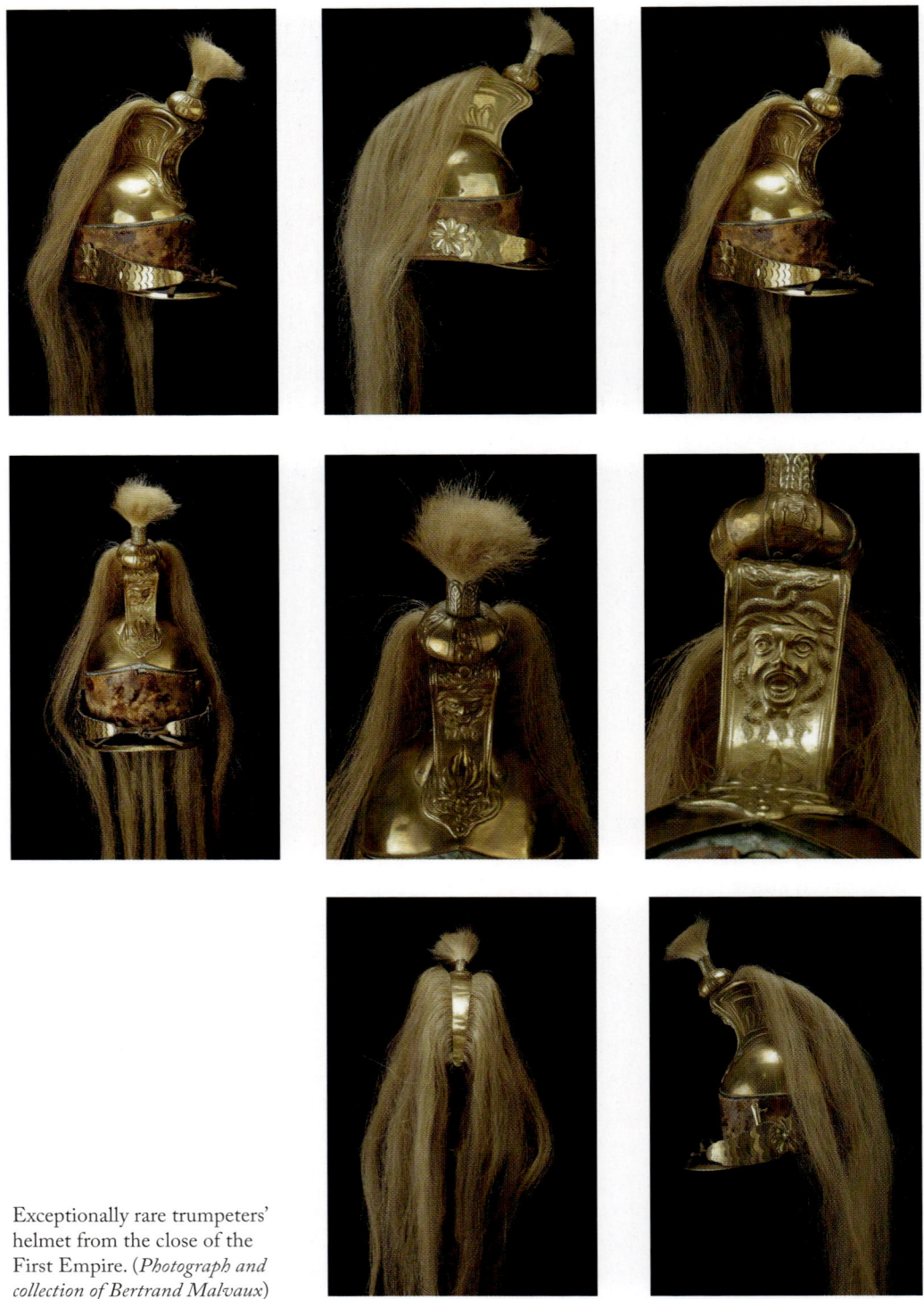

Exceptionally rare trumpeters' helmet from the close of the First Empire. (*Photograph and collection of Bertrand Malvaux*)

factories rather than made in house. Leather items were ordered from manufacturers, as were metal fittings including buttons. Headdress was also outsourced. If made in house or bought in, *marches* would be prepared for agreement by the regiment's administrative council, who would oversee the work and inspect the quality of the workmanship or materials.

The *Messe d'Habillement* also covered sundry items such as the epaulettes of the *adjutant-sous-officiers*, lace for rank stripes, service chevrons, musicians and drummers' lace, plumes and pompoms. The fund was to provide a soldier with his full issue of uniform and equipment. A soldier, in addition to his basic issue, needed more than a single shirt, stock and pair of shoes. This was paid for with more stoppages from his pay being sent to the Linen and Shoe Fund. The fund was paid for at the rate of 12 centimes a day for *sous-officiers* and 7 centimes for other ranks.[3] The men were paid, in theory, weekly, according to rank and status. In all cases, the pay was subject to a number of deductions for communal funds (masses), which left very little actual pay. The purpose of the pay was actually not to give the soldier pocket money to spend on wine, women and gambling but so he could pay for fines, pay repair bills for his clothing and equipment, purchase soap and cleaning equipment and if needed buy new items of clothing. The paperwork for the 8[e] *Dragons* gives a good idea of the day-to-day equipment and clothing needs of a regiment of dragoons:

**1 June 1808**
100 bayonet scabbards. Total 50fr
39 helmets at 22fr 20 each. Total 865fr 80
48 musket slings. Total 73fr 80
36 *porte-bayonets*. Total 31fr 50
Copper fittings for buff work. Total 141fr 95
3 bayonet scabbard fittings in copper. Total 25fr 50
9 pairs of chinscales for helmets. Total 18fr
11 pairs of chinscales. Total 22fr
7 pairs of rosettes for chinscales. Total 8fr 75
Rosette for helmet. Total 4fr 40

**30 September**
30 waistbelts in buff leather. Total 270fr
34 long sword slings. Total 25fr 35
53 small sword slings. Total 23fr 25
340 helmets with *crinieres*. Total 5,091fr 20
350 red plumes. Total 1,066fr
15 dozen pairs of spurs. Total 266fr 25
294 pairs of *manchettes de botte*. Total 1,323fr
300 pairs of *manchettes de botte*. Total 1,358fr
600 pairs of *manchettes de botte*. Total 540fr
5 ounces of silver lace for *sous-officiers*. Total 40fr 25

  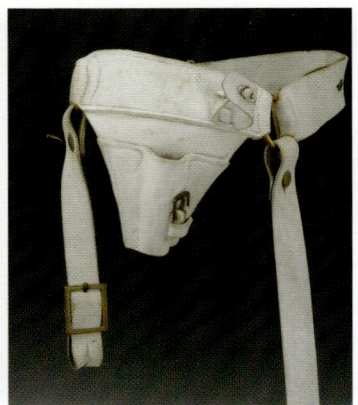
 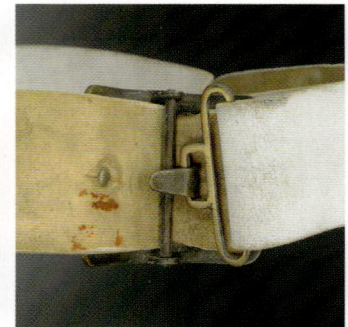 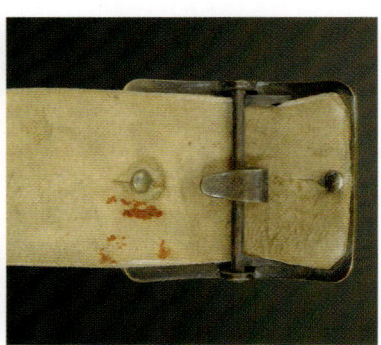

Troopers' waistbelt from the middle years of the First Empire. (*Photograph and collection of Bertrand Malvaux*)

33 ounces of linen lace for corporals. Total 22fr 40
300 stocks in black silk. Total 630fr
60 pairs of black gaiters. Total 285fr
60 stock buckles. Total 18fr.

**6 January 1809**
20m 50 silver lace for *sous-officiers*. Total 145fr 50
364 pairs of boots. Total 7,644fr
130 pairs of spurs straps. Total 50fr 65
200 pairs of gauntlets. Total 800fr
100 red plumes at 4fr 55 each. Total 455fr
310 waistbelts. Total 2,480fr
360 musket slings. Total 430fr
160 helmets at 16fr 20 each. Total 2,592fr
100 *crinieres* for helmets at 2fr 50 each. Total 250fr
100 peaks for helmets at 1fr 50. Total 150fr

Grenades for *gibernes*, buttons for musket slings, rosettes for helmets, bayonet ferrules, '*fleurones de plaques des gibernes*', buckles for sword slings. 650fr

Dragoon Uniforms 7

Sample of original *vert dragon* broadcloth. It is exceptionally dark in hue. (*Collection KM*)

Sample of original scarlet broadcloth. (*Collection KM*)

Sample of original crimson broadcloth. (*Collection KM*)

Sample of original *rose* broadcloth. (*Collection KM*)

Sample of original yellow broadcloth. (*Collection KM*)

80 bits. Total 400fr
52 saddle blankets at 14fr each. Total 728fr
132 *housses* and *chaperons* at 20fr 60 a set. Total 2,719fr 20
21 pairs of girths at 3fr each. Total 63fr
1 head collar. Total 4fr
51 watering bridles at 4fr 25. Total 174fr 25

**1 January 1810**
Pair of epaulettes for *adjutant-sous-officier*. Total 52fr 50

  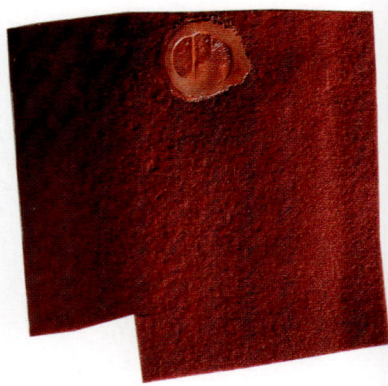

Sample of original aurore broadcloth. Note it is a shade of orange and not yellow. (*Collection KM*)

Sample of original *bleu de ciel* broadcloth. Note is it a much darker hue than traditionally ascribed for this colour. (*Collection KM*)

Sample of original *garance* broadcloth. (*Collection KM*)

**1 January 1811**
60 pairs of gauntlets. Total 240fr
7 pairs of gauntlets. Total 28fr
20 combs. Total 7fr 50
20 brushes. Total 25fr
15m 68 crimson serge to line *manteaux*. Total 34fr 50[4]

We assume that the red plumes and grenades for the *gibernes* were restricted to the regiment's elite company. We also see that helmets came as a kit of parts, with the peak, chinscales and *criniere* all to be added to the basic shell, which we assume had the turban fitted. The tailoring bill paid to the regiment's master tailor was as follows:

**31 March 1808**
22 *surtouts* at 2fr 45 each. Total 53fr 10
30 pairs of black gaiters at 1fr 40 a pair. Total 42fr
18 *bonnets de police* at 75 centimes. Total 13fr 50

**1 June**
8 *surtouts* at 2fr each. Total 16fr
15 stable coats at 1fr 40. Total 21fr
1 *bonnet de police* for *sous-officier*. Total 95 centimes

**30 September**
45 *habits* at 2fr 75 each. Total 123fr 75
74 plume covers. Total 14fr 63
64 *bonnets de police* for dragoons at 50 centimes each. Total 32fr

**6 January 1809**
36 *manteaux* at 1fr 50 each. Total 84fr
85 pairs of black gaiters at 4fr 75 each. Total 403fr
85 *bonnets de police* at 50 centimes, 46 *manteaux*, 210 plume covers. Total 290fr 25
88 *manteaux* at 1fr 50 each. Total 132fr
37 *porte-manteaux* at 3fr 20 each. Total 118fr
119 *manteaux* at 1fr 50 each. Total 178fr 50
175 *porte-manteaux* at 3fr 20. Total 792fr

**1 January 1810**
11 *manteaux*. Total 16fr 50
50 *bonnets de police*. Total 25fr
60 *bonnets de police*. Total 30fr

**1 June**
119 *manteaux* at 1fr 50 each. Total 178fr 50
132 *porte-manteaux* at 3fr 20. Total 422fr 40

**1 January 1811**
5 pairs of gaiters from black broadcloth at 4fr 75 each. Total 23fr 75[5]

We wonder as to the destination of the *surtouts* – perhaps for trumpeters? The three differing qualities of *bonnets de police* also raises questions. The 50 centimes version are clearly for rank and file and the 95 centimes version for a *sous-officier*, perhaps *adjutant-sous-officier*? The mid-price examples for trumpeters and or *sous-officiers*? Also, of interest gaiters were made from black tricot, but by 1811 they were made from black broadcloth, a superior and costlier fabric.

If clothing and equipment became damaged, repairs were carried out under the auspices of the *caporal-fourrier*. Minor repairs were to be carried out to clothing and equipment by the soldier, for more major repairs, the *caporal-fourrier* took the soldier and his damaged items to the captain clothing officer, who authorised the regimental workmen to undertake the repair. If the repair was judged to be due to the negligence of the soldier, he had to pay for the work or a replacement item from his pay.[6]

The definition of negligence and clothing simply falling to bits because it was badly made was a fine line. The company quarterly inspections of the 5ᵉ *Dragons*, unique at the time of writing in that the paperwork still survives into the modern era, demonstrates beyond any reasonable doubt that even in the midst of the Peninsular War an 'anything goes' attitude simply did not exist, and the nature of costs incurred by the men to serve in the army. For example, in 1ᵉ squadron 5ᵉ company in the first quarter of 1813, the following fines were paid for repairs to damaged items of equipment:

### Trooper Penin
A hook and buckle on the back of the *cimier*. 40 centimes
Two buckles and keepers. 40 centimes
A *jonc* – brass edging – for the peak of the helmet. 25 centimes

### Trooper Sexant
A pistol ram rod. 75 centimes
A body brush. 30 centimes

### Trooper Wasselin
A buckle. 25 centimes
A sabre belt ring for suspending a sword sling. 15 centimes
Fitting a new sabre belt buckle. 60 centimes

### Trooper Comil
A sabre scabbard chape. 1fr 50
Screws for the musket. 25 centimes

### Trooper Bidaut
One ramrod. 35 centimes
One brush. 30 centimes
Two side plates for the helmet crest. The regiment will pay 50 centimes for labour and 2fr for parts
One helmet peak. 25 centimes
Fixings for the helmet. The regiment will pay 35 centimes
One buckle for the helmet. 60 centimes

### Trooper Hoyosse
Two side plates for the helmet. The regiment will pay 50 centimes
4 fixings for the helmet. The regiment will pay 80 centimes
Two bosses for the helmet. 50 centimes[7]

The report goes on to list another 40 troopers who had damaged or lost items of kit that quarter. By the end of the quarter, the men in the company were out of pocket to the tune of 33fr 55 and the regiment had forked out 38fr 25 on repairs of harness and equipment. The repair reports deal with harness and saddlery, helmets and weapons and equipment, sadly nothing on clothing. Also preserved are the bills for shoeing the regiment's horses, some 1,305fr being spent in the first quarter of 1813 alone.[8] These returns broken down by company and by quarter allow us to reconstruct the shoeing system employed by the regiment's farriers, and the expenses on coal and iron. The staff was busy keeping their records in the midst of the campaign and the regimental adjutant-major had to buy from 'The sign of the Eagle', a printing and stationary stockist in Madrid, 50 pre-printed folios for inspecting regimental clothing at 1fr 20 each, 50 pre-printed inspection returns for the regimental horses at 80 centimes each, 10 folios for the staff to record expenses at 3fr each: a total expenditure of 130fr, paid in cash on 9 March 1813.[9] Pens and ink were also needed by the regiment's staff: 3 packets of feathers costing 4fr 50 were purchased, 1 ream of paper for 10fr, 1 ream of fine writing paper at 15fr, 4 balls of ink at 12fr and 2 bottles of ink at 2fr 60.[10]

The paybook of Trooper Clavieux of the 28e *Dragons* attests to the costs he incurred:[11]

| | | |
|---|---|---|
| 1/1/1810 | Boot repairs. 9fr | |
| 19/1 | A pair of shoes. 6fr | |
| 10/2 | A pair of overalls. 6fr 50 | |
| 18/2 | Leather wax and harness buckles. 0fr 85 | |
| 25/2 | A pair of gaiter straps. 0fr 62 | |
| 26/2 | One harness buckle, a tin of grease, a grease brush. 1fr 29 | |
| 7/3 | A sponge. 0fr 80 | |
| 16/3 | A copper brush and boot repairs. 0fr 75 | |
| 24/3 | A pair of scissors. 0fr 98 | |
| 03/4 | A pair of grey gaiters. 2fr 20 | |
| 04/4 | Boot repairs. 0fr 75 | |
| 11/4 | A pair of shoes. 6fr | |
| 27/5 | One horse brush and a scabbard. 6fr 25 | |
| 26/5 | Headband for helmet 0fr 35; one tin of grease and brush 2fr 79; one plume holder, two scales and rosacea for chinscales 0fr 95; one feed bag 2fr; repairs to bed linen 0fr 10; repairs to musketoon 0fr 37; soldiering new guard to sabre 1fr 25 | |
| 10/7 | A new shirt. 4fr | |
| 14/7 | Resoling of shoes 2fr 50; grease, shoe repairs and attachment to the horsecloth. 0fr 70 | |

Clearly shoes and footwear were a major source of expense. Based on this list of expenses, the heady mix of horse muck and urine, then as now, rapidly destroyed the shoes worn for stable duties. Clavieux got just four months' wear from a pair of shoes the army expected to last for a year! Thus in 26 weeks, Clavieux was out of pocket 46fr 08. When we add in his punishment fines, he was down 126fr against an income of 54fr 60! Thus, if Clavieux was a typical soldier, it was clearly very difficult to serve in the army and not to have to pay for the privilege!

What these two documents show is how the army, even in the midst of campaign, actually operated. It shows that on campaign it was as rigorous in making sure the men maintained their clothing, equipment, weapons and harness as much as they would have done on a peacetime footing in barracks. The whole notion of 'campaign dress' or 'campaign look' adored by re-enactors, figure painters and artists can be shown categorically to be wrong. These were professional soldiers who had to maintain their kit: their lives depended on it.

# Chapter 2

# Change and Change Again

As first Consul, Bonaparte had the time – a period of relative peace and plenty – during the Peace of Amiens and 'phony war' that followed to remake the army in the image he desired it to take. The decree of *1 Vendémiaire An XII* (24 September 1803), expanded the number of regiments to 30 with a 'shake-up' of how the cavalry was organised. Under the terms of the decree the remaining regiments were disbanded:

13$^e$ *Cavalerie* became the 22$^e$ *Dragons*
14$^e$ *Cavalerie* became the 23$^e$ *Dragons*
15$^e$ *Cavalerie* became the 24$^e$ *Dragons*
16$^e$ *Cavalerie* became the 25$^e$ *Dragons*
17$^e$ *Cavalerie* became the 26$^e$ *Dragons*
18$^e$ *Cavalerie* became the 27$^e$ *Dragons*
19$^e$ *Cavalerie* disbanded into 9$^e$, 10$^e$ and 11$^e$ *Cuirassiers* and 2$^e$ *Carabiniers*
20$^e$ *Cavalerie* disbanded into 12$^e$ *Cuirassiers* and 23$^e$ *Dragons*
21$^e$ *Cavalerie* disbanded into 24$^e$ and 25$^e$ *Dragons*
22$^e$ *Cavalerie* disbanded into 9$^e$ and 12$^e$ *Cuirassiers*
23$^e$ *Cavalerie* disbanded into 5$^e$, 6$^e$ and 7$^e$ *Cuirassiers*
24$^e$ *Cavalerie* disbanded into 1$^e$ and 8$^e$ *Cuirassiers*
25$^e$ *Cavalerie* disbanded into 2$^e$, 3$^e$ and 4$^e$ *Cuirassiers*
7$^e$ Bis *Hussard* became 28$^e$ *Dragons*
11$^e$ *Hussard* became 29$^e$ *Dragons*
12$^e$ *Hussard* became 30$^e$ *Dragons*

The changeover took time. Under the terms of the decree, each regiment was to have five squadrons, each to comprise of two companies. Each company was to total 54 mounted men, and 36 dismounted, 1 trumpeter, 1 drummer, 8 corporals, 4 sergeants, 1 *fourrier* (clerk), 1 sergeant major as well as 2 sub-lieutenants, 1 lieutenant and a captain. Each squadron was headed by a squadron commander assisted by one or two adjutants. The regiment was commanded by a colonel. The decree of 9 *Prairial An 13* (24 May 1804) increased each squadron to 300 men in the 2 mounted squadrons, the 3rd and 4th squadrons were designated as foot dragoons. The 5th was the depot squadron.

## Foot Dragoons

Under the decree of *1 Vendémiaire* (23 September 1803) regiments of dragoons were to have a dismounted company. Rather than keep these dismounted men with the parent regiment, at the camp of Boulogne, the various companies of foot dragoons were assembled into complete regiments, *20 Prairial An 13* (9 June 1805) and hastily grouped into four brigades with the decree of *7 Fructidor An 13* (25 August 1805). These regiments were dressed identically to their parent units, but swapped their boots for gaiters and were issued infantry *havresacs* and greatcoats. The 1st Division was commanded by General Klein: the 1st regiment was led by Colonel Prive, drawn from the 1$^e$, 2$^e$, 14$^e$, 19$^e$ and 20$^e$ regiments, with the 2nd regiment headed by Colonel Walther drawn from the 4$^e$, 13$^e$, 10$^e$ and 11$^e$ regiments. Baraguay des Hilliers led the 2nd Division: Lebaron led the 1st regiment drawn from the 3$^e$, 5$^e$ and 6$^e$ regiments, the 2nd was commanded by Beckler, drawn from the 8$^e$, 9$^e$, 12$^e$ and 21$^e$ regiments, with the 3rd regiment led by Colonel Barthelemy comprising men from the 15$^e$, 16$^e$, 17$^e$ and 18$^e$ regiments. This was replaced with a new formation on *3 Vendémiaire* (25 September 1805) when four regiments were created, each of two battalions:

These foot dragoons were observed in Germany sometime in early 1807.

**1st regiment.**
1st battalion: 1$^e$, 2$^e$, 20$^e$ *Dragons*. 2nd battalion: 4$^e$, 14$^e$, 26$^e$ *Dragons*

**2nd regiment.**
1st battalion: 10$^e$, 13$^e$, 22$^e$ *Dragons*. 2nd battalion: 3$^e$, 6$^e$, 11$^e$ *Dragons*

**3rd regiment.**
1st battalion: 5$^e$, 8$^e$, 12$^e$ *Dragons*. 2nd battalion: 9$^e$, 16$^e$, 21$^e$ *dragons*

**4th regiment.**
1st battalion: 15$^e$, 17$^e$, 25$^e$ *Dragons*. 2nd battalion: 18$^e$, 19$^e$, 27$^e$ *Dragons*

The conversion of *cavalerie* regiments to *dragons* from 1803 meant thousands of items of clothing in blue had been to phased out. This was simply not possible to achieve before the army marched to war in summer 1805. Many regiments, like the 26ᵉ *Dragons*, had green and blue clothing in use until 1806, as this artist correctly depicts. Of interest are the copper fish scale *contre-epaulettes*, which we know became common from 1808.

Standard bearer of the 1ᵉ *Dragons* c.1807. The colour is rather fanciful, unless it is a squadron marker of some sort.

On *1 Brumaire* (23 October 1805) captured Austrian horses with the capitulation of Ulm were to be issued to the foot dragoons. We have no trace of these units after 2 December.[1]

This was not the end of the experiment, however, on 13 September 1806, the Emperor wrote from Saint-Cloud to Bessières that it was his intention of forming an additional six battalions of foot dragoons, each of six companies. Each regiment of dragoons was to furnish two companies, each to be of 100 *sous-officiers* and men. The officers were to be drawn from the *Vélites* of the *Garde Impériale*. The six battalions, considered a corps, were attached to the *Garde Impériale*. Change followed on 15 September, when the scheme was scaled back to four battalions, each of four companies, each to comprise 1 captain, 1 lieutenant, 2 sub-lieutenants, 1 sergeant major, 4 sergeants, 8 corporals, 2 drummers and 130 troopers. General Dorsenne of the *Grenadiers à Pied* was placed in charge of organising the 1st and 2nd battalions at Mayence, and Major Friederichs of the *Chasseurs à Pied* had charge of the 3rd and 4th. The 1st battalion was created from the 2ᵉ, 14ᵉ, 20ᵉ and 26ᵉ regiments, the 2nd battalion from the 6ᵉ, 11ᵉ 13ᵉ and 22ᵉ regiments. They formed

Change and Change Again 15

Elite company trooper wearing campaign dress c.1807. The *surtout* is correctly shown as entirely green. The yellow waistcoat is surprising, but not improbable.

Farrier of a unknown regiment of *dragons*. The use of grey overalls is attested to in period documentation. The *sapeur* dressed in blue may be from a *dragon* regiment such as the 26ᵉ, which had some blue clothing in 1806.

the 1st Division. The 2nd Division was drawn from the 8ᵉ, 12ᵉ, 16ᵉ and 21ᵉ regiments in the 3rd battalion and the 4th from the 17ᵉ, 18ᵉ, 25ᵉ and 27ᵉ regiments. Men from the 1ᵉ, 3ᵉ, 4ᵉ, 5ᵉ, 9ᵉ, 10ᵉ and 15ᵉ regiments were sent to furnish a 200-man-strong squadron attached to the Legions of the Reserve. The four battalions were formally allocated on 23 October 1806 to the equipment train of the *Garde Impériale*.[2] The ephemeral organisation still existed by the start of 1807: with the disbandment of the 4th battalion of the 2ᵉ *Régiment de la Ligne*, the officers and elite company, along with cadre, were sent to the *dragons à pied de la Garde Impériale*.[3] Based on extant paperwork, the men were sent back to their parent units, mounted on Polish or Prussian horses in the wake of the action at Eylau. The officers and cadre were allocated to the newly levied *Dragons de Garde Impériale* as replacement officers and *sous-officiers*.[4]

## Blue or Green?

One of the perennial issues of the dragoons' uniform was the cost of the dyes for the green broadcloth. In 1798 it had been proposed to dress dragoons in *bleu de ciel* due to the cost of indigo dye and a good yellow dye that was fade resistant. The green broadcloth rapidly faded to blue as the yellow dye was lost due to UV exposure. *Bleu de ciel* was dyed from woad rather than indigo, and was, at least in theory, cheaper and more stable than troublesome green. On *18 Vendémiaire An 7* (9 October 1798), the War Ministry ordered dragoons to wear a *bleu de ciel habit* with distinctive colours:

Scarlet: 1<sup>e</sup> and 10<sup>e</sup>
Rose: 2<sup>e</sup> and 11<sup>e</sup>
Crimson: 3<sup>e</sup> and 12<sup>e</sup>
Light Yellow: 4<sup>e</sup> and 13<sup>e</sup>
White: 5<sup>e</sup> and 14<sup>e</sup>
Daffodil Yellow: 6<sup>e</sup> and 15<sup>e</sup>
Mouse Brown: 7<sup>e</sup> and 16<sup>e</sup>
Violet: 8<sup>e</sup> and 17<sup>e</sup>
Aurore: 9<sup>e</sup> and 18<sup>e</sup>

How far this idea progressed is almost impossible to say. Below are the units known to have adopted blue, and then re-appropriated the cloth to equip the trumpeters and drummers once green had been confirmed as the base colour for uniforms:

### 2<sup>e</sup>
The inspection of 30 April 1802 reports 24m of blue broadcloth had been used.[5] By the time of the 23 September 1804 review, a further 4m 20 of blue broadcloth had been used to make trumpeters' clothing.[6]

### 7<sup>e</sup>
Reviewed 6 August 1803, of the 32m of blue broadcloth in stores, 18m 26 had been used, we assume, on trumpeters' clothing.[7] Inspected 10 January 1805, we report 13m 74 of blue broadcloth had been used to make, presumably, trumpeters' clothing.[8]

### 10<sup>e</sup>
At the review of 19 July 1803, the inspector, General Emmanuel de Grouchy, commented the unit had 56 bearskins with the elite company, and all the sheepskin *schabraques* had been removed from use. Stores held 19m 30 of blue broadcloth, which had been purchased in April 1802.[9] Reviewed 19 October 1804, the regiment had 189 dismounted men with 8 drummers and 548 mounted with 4 trumpeters. The dismounted men had black twill gaiters, *havresacs* and *capotes*, which like the *manteaux* were made from *blanc picque de bleu* broadcloth. We note 701 *habits* were in use and 739 *surtouts*, 447 *manteaux* and 127 bearskins for the elite company. The horses were equipped with *chaperons* and *housses*. Regimental accounts report 19m 90 of blue broadcloth had been used to cloth the trumpeters and drummers.[10]

### 12<sup>e</sup>
The regiment was reviewed 23 August 1805. The report notes 11m 08 of blue broadcloth had been used to make trumpeters' clothing and over 73m remained in stores.[11]

### 13ᵉ
The regimental archives show that between 13 February 1802 and 16 May 1803 stores had used 188m 87 of blue broadcloth and not an inch of green to make 61 *habits*, 87 *surtouts* and 158 *housses*.[12, 13] Inspected 25 July 1805, scheduled for replacement were 25 blue habits no doubt worn by trumpeters and drummers.[14]

### 14ᵉ
Reviewed 14 October 1804, we note stores had held 33m 60 of blue broadcloth in 1803, a further 45m 70 had been purchased, of which 59m 64 had been used, leaving 19m 70 in stores.[15] Reviewed again 19 August 1805, over the preceding year more blue broadcloth had been bought, making a total of 37m 40 of blue broadcloth, of which 23m 80 had been used to make, we assume, trumpeters' clothing.[16] Inspected 26 December 1807, since 1805 a further 77m 56 of blue broadcloth had been purchased, and 37m 50 being used, leaving 37m 46 in stores.[17]

### 15ᵉ
Reviewed 14 July 1803, 15m of blue broadcloth had been used since 1802 for, we assume, trumpeters' clothing.[18]

### 16ᵉ
A report of 12 November 1802 implies one company was dressed in blue.[19]

Dragoons in blue was far more common than heretofore assumed. It also means that before 1808, eight regiments had trumpeters not in reversed colours, but blue.

With the conversion of *cavalerie* regiments to dragoons, the realisation of the huge number of men to be clothed sent the War Ministry into 'panic mode' over the costs, and a hasty compromise scheme was created.

Thousands of men had to be totally reclothed, many having just received a new blue *habit*. The cost of green dye, and also the cost of replacing a lot of brand-new clothing, resulted in General Bourcier resurrecting the idea to dress dragoons in blue, which was included in the decree of *1 Vendemiaire An XII* (24 September 1803). Change took time as many dragoon regiments had large stocks of green cloth and uniforms. The uncertainty about the colour of uniforms led to a note being sent to the Emperor on 20 January 1805 seeking clarity. The response came on 27 February 1805 with an order for the 27ᵉ *Dragons* to adopt a new model of uniform, which sought to unify the dress of the dragoons, with the *cuirassiers* wearing dark blue and adopting a *cuirassier* helmet: both arms were to be dressed identically, bar the *cuirass* of course. Yet green clothing was still being produced. At the same time the 4ᵉ and 18ᵉ de Ligne were ordered into white. We have no fixed date when blue uniforms were abandoned for dragoons, we can only assume the idea was quietly dropped, although some regiments had purchased blue broadcloth, which was no doubt hastily used to dress the trumpeters.[20] These were the 21ᵉ, 22ᵉ, 23ᵉ, 25ᵉ, 26ᵉ, 27ᵉ, and 30ᵉ, making 15 regiments having trumpeters dressed in blue, or had blue on their uniform: in basic terms, 50% of trumpeters wore blue somewhere on their uniform and not reversed colours of myth. I know of no contemporary iconography showing these uniforms, alas.

## 1807 Reviews

The uniform of the dragoons underwent very few modifications. The decree of 23 March 1806 allowed both a *surtout* and *habit*. It left the dress of the *dragon* regiments unchanged but did confirm green as the base colour of uniforms: the short-lived experiment with blue was over. Following Jena, the dragoons found themselves heavily committed to action in the pursuit of the Prussian army. By new year 1807 many regiments needed refitting and were allocated the following items by the decree of 15 January 1807:

| Regiment | Habit | Vestes | Culottes en drap | Capotes | | Pairs of shoes | Shirts | Pairs of boots | Manteaux |
|---|---|---|---|---|---|---|---|---|---|
| | | | | Ready made | To sew | | | | |
| 1$^e$ | | | | 3 | | 126 | 432 | 27 | 81 |
| 2$^e$ | 168 | 518 | | | | 138 | 436 | 936 | 957 |
| 3$^e$ | 157 | 500 | | 25 | | 103 | 453 | 45 | 81 |
| 4$^e$ | 210 | 500 | | 2 | | 74 | 433 | 210 | 248 |
| 5$^e$ | 250 | 500 | | 41 | | 679 | 120 | 36 | 112 |
| 6$^e$ | 171 | 500 | | 20 | | 31 | 426 | 147 | 66 |
| 8$^e$ | 250 | 500 | 56 | | | 152 | 308 | 408 | 46 |
| 9$^e$ | 250 | 500 | 73 | | | 185 | 158 | 50 | 94 |
| 10$^e$ | 209 | 500 | | 29 | | 64 | 431 | 14 | 26 |
| 11$^e$ | 200 | 500 | | 9 | | 71 | 407 | 349 | 79 |
| 12$^e$ | 250 | 500 | | 52 | | 184 | 149 | 186 | 105 |
| 13$^e$ | | | | 11 | | 29 | 708 | 146 | 246 |
| 14$^e$ | 171 | 500 | | 9 | | 274 | 432 | 225 | 199 |
| 15$^e$ | | | | 36 | | 36 | 300 | 10 | 31 |
| 16$^e$ | 250 | 500 | | 27 | | 130 | 36 | 135 | 60 |
| 17$^e$ | 250 | 500 | | 106 | | 14 | 411 | 93 | 46 |
| 18$^e$ | 250 | 500 | | 9 | | 71 | 454 | 136 | 30 |
| 19$^e$ | 500 | 500 | | 12 | | 53 | 499 | 76 | 96 |
| 20$^e$ | | 500 | | 75 | | 138 | 436 | 203 | 42 |
| 21$^e$ | 250 | 500 | | 54 | | 191 | 14 | 416 | 127 |
| 22$^e$ | 250 | 500 | | 12 | | 23 | 510 | 197 | |
| 23$^e$ | | | | 1 | | 1 | | | |
| 25$^e$ | 250 | 500 | | 22 | | 26 | 163 | 91 | 140 |
| 26$^e$ | 5 | | | 6 | | 60 | 480 | 96 | 52 |
| 27$^e$ | 528 | 500 | | 24 | | 51 | | 1 | 2 |

These items were all produced from cloth captured at Glogau or Warsaw, as well as Prussian stores. Also issued were 325 pairs of *culottes de peau* to the 1ᵉ regiment, 50 to the 3ᵉ, 59 to the 6ᵉ, 135 to the 8ᵉ, 56 to the 10ᵉ, 5 pairs to the 12ᵉ, 22 pairs to the 22ᵉ, 8 pairs to the 17ᵉ and 12 to the 23ᵉ, who also received 4 helmets. From Prussian stocks the 1ᵉ *Dragons* received 900 *porte-gibernes* and *gibernes*, 1,000 musket slings and 1,500 *banderole-porte-mousqueton* and the same number of captured Prussian carbines, and 500 Prussian saddles and bridles. The 13ᵉ also received 500 Prussian carbines and belts. The 27ᵉ were issued 100 pairs of *pantalons en drap brun*.[21]

The rigours of campaign life meant that many items issued after Eylau were life expired by the summer and many colonels had adopted non-regulation items of clothing better suited to the needs of a regiment on campaign, rather than what the War Ministry felt was the best item to wear. An idea of allocation, and the overall shabby condition of the dragoons at the end of the Heilsberg campaign, can be gained from a wide-ranging review of dragoon regiments made in Germany in July 1807:[22]

| Regiment | Item | In good repair | In need of repair | To be replaced | Total | Observations |
|---|---|---|---|---|---|---|
| 1ᵉ *Dragons* | Habits | The regiment has none | | | | The regiment is missing 24 bayonets. The clothing issued from the stores is badly cut and sewn. |
| | Surtouts | 461 | | 50 | 511 | |
| | Gilets en drap | The regiment has none | | | | |
| | Gilets d'écurie | 508 | | | 508 | |
| | Culottes de peau | 330 | | 194 | 524 | |
| | Bearskins | 25 | | 47 | 72 | |
| 2ᵉ *Dragons* | Habits | The regiment has none | | | | The regiment is missing 47 bayonets, 74 dragoon muskets and 160 pistols. |
| | Surtouts | 606 | | 162 | 768 | |
| | Gilets en drap | 1164 | | 106 | 1270 | |
| | Gilets d'écurie | 508 | 556 | 171 | 727 | |
| | Culottes de peau | 705 | | 97 | 802 | |
| | Bearskins | 58 | | 29 | 87 | |
| 3ᵉ *Dragons* | Habits | 462 | | | 462 | The regiment is missing many *habits*, and *gilets d'écurie*. |
| | Surtouts | 515 | | | 515 | |
| | Gilets en drap | 460 | | | 460 | |
| | Gilets d'écurie | 291 | | | 291 | |
| | Culottes de peau | 515 | | | 515 | |
| | Bearskins | 119 | | | 119 | |
| 4ᵉ *Dragons* | Habits | 243 | 24 | 213 | 300 | The clothing is generally in good condition. The men all need new boots. |
| | Surtouts | 35 | 6 | 412 | 453 | |
| | Gilets en drap | 82 | 36 | 72 | 190 | |
| | Gilets d'écurie | The regiment has none | | | | |
| | Culottes de peau | 482 | | 17 | 499 | |
| | Bearskins | The regiment has none | | | | |

| Regiment | Item | In good repair | In need of repair | To be replaced | Total | Observations |
|---|---|---|---|---|---|---|
| 5ᵉ *Dragons* | *Habits* | The regiment has none | | | | 257 plumes are used by the 1st squadron. |
| | *Surtouts* | 323 | 145 | | 467 | |
| | *Gilets en drap* | 433 | | | 433 | |
| | *Gilets d'écurie* | 214 | 269 | | 483 | |
| | *Culottes de peau* | 311 | 171 | | 482 | |
| | Bearskins | The regiment has none | | | | |
| 6ᵉ *Dragons* | *Habits* | 542 | | | | The clothing is generally in good condition. |
| | *Surtouts* | 668 | | | | |
| | *Gilets en drap* | 682 | | | | |
| | *Gilets d'écurie* | 139 | | | | |
| | *Culottes de peau* | 676 | | | | |
| | Bearskins | 105 | | | | |
| 8ᵉ *Dragons* | *Habits* | The regiment has none | | | | *Pantalons d'écurie* made in broadcloth reinforced with leather are used. |
| | *Surtouts* | 527 | 100 | | 627 | |
| | *Gilets en drap* | 600 | 27 | | 627 | |
| | *Gilets d'écurie* | 378 | 100 | | 408 | |
| | *Culottes de peau* | The regiment has none | | | | |
| | Bearskins | | | | | |
| 9ᵉ *Dragons* | *Habits* | 212 | 250 | | 462 | 462 plumes are in use. In lieu of *culottes de peau*, *pantalons d'écurie* made in broadcloth reinforced with leather are used. |
| | *Surtouts* | 515 | | | 515 | |
| | *Gilets en drap* | 462 | | | 462 | |
| | *Gilets d'écurie* | 174 | | | 174 | |
| | *Culottes de peau* | | 74 | | | |
| | Bearskins | The regiment has none | | | | |
| 10ᵉ *Dragons* | *Habits* | 397 | | | | The clothing issued from Potsdam is very low quality due to issues of sending clothing from France. The sabre knots are made from blackened cow hide and yellow buff. |
| | *Surtouts* | 390 | | | | |
| | *Gilets en drap* | 405 | | | | |
| | *Gilets d'écurie* | | | | | |
| | *Culottes de peau* | 372 | | | | |
| | Bearskins | 103 | | | | |
| 11ᵉ *Dragons* | *Habits* | 697 | | | | The clothing is in good condition and complete. |
| | *Surtouts* | 676 | | | | |
| | *Gilets en drap* | 947 | | | | |
| | *Gilets d'écurie* | 158 | | | | |
| | *Culottes de peau* | 931 | | | | |
| | Bearskins | 118 | | | | |

| Regiment | Item | In good repair | In need of repair | To be replaced | Total | Observations |
|---|---|---|---|---|---|---|
| 12ᵉ Dragon | *Habits* | 250 | | | 250 | In lieu of *culottes de peau*, *pantalons d'écurie* made in broadcloth reinforced with leather are used. |
| | *Surtout* | 221 | 405 | | 626 | |
| | *Gilets en drap* | 500 | | | 500 | |
| | *Gilet d'écurie* | 176 | 376 | | 552 | |
| | *Culottes de peau* | 297 | | | 297 | |
| | Bearskins | The regiment has none | | | | |
| 13ᵉ Dragon | *Habit* | The regiment has none | | | | The clothing is in bad condition, especially the *gilets d'écurie* and *bonnets de police*. |
| | *Surtout* | 550 | 200 | 29 | 779 | |
| | *Gilets en drap* | The regiment has none | | | | |
| | *Gilets d'écurie* | | | | | |
| | *Culottes de peau* | 600 | 150 | 130 | 762 | |
| | Bearskins | | | 93 | 93 | |
| 14ᵉ Dragon | *Habits* | 594 | | | 594 | The regiment has 216 plumes. Every man needs a new pair of boots, the *portemanteaux* are in terrible condition and lack uniformity. |
| | *Surtouts* | 391 | | 401 | 792 | |
| | *Gilets en drap* | 619 | | | 619 | |
| | *Gilets d'écurie* | The regiment has none | | | | |
| | *Culottes de peau* | 923 | | 47 | 970 | |
| | Bearskins | 96 | 28 | | 122 | |
| 15ᵉ *Dragons* | *Habits* | The regiment has none | | | | The cloth is in the worst condition imaginable. |
| | *Surtouts* | 408 | 184 | 352 | 944 | |
| | *Gilets en drap* | The regiment has none | | | | |
| | *Gilets d'écurie* | | 35 | 18 | 73 | |
| | *Culottes de peau* | 460 | | | 460 | |
| | Bearskins | | 49 | 39 | 88 | |
| 16ᵉ Dragon | *Habits* | 461 | 100 | | 561 | In lieu of *culottes de peau*, *pantalons d'écurie* made in broadcloth reinforced with leather are used. |
| | *Surtouts* | 120 | 569 | | 689 | |
| | *Gilets en drap* | 500 | 72 | | 572 | |
| | *Gilets d'écurie* | | 336 | | 336 | |
| | *Culottes de peau* | 159 | | | 159 | |
| | Bearskins | The regiment has none | | | | |
| 17ᵉ Dragon | *Habits* | 251 | | | 251 | For immediate needs the regiment requires 81 *surtouts*, 138 *gilets d'écurie*, 161 *manteaux*, 173 pairs of *culottes de peau*, 11 bearskins, 130 pairs of gauntlets, 264 pairs of boots. |
| | *Surtouts* | 428 | 218 | | 646 | |
| | *Gilets en drap* | 501 | | | 501 | |
| | *Gilets d'écurie* | 324 | 265 | | 589 | |
| | *Culottes de peau* | 324 | 230 | | 554 | |
| | Bearskins | 82 | 11 | | 89 | |

| Regiment | Item | In good repair | In need of repair | To be replaced | Total | Observations |
|---|---|---|---|---|---|---|
| 18ᵉ *Dragons* | *Habits* | The regiment has none | | | | In lieu of *culottes de peau*, *pantalons d'écurie* made in broadcloth reinforced with leather are used. The *gibernes* and belts are all missing. |
| | *Surtouts* | 600 | | 165 | 765 | |
| | *Gilets en drap* | The regiment has none | | | | |
| | *Gilets d'écurie* | 400 | | 385 | 765 | |
| | *Culottes de peau* | The regiment has none | | | | |
| | Bearskins | | | | | |
| 19ᵉ *Dragons* | *Habits* | The regiment has none | | | | For immediate needs the regiment requires 35 *surtouts*, 65 *manteaux*, 48 pairs of stable trousers. In lieu of *culottes de peau*, *pantalons d'écurie* made in broadcloth reinforced with leather are used. |
| | *Surtouts* | 469 | | 250 | 719 | |
| | *Gilets en drap* | The regiment has none | | | | |
| | *Gilets d'écurie* | | | | | |
| | *Culottes de peau* | | | | | |
| | Bearskins | 69 | | 31 | 100 | |
| 20ᵉ *Dragon* | *Habits* | 509 | 71 | 179 | 759 | To complete the regiments clothing, there is needed 213 *vestes*, 592 *surtouts*, 663 *gilets d'écurie*, 174 helmets, 130 *manteaux*, 408 pairs of *culottes de peau*, 171 sabre belts, 255 *gibernes* and belts. Missing are 58 bayonets, 8 dragoon muskets, 225 pistols and 253 sabres are to be written off. |
| | *Surtouts* | 31 | 59 | 161 | 251 | |
| | *Gilets en drap* | 470 | | 48 | 518 | |
| | *Gilets d'écurie* | | 20 | 7 | 27 | |
| | *Culottes de peau* | 408 | 30 | 68 | 506 | |
| | Bearskins | 80 | 6 | 20 | 106 | |
| 21ᵉ *Dragon* | *Habits* | The regiment has none | | | | 666 plumes are in use. |
| | *Surtouts* | 566 | 100 | | 666 | |
| | *Gilets en drap* | 460 | 206 | | 666 | |
| | *Gilets d'écurie* | 480 | 186 | | 443 | |
| | *Culottes de peau* | | 595 | | 595 | |
| | Bearskins | The regiment has none | | | | |
| 22ᵉ *Dragon* | *Habits* | The regiment has none | | | | The regiment is in the worst condition imaginable. The uniforms and equipment are missing or entirely need replacing. Many saddles are broken. |
| | *Surtouts* | 285 | | 325 | 693 | |
| | *Gilets en drap* | The regiment has none | | | | |
| | *Gilets d'écurie* | | | | | |
| | *Culottes de peau* | 644 | | | 644 | |
| | Bearskins | 30 | | 74 | 94 | |

## Change and Change Again   23

| Regiment | Item | In good repair | In need of repair | To be replaced | Total | Observations |
|---|---|---|---|---|---|---|
| 23ᵉ *Dragons* | *Habits* | The regiment has none ||| | The regiment is in the worst condition imaginable. The uniforms and equipment are missing or need entirely replacing. Many saddles are broken. |
| | *Surtouts* | 582 | | 111 | 692 | |
| | *Gilets en drap* | The regiment has none ||| | |
| | *Gilets d'écurie* | 220 | | 172 | 392 | |
| | *Culottes de peau* | 690 | | 8 | 698 | |
| | Bearskins | 80 | | 20 | 100 | |
| 26ᵉ *Dragon* | *Habit* | 402 | 81 | 54 | 537 | Needed to complete the clothing of the regiment are 317 *habits*, 298 *vestes*, 402 *surtouts*, 500 *gilets d'écurie*, 87 *casques*, 589 pairs of *culottes de peau*. The regiment has refused to receive items that are badly made. Also missing are 192 sabre belts, 133 *gibernes* and belts, 206 pairs of boots, 83 *portemanteaux*, 131 bayonets. In lieu of *culottes de peau*, *pantalons d'écurie* made in broadcloth reinforced with leather are used. |
| | *Surtout* | 156 | 242 | 391 | 789 | |
| | *Gilets en drap* | 458 | 44 | 64 | 566 | |
| | *Gilets d'écurie* | The regiment has none ||| | |
| | *Culottes de peau* | 174 | 37 | 106 | 317 | |
| | Bearskins | 94 | | | 94 | |
| 27ᵉ *Dragons* | *Habits* | 250 | | | 250 | For immediate needs the regiment requires 524 *habits*, 86 *surtouts*, 274 *vestes*, 113 *gilets d'écurie*, 148 *manteaux*, 774 pairs of *culottes de peau*, 624 pairs of gauntlets, 95 pairs of boots. The regiment has *pantalons d'écurie* made from drap reinforced with leather. It has 641 dragoon muskets, and 110 infantry muskets in good condition. In lieu of *culottes de peau*, *pantalons d'écurie* made in broadcloth reinforced with leather are used. |
| | *Surtouts* | 375 | | 313 | 688 | |
| | *Gilets en drap* | 500 | | | 500 | |
| | *Gilets d'écurie* | 477 | | 184 | 661 | |
| | *Culottes de peau* | The regiment has none ||| | |
| | Bearskins | 89 | | 3 | 92 | |

At the end of the 1807 the dragoon regiments must have looked incredibly shabby with a huge variety of what was considered 'uniform'. We can see that not every man had a *habit* and a *surtout*, it was a case of either or. Again, not every man had a *gilet d'écurie*, and the most common form of legwear were *pantalons à cheval*, copied directly from the dress of the light cavalry. This was a practical solution to the problem of the *culottes de peau* being almost useless on campaign: in the summer they are hot and sweaty, in the winter and rain they get water-logged, cold and heavy, and they take 'an age' to dry out if the leather and stitching is not to be damaged. These grievances would occur again and again over the course of the Empire about these items. Thus, colonels took a pragmatic approach to give their men a practical and hard-wearing type of legwear. We imagine that every regiment had its men with feather plumes: largely based on the artwork of Aaron Martinet, who gives each regiment such an ornament in his plates. However, the reality seems to have been that plumes were worn very infrequently, and not every elite company had bearskins. Based on this wide-ranging inspection, the dragoons presented a far from uniform, and regulation, image on parade at the end of almost three years' active service.

Confirming the rather shabby appearance of the dragoons on active service, the orders for General La Houssaye provide a wealth of details of how a division approached issues of resupply. From the orders, we know in October 1807 red broadcloth was purchased to make repairs on the sheepskin *schabraques* across the division (17e, 18e, 19e and 27e regiments) – presumably the festoon on the edging. Yet these items in theory had been abolished in 1802: we assume these items had been issued from captured stocks of Prussian equipment. The only unit in the division with sheepskin *schabraques* according to the regiment's archive was the 18e, which in 1808 had 46 *schabraques*, all obtained after summer 1805.[23] At the end of the same month, La Houssaye was informed that the saddles of the 19e regiment were in a very bad state of repair.[24]

The same archive document gives us some very interesting details concerning the appearance of regiments in the division. On 21 October 1807, General La Houssaye sent the following memorandum to his colonels:

> I want the regiments under my command to adopt for use on foot as well as when mounted, the sabre worn bandolier style. Aside from the obvious advantages that this has over wearing it as a waistbelt, it will make things much easier for a dragoon when he has to dismount and take up duties on foot … give me your opinions on this idea which is already in practice with some two divisions of dragoons in the army.[25]

And on the 26th of the same month he ordered: 'It is decided that regiments will wear the sabre belt bandolier style mounted as well on foot.'[26] It seems in the division, there was a great deal of laxity towards dress.

In the 17e *Dragons*, the *culottes de peau* had been replaced with beige broadcloth *pantalons*, which were 'were so baggy, that the regimental tailors had to pleat them at the knees' to enable them to be worn under the boots, and moreover their horses were always overloaded with odd items of equipment, Houssaye remarked. Houssaye added that when mounted he noted that many, 'dragoons wear their helmets tilted backwards with the chin-straps raised on the peak [...] non-regulation *porte-manteaux* are in service and various other items are slung from the saddle.'

For the 18e *Dragons*, Houssaye tells us the 'boots were cut very short, and did not reach the back of the knee' and that 'the plume was always worn in the wrong place' but alas does not say where, possibly the right side of the helmet not the left.

Further, Houssaye tells us the 19e carried their *porte-manteaux* in a non-regulation style and wore trouses made from brown broadcloth and neck cloths of varying colours rather than the regulation stock.

The best regiment in the division was the 27e, it seems, who came in for praise because they wore the correct uniform and were generally well turned out except for their *porte-manteaux*, which were in a bad state of repair.

Clearly, a lot of improvised clothing had been taken into use since the regiments had left for campaign two years or more earlier. A document of 17 September 1807 allowed trumpeters white epaulettes and helmet *criniere* to conform to the other divisions of dragoons.[27] Clearly, the white *criniere* was not uniform until, we assume, 1808, and the division had not had these items in earlier campaigns.

## 1810 Regulation

Nothing further was issued by the War Ministry concerning uniforms until March 1810. In order to make the cost of equipping a dragoon cheaper, the *surtout* was eliminated from use and a new *habit* was designed that had considerably shorter tails than before, in essence presaging the changes wrought by the Bardin regulations:[28]

| Item | Cloth | Old Specification | New Specification 1810 |
|---|---|---|---|
| *Habit* | Green broadcloth | 2m 08 | 1m 52 |
| | Facing colour serge | 3m 26 | 2m 12 |
| | Facing colour broadcloth | 0m 23 | 0m 26 |
| | Linen | 0m 89 | 1m 09 |
| | Large buttons | 11 | 11 |
| | Small buttons | 22 | 22 |
| *Surtout* | Green broadcloth | 1m 73 | This garment removed from service in 1810 |
| | Facing colour serge | 3m 26 | |
| | Linen | 0m 89 | |
| | Large buttons | 10 | |
| | Small buttons | 6 | |
| Stable coat | Green broadcloth | This garment was previously made from the old *surtouts*. No tariff exists for its production. | 1m 09 |
| | Linen | | 1m 30 |
| | Small buttons | | 24 |

| Item | Cloth | Old Specification | New Specification 1810 |
|---|---|---|---|
| *Veste* | White broadcloth | 1m 19 | 1m 15 |
| | White serge | 2m 52 | |
| | Linen | 0m 29 | 1m 40 |
| | Small buttons | 12 | 12 |
| *Bonnet de police* | Green broadcloth | Materials were previously recovered from the old clothing. No tariff exists for its production | 0m 25 |
| | Linen | | 0m 12 |
| *Manteaux* | *Blanc picque de bleu* broadcloth | 4m 75 | 4m 75 |
| | Serge | 1m 48 | 1m 47 |
| *Housses et Chaperons* | Green broadcloth | 0m 59 | 0m 59 |
| | 45mm wide white worsted lace | 5m 95 | 5m 95 |
| *Porte-manteaux* | Green tricot | 1m 34 | 1m 34 |
| | *Treillis* | 1m 73 | 1m 73 |
| | Leather | | 0m 2 |
| | 27 mm wide white worsted lace | 2m 97 | 1m 34 |

From the tariff, we see the white *gilet* that formerly had serge lining to the body and a small amount of linen for the button stands and sleeves, became entirely lined in linen – no doubt as linen was far cheaper than serge. The stable coat is a bit of an enigma as officially until 1809 it had no cloth allowed for it – this had been made by simply cutting the tails off the old *surtout*, according to the notes in Les Gupil. The notes to the tariff also state that the *manteaux* had the collar and *rotonde* – shoulder cape – lined in the same cloth as the body and that the serge was used to line the body.

Nothing further was issued by the War Ministry until 1811. In February, the *habit* and stable coat had to last three years rather than two as a matter of economy.[29] Economy was at the forefront of War Ministry thinking as in March, as a cost-cutting measure, the *habit* was to cost no more than a *surtout* and the *porte-manteaux* were to be reduced in dimensions and to contain the barest of essential items.[30] After adopting this stopgap measure, a commission set to work to examine the dress of the army in detail. Less than six weeks after being convened, the commission reported to Marshal Berthier on 30 April 1811:

> the commission has recognised that the line infantry's uniform habit is too tight and not large enough in the arms; the habit is too short and leaves the loins and upper hips uncovered, the pockets are too small and only allow the soldier to have access to them with great difficulty. Consequently, the habits fit badly and its general appearance is one of not clothing the soldier in a decent manner. Under the old specifications, a jacket used 1m71 worth of broadcloth for the body. The

directive of 9 February 1810 reduced that amount to 1m34. The materials used for these models were reduced further to 1m18. Both these reductions represent a loss of 51cm or two-thirds …

With regards to the details of construction, the lapels are expensive and absolutely useless for their intended purpose since it is impossible for the soldier to close them across the chest. What is needed is:

> that the revers are stitched directly to the habit in order to preserve uniform distinctions.
> to adopt squared revers, that are cut lower to cover the top of the pantalons.
> to get rid of the revers, by buttoning up the habit down the centre.

Furthermore, the neckline of the habit is too low, due to a design issue. The collar itself is not high enough, which is detrimental to the health of the soldier because of his short hair. The lining of the habit, which is made from linen, should be cut squarely to the top of the pockets and covered by a serge lining, in order to make it more durable … The madder red colour of the cuffs is often inconsistent, scarlet red should be preferred. The culottes are lined with linen which makes them unbearably hot during the marches in the summer and difficult to keep clean. The lining of the culotte should be abolished and replaced by underwear. The sleeves of the capote seem to be a little narrow and a little too short.

The light infantry habit has the same disadvantages as the one for the line infantry. That is to say that it is too short and too tight … The neckline is also too shallow, the tails should be lined with serge as those lined with bay are chafed easily, which immediately gives the habit a ragged look. The use of *pantalons* de tricot in the light infantry has allowed some saving to be made and the extra cloth has been used on the habits to line the tails with wool broadcloth which looks better and needs less maintenance.

Cavalry: the same general observations as those regarding the line and light infantry. This leads us to the conclusion that it is crucial to adopt a new model of uniform that will give the soldier greater freedom in his movements and dress him well. Habits of a larger size, cut longer and with squared revers descending over the waistband of the *pantalons* will satisfy these criteria and will better protect the soldier's health. With regards to certain proposed changes, it will not be permissible to allow them without the inconvenience of touching upon the uniform distinctions that certain units have benefitted from for a long time now.[31]

On the strength of the report, Berthier ordered General Antoine Bourcier, Inspector General of Cavalry, in July 1811 to head a new commission that was tasked by the Minister of War to determine a new uniform for all branches of the army. General Sorbier represented the artillery; Colonel Dautancourt the cavalry; Major Bardin the infantry, who also acted as secretary; and Intendant General Dufour represented the administration and staff.[32] The commission worked with great speed, and any attempt to hinder or obstruct the work largely failed once the initial idea to also reclothe the Imperial Guard had been dropped. Imperial Livery was actually not part of Bardin, and had been introduced to the army on 15 May 1811 when the War Ministry authorised a trumpeter's *habit* to have wool lace 24mm wide, and required 15m 30 of lace of a model yet to be determined.[33] Something more formal about the dress of the trumpeters was enacted with the decree of 30 December 1811:

1. The habits of drummers and trumpeters were to be laced with 2m 70 of lace 27mm wide, to be sewn on to the habit conforming to the decree of 1 October 1786.
2. The habits of drum majors, trumpet majors and master musicians are to be no longer laced in gold or silver; the drum majors and trumpet majors will not be distinguished, but the master musicians will be by a double row of silver lace 22mm wide at the cuff, and the musicians by a single row in the same place.

The body of the habit will be green. The lining of the habit, the cuffs, the revers, the collar, veste or gilet, the culotte or pantalons will retain the colours of their corps and are not to be affected by these changes. No further changes to the remainder of the uniform, such as pompoms, retroussis etc. are to be made.[34]

Major Bardin notes that the 1811 decree was not enforced rigorously.[35]

On 2 January 1812, the Minister of War wrote to Napoléon informing him that he had received the conclusions of the commission appointed to review changes in the army's uniforms.[36] The Emperor, seemingly in agreement with the proposed new uniform regulations, asked the Ministry of War to draft a decree, which he signed on 19 January 1812 and a second decree of 7 February was issued that concerned the mounted troops for implementation by February 1813.

# Chapter 3
# Bardin Regulation

Donated by Madam Millot in 1901 to the *Musée de l'Armée* is Major Bardin's working copy of the manuscript. The text, after being presented to the Emperor, went through many edits, and it is filled with notes, comments and major changes to the regulations in April 1813. We have used Bardin's own notes as the basis for our work. We have endeavoured to present the text as it is written down by Bardin, including corrections and annotations. Where words are struck out in the text we have done so, ~~comment~~; where words are added in later, we have used superscript, <sup>comment</sup>; where Bardin has added in notes, we have italicised these words, *comment*. The heavy redaction appears to date from April 1813. In some places he adds notes with a date, simply signed Bdn. It is hard to untangle the various edits to recover the original intention of Bardin, as in many places he pasted new sheets of paper over the original text. The text is therefore presented in its final form from April 1813, warts and all.

In theory, the An X and 1810 regulation was swept away in 1812. About the clothing for the other ranks, the regulations state:

### Art 1. Clothing

1019. The clothing of the sous-officiers and dragoons will comprise ~~a habit-veste in broadcloth, a gilet without sleeves in broadcloth, a veste d'écurie in green tricot, a pair of culotte de peau, a pair of Surculotte, pair of pantalon de treillis, a manteau a manche.~~ *of the prescribed general dispositions Viz No. 297*

1020. The *habit* is cut from dark green broadcloth <sup>see table of uniforms No. 1084</sup> and conform to the general model no. 4 ~~except that there will be a piping of the distinctive colour to the epaulettes, to the front and pockets. The piping to the cuff flaps, the cuff facings and to the collar is green. The pockets, revers are figured in the distinctive colour Viz the table of uniforms No. 1084.~~ The pocket flaps are to conform to the engraving no. 1021 and are figured with piping except where they attach to the habit. They conform to the dimensions of the retroussis and are to be inset 20mm from each extremity. Each pocket is 120mm at its deepest point, the top edge is placed parallel to the bottom of the habit, and is 140mm at the narrowest part; three buttons are place in each of the points 20mm from the piping, From the extremity of one point to another is 140mm, piping included; the depth of the pocket in the middle is 20mm greater than those on the outside. The piping does continue on to the exterior edges of the pocket which mirror the form of the retroussis by a distance of 15 to 20mm. The flap is 55mm deep at the shallowest part. The vertical pockets conform to the model Viz. No. 1240. <sup>The buttons are of the colour indicated in table No. 1087.</sup>

1022. The *gilet* has no sleeves and conforms to the general model Viz. No. 301. The buttons are of the colour indicated in table No. 1087.

1023. The *veste d'écurie* is made from green tricot and will conform to the general model No. 302.

1024. The breeches are made from sheep or doe hide, and conform to the general model. No.303.

1025. The *pantalon de treillis* will conform to the general model No. 311.

1026. The manteau will be made from blanc picque de bleu broadcloth and will conform to the general model Viz. No. 313.

**Art 2. Headdress**
1027. The headdress of the *sous-officiers* and dragoons will consist of a helmet, of the dimensions given and a *bonnet de police* in green broadcloth of the general model; Viz. No. 45.

1028. The helmet is comprised of the *calotte* or *bomb* in copper, the *cimier* [crest] the *criniere* and the turban see the engraved design No. 1028.

1029. The *bomb* is the same as for the light horse [illegible]. The chinscales will conform to the engraved design No. 1029.

1030. The *cimier* is the same as the light horse [illegible] and will conform to the engraving No.1030. The flanks are the same as those of the light horse except that it is joined by three bolts and not two.

1031. The *criniere* is the same as for the *cuirassier*.

1032. The *bonnet de police* is made from green broadcloth and is made according to the general model (Viz. 45).

**Art 3. Distinctive Marks**
1033. The distinctive marks for the *sous-officiers* and corporals will conform to the general dispositions Viz. No. 335 to 337.

1034. The bonnets de police are of the regiment.

1035. [the first part of this section is lost or has been totally redacted] ~~The trumpeters may wear in the helmet a criniere in white horse hair.~~

For the regiments with horizontal pockets, the lace will follow the piping, at each of the three buttons will be a button loop of lace, folded back and extending into the points. The button loop is 110mm long. The middle point is 95mm, that of the outside edge is 80mm. The lace will figure the buttons at the small of the back to the same height as the button loops.

1036. The distinctions of the elite companies will be an aigrette and epaulettes. They will wear a helmet like the other dragoons.

### Art 4. Armament and Equipment
1037. The armament of the corporals and dragoons will comprise a sabre, a musket with bayonet and a pistol. The sergeants, fourriers, trumpeters and farriers will be armed with two pistols and will not carry the musket. Their arms will be of the regulation model and will be issued from the arsenals of the Empire.

1038. The equipment of the sous-officiers and dragoons will be the same as the carabiniers; however, the buff work will be whitened and will lack the lace edging. Their boots will be à l'écuyère and not the bottes fortes used by the carabiniers. There will be carried from the saddle in lieu of a pistol a hatchet or cycle as described later.

### Art 5. Petit Equipement
1060. The petit équipement of the dragoons ~~will comprise a musette, a pair of black gaiters, three shirts, two black stocks, three rabats, a handkerchief,~~ [illegible] ~~a pair of manchettes du botte~~ will be as for the general dispositions No. 373.

### Art 6. Harness
1061. The harness of the dragoons will be the same as for the carabiniers and cuirassiers with the following exceptions.

1062. The seat of the saddle will be 20mm smaller, as will be the panels.

1063. The housse is made from green broadcloth, and will be 80mm less in the measurement of width and length. The number of saddles that carry a pistol is indicated by the decree of the minister of war; there will be on the left side a font [pistol holster ed] and on the right a case for the tool; the font and tool case are attached to a joining strap. The axe case is made from 'cuir de hongre [alum tanned leather]'.[1]

Under Bardin, dragoons adopted the same *habit* as the line infantry. The regulation further states that the *gilet*s were to be cut in the same form as the infantry, but with no sleeves, the *gilet d'écurie* to pattern No. 302 [the generic cavalry pattern], and to be cut so as to be able to be worn over the *gilet*.[2] The *gilets, gilets d'écurie*, legwear, boots, horse equipment, *bonnets de police* and *manteaux* were all the same design as for the *cuirassiers*, with dragoon green replacing blue in all respects. In the first state of Bardin, we are led to believe the trumpeters wore the same *habit* as the other ranks, with but Imperial livery to collar, cuffs, pockets, tails, taille and around the *revers*. This uniform was abolished to issue a single uniform coat for all drummers, voltigeur hornists and trumpeters in April 1813.[3] The clothing tariff for the dragoons in 1812 was as follows:[4]

| Item | Cloth | 1812 |
| --- | --- | --- |
| *Habit* | Green broadcloth | 1m 49 |
| | Serge | 1m 03 |
| | Facing cloth | 0m 37 |
| | Linen | 1m 44 |
| | Large buttons | 8 |
| | Small buttons | 22 |
| *Surculotte* | Grey broadcloth | 0m 93 |
| | Linen | 0m 30 |
| | Bone buttons | 24 |
| *Gilet d'écurie* | Green broadcloth | |
| | Green tricot | 1m 81 |
| | Linen | 1m 30 |
| | Small buttons | 16 |
| *Veste* | White broadcloth | 1m 15 |
| | White serge | 0m 66 |
| | Linen | 0m 70 |
| | Small buttons | 10 |
| *Bonnet de police* | Green broadcloth | 0m 28 |
| | Facing cloth | 0m 02 |
| | Linen | 0m 21 |
| *Manteaux* | *Blanc picque de bleu* broadcloth | 5m 35 |
| | Facing colour serge | 1m 47 |
| *Housses et Chaperons* | Green broadcloth | 0m 59 |
| | 45mm wide white worsted lace | 4m |
| *Porte-manteaux* | Green tricot | 1m 34 |
| | *Treillis* | 1m 73 |
| | Leather | 0m 2 |
| | 27mm wide white worsted lace | 1m 34 |

When we compare the 1812 tariff with that of 1810, we see just 2cm of cloth difference between the 1810 and 1812 regulation, which proves the 1810 *habit* was short tailed.

*Officers*
The dress of the officers was not forgotten either:

**Section 8: The clothing and headdress of the officers of cavalry of all arms.**
**Art 1. Clothing**
419. The clothing of the officers of carabiniers, cuirassiers, dragoons, artillery engineer and equipment train will comprise a habit, a gilet, a frac, a manteau, pair of culottes de peau made from whitened deer hide and a pair of gauntlets. They may also be allowed a redingote, a pair of surculotte and a pair of breeches in white broadcloth. The officers of carabiniers and cuirassiers will wear their habit under the defensive armour of their arm.

421. The habit of the officer's dragoons conforms to that of their arm.

423. The surculotte are made from grey broadcloth and are made in the same for as for the troop, except the cloth is superfine.[5]

Specific text for the dragoons were also prepared: the original text is lost and we have Bardin's later version glued over the top of the original text:

**Section 4: Dragoons**
**Art 7. Clothing and equipment of the Officers of dragoons**
1073. The clothing of the officers of dragoons will conform to the general dispositions Viz. 419. The habit is made from superfine green broadcloth and the pockets be they vertical or horizontal are in the form of the regiment. The habits will take the same form and cut as those of the officers of the infantry Viz. No. 199. The frac and the manteau are in green broadcloth and will be made according to the details Viz No. 423 and later.

1074. The headdress of the officers will conform to the general dispositions Viz. No. 439. The helmet is that of the troops except that it is gilded and the turban is covered in tiger skin. The chapeau and bonnet de police are detailed also in the general dispositions for the cavalry Viz. No. 447 to 450.

1075. The distinctive marks of the officers will conform to the general dispositions Viz. No. 450. The epaulettes, sword knot, sabre knot will be in silver and conform the details No. 451 to 453.

1076. The footwear of the officers will conform to the general dispositions Viz. No. 454 to 457.

1077. The armament of the officers of dragoons will conform to that prescribed by the general dispositions No. 459. The sabre will conform to the following descriptions.

1078. The sabre of the officers of dragoons will be the same as the officers of the carabiniers with the following differences: the hilt will conform to engraving 1076 and will not carry a grenade. The blade will only be 890mm long.

1079. The equipment of the officers will conform precisely to the general dispositions No. 465 to 470. The waistbelt buckle will be in gilded copper; it will be 10mm large and the corners will be chamfered; all other distinctions will conform to the engraved designed No. 1079.

1080. The harness of the officers will be the same as the dragoons, and will comprise a housse and chaperons, a curb bridle, a snaffle bridle.

1081. The saddle will be of exactly the same form and dimensions as the troop. It will be covered in green broadcloth and green lace ~~exactly the same as employed on the saddle of the officers of carabiniers. Viz. 959.~~ The housse and chaperons are in green broadcloth and in the same form, border and lace and of the dimensions fixed in No 977. All parts of the saddle, curb bridle, snaffle bridle, head collar will be exactly as described for the troops except that the buckles and bossettes are in copper that is silvered and will have the number of the regiment in the same manner as the uniform buttons.

1082. The officers of dragoons are authorised to use on route marches and undress a housse and chaperons in green broadcloth laced in green mohair Cul-de-dé lace 40mm wide for all ranks.[6]

The latter point is of interest, as most artists depict officers with black sheepskin *schabraques*, which is clearly an error.

### Bardin changes

Despite the Bardin decree being signed off in February 1812, no archive document could be located in 2023 that authorised the production of Bardin-regulation clothing. The only document that mentions Bardin with any certainty is the decree of 17 September 1812, which is frustratingly vague: it makes no mention of clothing, but does mention the adoption of trumpeters' lace, grenadiers' scarlet epaulettes and scarlet *aigrette* for the elite company, and a new-pattern helmet with a turban made from seal skin to be 101mm tall, and to be ornamented with a pompom in company colours.[7] On 30 August cloth *chaperons* were officially supressed in favour of sheepskin *schabraques*, and gaiters for stable duties were to be made from black worsted and not broadcloth. A new *manteau-capote* was authorised from 18 April 1813.[8] Realising regiments had hundreds of pairs of *chaperons* in stores, a decree of 10 July 1813 allowed both cloth *chaperons* and sheepskin *schabraques,* along with *housses* of the old and new model.[9] We are left to wonder how and when regimental colonels were informed about the new uniform model.

When the Bourbon monarchy was restored to power in 1814, they inherited a bankrupt and demoralised country, fatigued after almost 25 years of fighting. The army was ill equipped and under-strength. Some regiments were little more than a battalion or squadron strong. The army was to be consolidated around a hardcore nucleus of veterans.

The Royal decree of 12 May 1814 disbanded the Imperial Army.[10]

All three arms were culled. Only the senior regiments of cavalry and infantry were to be taken into the new Royal Army. The Royal decree of 12 May 1814 further declared that only the senior regiments of cavalry and infantry were to be taken into the new Royal Army. The cavalry was reduced from 110 regiments to 56. The 21$^e$ to 30$^e$ regiments were to be disbanded.[11]

The time of peace following the restoration allowed 'shakedown' inspections of the army to be made, and serious consideration given to new uniform regulations. To do so a committee of senior cavalry officers was convened, overseen by General of Division *Comte* de Saint Germain.

The first issue raised by the committee was quality control and standard of workmanship and materials used. The committee agreed that the use of private contractors to clothe and equip the army was a total failure: low-grade workmanship using 'cheap substandard materials' was harmful to the army, and the contractors had been able to inflate prices to maximise their profit, and had put many regiments into debt. Hence forward, everything would be made in the regimental workshops using regulated materials. In order to ensure standards were met, inspectors of review would check the materials and quality of workmanship rather than colonels. Instead of *culottes de peau*, they were to be replaced by *pantalons en drap* i.e., broadcloth. General *Comte* de Saint Germain proposed that the *dragons* were to adopt white broadcloth riding trousers that should be worn on parade, with long grey trousers for campaign use, 'to be worn outside the new model of boots, which should no longer have a knee piece'. The knee guards – *manchettes du botte* – were to be suppressed, and the money saved from their production be carried over to produce the *pantalons en drap*. Next up, the committee ordered that for the heavy cavalry, the *manteau*, which had formally been folded on the *porte-manteau*, was now to be carried at the front of the saddle. The broadcloth *housse* was to be abolished, and a sheepskin *schabraque* like the light cavalry used, which totally covered the saddle and saddle blanket, was to be adopted, along with the round *porte-manteau*. The last point the committee made was to officially authorise 'pockets to be made in the sheepskins to access the pistols': this is a very common-sense idea as it is on practical experience almost totally impossible to get to the pistols under the sheepskin! The committee's recommendations were signed off on 12 January 1815 by *Comte* Victor Latour-Maubourg.[12]

This was codified in the decree of 8 February 1815, stating that *dragon* clothing and equipment was to be:[13]

| | |
|---|---|
| Cloth for lining 104cm wide | 1fr 40 |
| Line for *pantalons* and *caleçons*, 89cm wide | 1fr 65 |
| Large buttons | 40 centimes a dozen |
| Small buttons | 24 centimes a dozen |
| Bone buttons | 6 centimes a dozen |

### Lace
| | |
|---|---|
| Silver for *sous-officiers* | 5fr 60 |
| In wool for corporals and chevrons | 55 centimes |
| In thread 28mm | 30 centimes |
| Livery for Trumpeters No. 1 | 90 centimes |
| Livery for Trumpeters No. 2 | 90 centimes |

### Epaulettes
| | |
|---|---|
| For adjutants | 25fr |
| Scarlet for grenadier | 3fr 40 |
| Epaulettes and *aiguillettes* for *régiment du Roi* | 5fr |
| Leather for breeches | 9fr 50 |
| Hooks and eyes | 10 centimes |
| Braces | 60 centimes |

### Labour cost
| | |
|---|---|
| *Habit-veste* | 2fr 45 |
| *Habit-veste* for trumpeters | 8fr 50 |
| *Gilet sans manche* | 1fr |
| *Gilet d'écurie* | 1fr 30 |
| *Bonnet de police* | 60 centimes |
| Sleeved cloak with hook and eye | 2f 80 |
| *Porte-manteau* with buckles and straps | 2f 50 |
| *Surculotte* with buckles | 1fr |
| *Culottes de Peau* | 3fr |
| *Pantalon du treillis dit d'écurie* | 80 centimes |

### Headdress
| | |
|---|---|
| Helmet | 11fr 75 |
| Pompom | 95 centimes |
| Scarlet *Aigrette* for Grenadiers | 3fr 50 |
| White plume and cover for *régiment du Roi* | 2fr |

For equipment, the regulations stated that:[14]

| | |
|---|---|
| Waistbelts with hook and bayonet frog | 7fr25 |
| *Giberne* | 4fr 55 |
| *Porte-giberne* | 5fr 10 |
| Musket sling and copper button | 1fr 15 |
| Boots and spurs | 24f |
| Gauntlets | 4fr 5 |
| Sword knot | 1fr |
| Trumpet with cords | 25fr 98 |

The regulations were framed on the Bardin regulation of 1812. It was the first time that the army had had a chance to be totally re-equipped with new-pattern clothing and equipment, although some regiments clung onto the old-style *habits*, and other idiosyncrasies. A huge reclothing programme began in spring 1815. The decree of 23 April 1814 ordered that all Imperial iconography was to be removed from use. Trumpeters were to be dressed in blue; their *habits* adorned with the King's Livery. *Fleur-de-lys* were to replace grenades, eagles or other devices on uniforms. The decree also outlined that any clothing not made to the regulation of 1812 was to be replaced forthwith.[15]

Any chance of rolling out the new regulation came to a juddering halt with Napoléon's return. The decree of 1 May reintroduced Imperial Livery for trumpeters and removal of Royalist iconography.[16]

How far the changeover was completed by the time Waterloo was lost is impossible to say. Certainly, the army in the 100 days' campaign would have presented a far from uniform appearance, with Royalist Livery worn side by side with brand-new Imperial Livery.

# Chapter 4

# Regulations in Practice

In order to assess how the various regulations were implemented, what follows is an overview of the paper archive for all 24 regiments of dragoons. The archives of some regiments are more complete than others, but overall, it does allow us to answer specific questions about the dress of the dragoons during the First Empire.

## 1ᵉ *Dragons*

Created in 1656, it was known as the *Dragons Etranger du Roi* as it was raised in Germany. It became the 1ᵉ *Dragons* in 1792. Inspected on 1 March 1802, the reviewing officer, General Canclaux, remarked that 'the regiment's buff work was all of the chasseur pattern and the regiment was armed with light cavalry carbines'. The regiment also had 'many sabres to be exchanged for the dragoon pattern'. We wonder as to how the regiment became so

Elite company trooper of the 1ᵉ *Dragons* from a plate by Parisian artist Aaron Martinet.

Centre company trooper of the 1ᵉ *Dragons* by Martinet.

## Regulations in Practice

Centre company trooper of the 1ᵉ *Dragons* in 1808. The regiment's paper archive confirms that on campaign the troopers wore light cavalry-style *pantalons à cheval*. (Collection KM)

*Sapeur* of the 1ᵉ *Dragons* in a gauche painting by an artist known as 'Otto' executed sometime in 1808. No *sapeurs* were present at the December 1807 inspection, so we assume they were added to the regiment in new year 1808. (Collection KM)

Trumpeter of the 1ᵉ *Dragons* c.1805. This image by Ernest Fort is based on an undoubtedly original image of Joseph Dupuy, an elite company trumpeter of the regiment. The image has also been copied by Boisselier and Rousselot, giving a helmet and white epaulettes. The original image is lost. Presumably by 1808 the trumpeters wore a reversed colour *habit* with white lace.

equipped! No man had a *habit*, but 534 *surtouts* were in use along with 55 white *vestes*. The men only had their stable trousers for legwear, noted as being light cavalry style pantalons a cheval. In addition, 505 stable coats were in use, 235 *manteaux*, 469 helmets and 435 *bonnets de police*. For the horses, 361 *housses* were in use, 65 pairs of cloth *chaperons* and 332 sheepskin *demi-schabraque*. General Canclaux authorised the immediate production of 243 *habits*, 300 *surtouts*, 111 *manteaux*, 243 *gilets*, 243 stable coats, 874 pairs of *culottes de peau*, 582 pairs of stable trousers, 111 helmets, and 394 *bonnets de police*. The regiment's leather work was, despite being the wrong model, in good condition and only 73 *gibernes* with belts, sabre belts, sword knots and other items were authorised for production, along with 111 *porte-manteaux* and 205 pairs of boots. He also authorised the purchase of 57 saddles, 113 saddle blankets, 183 *housses* and 183 pairs of *chaperons*. For the saddles, 28kg of best-quality leather was purchased, 20 shoulders of buff to make the belt part of the sabre belts – presumably the light cavalry slings were retained or were new slings made – and also to make the straps needed to carry the dragoon musket off the saddle.[1]

In an undated letter, Canclaux sent a report to the War Ministry stating that the regiment had 514 men and 311 horses. The regiment needed 103 men to bring it up to strength. Canclaux ordered the colonel to send a list of 66 names to him for the men to form the elite company and to inform the War Ministry of the officers sent to the company. He authorised furthermore 40 horses were to be purchased to mount the elite company.[2]

Inspected on 11 October 1804, the regiment mustered 590 other ranks. The men were wearing 843 *habits*, 946 *surtouts*

A trooper of the 7ᵉ *Cuirassiers*, accompanied by a centre company trooper and trumpeter of the 1ᵉ *Dragons* as observed in 1808. (*Collection KM*)

and the elite company had 107 bearskins. We note a huge shortfall in harness; 404 *housses* and 296 pairs of *chaperons* for 590 horses, which had just 337 saddles! The *manteaux* the inspector noted were made from *blanc picque de bleu* broadcloth.[3] This cloth was made from a mix of 7 white threads to 1 blue, giving a very light shade of blue.

When reviewed on 7 August 1805, since the previous inspection 181 *habits* had been made, and 707 pairs of *culottes de peau* and 150 helmets had been purchased. Furthermore, 250 pairs of boots, 530 *housses* and 700 sets of *chaperons* now existed. The men were issued 807 dragoon muskets and 1,011 pairs of pistols, 830 sabres and, for some odd reason, 844 bayonets.[4]

Inspected on 30 October 1807, 809 *habits* and 1,033 *surtouts* were in service, while the elite company had 91 bearskins. A mix of legwear was in use: 267 pairs of *pantalons à cheval*, 1,033 pairs of *culottes de peau*, and 497 pairs of stable trousers. As before, *chaperons* were in use, 799 pairs existing and 791 *housses*.[5] The regiment was disbanded in 1811 to form the 1ᵉ *Lanciers*.

## 2ᵉ *Dragons*

This unit was created in 1693 and given the title '*Enghien-Cavalerie*'. In 1746 the regimental title was changed to '*Cavalerie de Conde*', and the unit was re-formed as dragoons in 1776. As the 2ᵉ *Dragons*, it fought with the Grande Armée in 1805, served

Officer of the 2ᵉ *Dragons* by Martinet.    Centre company trooper by Martinet.

in Spain from 1808 and marched to Germany in summer 1813. The inspection of 30 April 1802 reports 24m of blue broadcloth had been used – for trumpeters? We also note the regiment had 379 light cavalry *mousquetons* in use carried from *banderole-porte-mousquetons*. The regiment was in the process of swapping from *schabraques* to *chaperons*.[6] By the time of the 23 September 1804 review, a further 4m 20 of blue broadcloth had been used to make trumpeters' clothing.[7] Reviewed on 20 August 1805, the trumpeters we note were armed with light cavalry *mousquetons*, as were the drummers in the foot company, 24 such weapons being issued. The elite company had 106 bearskins.[8] When inspected on 22 December 1807, the clothing and equipment was as follows:[9]

| Item | Good conduction | In need of repair | To be written off | Total | Number made since 25 July 1805 |
|---|---|---|---|---|---|
| *Habits* | 400 | 297 | 53 | 750 | 697 |
| *Surtouts* | 308 | 260 | 371 | 939 | 675 |
| *Manteaux* | 425 | 145 | 153 | 723 | 425 |
| *Gilets* | | | | 896 | 896 |
| *Gilets d'écurie* | 300 | 120 | 233 | 653 | 283 |
| *Culottes de peau* | 900 | | 91 | 991 | 991 |
| *Pantalons d'écurie* | 500 | | 177 | 677 | 677 |
| *Casques* | 600 | 100 | 95 | 795 | 225 |

| Item | Good conduction | In need of repair | To be written off | Total | Number made since 25 July 1805 |
|---|---|---|---|---|---|
| *Bonnets à poil* | | | 92 | 92 | |
| *Bonnets de police* | 900 | | 63 | 963 | 963 |
| *Ceinturons* | 889 | | | 889 | 252 |
| *Gibernes* | 591 | 200 | 132 | 923 | 408 |
| *Porte-gibernes* | 800 | 100 | 23 | 923 | 400 |
| *Bretelles de fusil* | 800 | 127 | | 927 | 546 |
| *Porte-manteaux* | 500 | 150 | 203 | 853 | 741 |
| *Bottes* | 300 | 200 | 200 | 700 | 589 |
| *Selles completes* | 400 | 200 | 116 | 716 | 417 |
| *Brides complete* | 500 | 103 | 70 | 673 | 630 |
| *Bridons d'abreuvoir* | 50 | 50 | | 100 | |
| *Licol et longe* | 304 | 200 | 248 | 752 | 511 |
| *Sangles* | 400 | 200 | 116 | 716 | 417 |
| *Housses* | 500 | 100 | 116 | 716 | 550 |
| *Chaperons* | 400 | 200 | 116 | 716 | 550 |
| *Couvertures* | | 200 | 41 | 241 | |

Of note, the elite company bearskins were all to be disposed of. Cloth used since 1805 and by 22 December 1807 was as follows:[10]

| Item | In *Dépôt* 1805 | Purchased since 1805 | Total | Amount Used | Remaining in *Dépôt* |
|---|---|---|---|---|---|
| Green broadcloth | 524m 15 | 4,892m 58 | 5,416m 73 | 5,365m 41 | 51m 31 |
| White broadcloth | 442m 23 | 882m 98 | 1,325m 21 | 1,315m 93 | 9m 28 |
| Scarlet broadcloth | 94m 19 | 184m 57 | 278m 76 | 220m 59 | 58m 17 |
| *Blanc picque de bleu* | 633m 29 | 1,434m 60 | 2,667m 89 | 2,067m 89 | nil |
| White serge | 716m 88 | 3,157m 57 | 3,874m 45 | 3,782m 27 | 92m 18 |
| Scarlet serge | 1,954m 38 | 2,635m 58 | 4,589m 96 | 4,003m 65 | 586m 31 |
| Green tricot | nil | 980m 60 | 980m 60 | 980m 60 | nil |
| *Treillis* | nil | 1,346m 55 | 1,346m 55 | 1,346m 55 | nil |
| Linen | 5m 71 | 4,080m 72 | 4,086m 43 | 3,998m 61 | 87m 82 |
| Leather | 82m | 363m | 445m 04 | 414m 20 | 30m8 0 |

Clothing existing in 1805, made since then and issued by 22 December 1807 was as follows:[11]

| Item | Issued New | Needing repairs | New unissued in *Dépôt* | To be written off |
|---|---|---|---|---|
| *Habits* | 697 | | | |
| *Surtouts* | 1,145 | | 264 | |
| *Manteaux* | 490 | 100 | | |
| *Gilets* | 2,005 | 88 | 91 | |
| *Gilets d'écurie* | 1,400 | | 556 | |
| *Culottes de peau* | 493 | 102 | 20 | |
| *Pantalons d'écurie* | 900 | | 28 | |
| *Casques* | 291 | 23 | 146 | |
| *Bonnets à poil* | 1 | | | |
| *Bonnets de police* | 1,269 | | 46 | |
| *Ceinturons* | 162 | 12 | 148 | |
| *Gibernes* | 431 | | 183 | |
| *Portes giberne* | 483 | | 180 | |
| *Bretelles de fusil* | 609 | | 34 | |
| *Porte-manteaux* | 637 | 174 | | |
| *Bottes* | 5,450 | 20 | 160 | |
| *Selles completes* | 487 | | 37 | 9 |
| *Brides complete* | 620 | | 37 | 10 |
| *Licol et longe* | 511 | | 96 | |
| *Sangles* | | | 452 | |
| *Housses* | 521 | | 6 | 40 |
| *Chaperons* | 502 | 33 | 8 | 46 |
| *Couvertures* | 688 | | 17 | |
| Pairs of scissors and combs | 492 | | 15 | |
| Oat bags | 537 | 33 | | |
| Wallets | 370 | | 120 | |
| Body brushes | 684 | | | |
| Curry combs | 661 | | 33 | |
| Shirts | 1,458 | | | |
| Black stocks | 1,172 | | | |
| Pair of gaiters | 824 | | | |
| Linen bags | 646 | | | |
| Cockades | | | 600 | |

Clothing needed for new issue and replacement in the year 1808 was to be the following items:[12]

| Item | Total Items | Duration of issue | To be replaced |
|---|---|---|---|
| *Habits* | 1,077 | 4 yrs | 269 |
| *Surtouts* | 1,077 | 9 yrs | 538 |
| *Manteaux* | 795 | 9 yrs | 88 |
| *Gilets* | 1,077 | 4 yrs | 869 |
| *Gilets d'écurie* | 1,077 | 2 yrs | 538 |
| *Culottes de peau* | 1,077 | 1 yr | 1,077 |
| *Pantalons d'écurie* | 1,077 | 1 yr | 1,077 |
| *Casques* | 970 | 10 yrs | 97 |
| *Bonnets à poil* | | | |
| *Bonnets de police* | 1,077 | | |
| *Ceinturons* | 1,065 | 20 yrs | 53 |
| *Gibernes* | 1,065 | 20 yrs | 53 |
| *Portes giberne* | 1,065 | 20 yrs | 53 |
| *Bretelles de fusil* | 1,065 | 20 yrs | 53 |
| *Porte-manteaux* | 1,065 | 9 yrs | 118 |
| *Bottes* | 1,065 | 3 yrs | 355 |

Of note, the elite company from January 1808 onwards does not seem to have regained its bearskins. The trumpeters were issued *gibernes* and belts and were armed with 14 light cavalry *mousquetons*.[13]

In Spain from 1808, the regiment marched to Germany, where they arrived on 1 August 1813. The 3ᵉ and 4ᵉ squadrons were couped up in besieged garrison towns of Magdeburg and Danzig. Hardly any money was spent on clothing: 792fr on men in the *dépôt* and 192fr on the war squadrons between 1 January 1813 and 20 June 1814. Clearly the men were wearing whatever they had been from 1812 and earlier, and therefore had not adopted Bardin regulation.[14] Disbanded in summer 1814, the remaining men merged with Royalist Volunteers to form the *Dragons du Roi*. We know nothing absolute about the dress of the regiment after the 1807 review.

## *Officers' uniforms*

We are fortunate that the regiment's paper archive is very thorough: we have several inspection returns and regimental standing orders that shed great light on the dress of the regiment. In the new year of 1806, Colonel Ythier-Sylvain Privée issued the following standing orders for the dress of the regiment:

> The officers when off duty will wear:

> The chapeau, cut in military style, the right-hand corner may be positioned in front of the right eye, and the other behind the left eye by half an inch.
> 
> A black cravat with the knot entirely concealed to conceal all the collar of the shirt and may reach to the chin.

The surtout to be buttoned closed with 9 buttons down the chest, cut to show just the bottom-most buttons of the waistcoat.

The waistcoat to be made from white broadcloth and fitted with uniform buttons, or a waistcoat made from white polished cotton with buttons covered in the same material.

The culotte to be made from black Casimir with black silk stockings, and in the summer from nankeen with white stockings. The shoes are to have silver buckles.

The regulation epee to be worn with the sword knot in white linen. The gloves are to be in chamois.

In full dress the officers will wear, unless the commanding officer orders otherwise; the chapeau with plume, a white stock, the uniform habit, a waistcoat from white broadcloth or polish cotton, culotte in white broadcloth, white stockings, shoes with buckles, epee with gold lace sword knot, chamois gloves.

The officers when on active service will wear the helmet and sabre belt worn across the body when on foot, and around the body when mounted, the habit or surtout may be worn at the discretion of the commanding officer, the waistcoat and culotte to be in white broadcloth, knee guards, riding boots, bronze spurs. In undress, the sabre is to have a white linen sword-knot. In full dress the sword-knot is to be gold. On foot duty the boots and gloves are to be à l'écuyère [i.e. semi soft knee boots and wrist gloves] and in full dress stiff riding boots and gauntlets to be worn.

The officers may wear in the morning the redingote and bonnet de police, but past the hour of 10 o'clock in the morning they will wear the order of dress to be described: in wet weather or when it is cold, the redingote may be worn over the uniform, but not buttoned up. The redingote will have a stand and fall collar, it will close across the chest and fasten with two rows of 9 buttons. It will descend to the largest part of the calf, the bottom of the sleeves are to be open and closed with two small uniform buttons.

The epaulette retaining straps on the habit are to be the same on the redingote at the point of the shoulder … when the regiment is on foot under arms, on the march or to ride for instruction, the officers are to wear the redingote fully buttoned closed, the epaulettes to be worn, green broadcloth culotte are to be worn with the chamois wrist gloves; on line of march the helmet to be worn, in garrison the chapeaux.

The sous-officiers and dragoons are to habitually wear, like the officers, when off duty the chapeaux, and as for the officers, a black stock will be worn with white piping 3mm wide, the surtout, waistcoat in white broadcloth, culotte de peau, white linen stockings, shoes with buckles.

When the regiment is mounted for instruction, the sous-officiers will wear the surtout and chapeaux, the dragoons will wear their stable coats and bonnet de police, the culotte will be covered with white canvas over trousers, the saddle without equipment.

When the regiment is under arms on foot in undress, the sous-officiers and dragoons will wear the helmet and the sabre across the body, black gaiters, chamois sheepskin wrist gloves, in full dress the plume will be worn in the helmet.

When the regiment is mounted under arms in undress, the saddle will be fully equipped, the manteaux will be folded with the lining on the inside, the sous-officiers and dragoons will wear the sabre belt at the waist, and the chamois wrist gloves; in full dress the manteaux will be folded with the lining on the outside, the gauntlets will be worn, and the plume will be worn on the helmet.[15]

Colonel Privée further made it clear that the men were not to wear the boots for stable duties or around the barracks. Coloured neck cloths, waistcoats cut round at the bottom [i.e., flat] or closed with three rows of buttons were forbidden to be worn, *hussard* boots, jockey-style boots, and Suvorov boots were all forbidden. Non-regulation shoes, coloured stockings, and silvered spurs were all strictly forbidden to be worn, which of course must mean that these items *had* been worn.[16]

## 3ᵉ *Dragons*

Levied in 1649, the regiment was wearing on 1 August 1805 894 *habits*, 894 *surtouts*, 894 helmets, 740 green broadcloth *manteaux*, and 481 sets of *housses* and *chaperons* were in use. Of the regiment's 24 trumpeters, 8 were armed with light cavalry *mousquetons*.[17] When reviewed on 30 October 1807, 1,001 *habits* and *surtouts* were in use and 996 pairs of *pantalons à cheval*. The elite company had no bearskins, and we note 996 *housses*,

Officer of the 3ᵉ *Dragons* painted in spring to summer 1808 by Otto, copied here by Rousselot. (*Collection KM*)

Trooper of the 3ᵉ *Dragons* by Otto, copied here by Rousselot, showing the regiment in the first half of 1808. (*Collection KM*)

## Regulations in Practice 47

Trooper of 3ᵉ *Dragons* by Martinet.

Trumpeter of the 3ᵉ *Dragons* by Rousselot, based on the Markholsheim manuscript. Presumably the same uniform was worn by elite company trumpeters. As with all images from the series, it is worth pointing out that archive and other contemporary sources can neither confirm or deny the uniform shown. For a discussion of the manuscript, I recommend readers to the work of Vincent Bourgeot and Yves Martin on the trumpeters of the First Empire. All images from this manuscript are not fact, but possibilities. (*Collection KM*)

996 pairs of *chaperons* and 675 sheepskin *schabraques* were in use, 666 pairs being delivered since 1805. The *chaperons* were to be withdrawn, the inspector noted. The elite company *gibernes* were decorated with a copper grenade badge, 709 smocks were issued, 2 pairs of green broadcloth knee breeches and 227 infantry greatcoats.[18]

The decree of 18 June 1811 transformed the 1ᵉ, 4ᵉ and 7ᵉ companies into the 2ᵉ *Lanciers*. Remaining cadres were sent to the 6ᵉ and 11ᵉ Dragoons. The conversion process was to be overseen by General Bourcier. Transferred to the new regiment were 17 officers and 156 other ranks with 38 officer's mounts and 117 troop horses. The clothing sent to the 6ᵉ *Dragons* was as follows:[19]

Trumpeter of the 3ᵉ *Dragons* in action against Austrian troops during the 1805 campaign. Note the uniform is scarlet with blue collar, cuffs and epaulettes. The helmet *criniere* is black – white was only adopted at the end of 1808. The troopers we note have cloth *schabraques*, carry light cavalry *mousquetons*, and wear a mix of *pantalons* and *culottes de peau*, both of which garments are recorded in regimental archives. Interestingly, the elite company men do not have bearskins and are marked out solely by their epaulettes. (*Private collection*)

Regulations in Practice  49

38 *Habits* and *bonnets de police*
38 *vestes*
72 stable coats
16 helmets
72 bearskins
Total: 2,650fr 13

The elite company of the 6ᵉ *Dragons* we assume already had bearskins, or did they adopt them after this date? Clearly, that of the 3ᵉ had bearskins. The 2ᵉ *Lanciers* were reimbursed for this cost, and also for harness and saddlery, for the sum of 1,923fr 67. Also transferred were:[20]

58 complete saddles, with bridles and filet. Total 3,383fr 40
58 headcollars. Total 121fr 90
58 *housses*. Total 566fr 66
58 sheepskin *demi-schabraques*. Total 278fr 98
24 new *manteaux*. Total 876fr
34 *manteaux*. Total 1,757 fr 80
Total: 6,984fr 64

The items of clothing passed to the 11ᵉ *Dragons* comprised:[21]

37 *Habits* and *bonnets de police*
37 *vestes*
37 stable coats, in bad condition
14 helmets
39 bearskins at 34fr each
Total: 2,608fr 90

Also transferred to the 11ᵉ *Dragons* were:[22]

57 complete saddles, with curb and snaffle bridles. Total 3,351fr 60
57 headcollars. Total 119fr 70
57 *housses*. Total 556fr 89
587 sheepskin *demi-schabraques*. Total 274fr 19
24 new *manteaux*. Total 876f
33 *manteaux*. Total 1,706fr 10
Total: 6,884fr 46

Unfortunately, we have no further detail on the uniform of the regiment.

## 4ᵉ *Dragons*

Levied in July 1667, it was converted to a dragoon regiment in 1776. It served with the Grande Armée from 1805, thence in Spain from 1807. We note that on 30 January 1802, white worsted lace was purchased for *bonnets de police*, 536 plumes of undetermined colour and that the regiment's *surtouts* were lined in white serge rather than the expected green or scarlet. The men were issued light cavalry carbines and belts.[23] Inspected on 20 July 1805, we note the elite company had 107 bearskins, and the men were issued 784 *habits* and 764 *surtouts*. Just 378 *manteaux* were issued, made from *blanc picque de bleu* broadcloth. No sheepskin *schabraques* were in use. The inspector reported that 36 pairs of grey linen gaiters and 87 pairs of white gaiters were in use alongside 245 of black for the foot companies. The men were issued dragoon muskets.[24] When reviewed on 27 November 1807, the men were wearing 829 *habits*, 1,031 *surtouts*, and notably 707 green broadcloth *manteaux*. We also note 749 sets of *housses* and *chaperons* were in service, along with 1,048 pairs of shoes, 1,049 pairs of gaiters, and we also observe the trumpeters were armed with 16 light cavalry *mousquetons*, and were issued *giberne*s and belts. The elite company had no bearskins, presumably lost on campaign, if they existed.[25]

The regiment's archive is almost entirely bereft of documents relating to its clothing. Among the papers of Lucien Rousselot, we find a document copied from the Archives Nationales:

> Items dispatched from Bayonne de 7bre 1811 to the Army of the Midi
> 4ᵉ *Dragons*. 455 *habits*, 492 *culottes de peau*, 150 pairs of boots, 500 pairs of shoes, 480 red plumes, 731m green broadcloth, 4 helmets, 2 bearskins.[26]

Clearly the elite company wore bearskins and all ranks wore red plumes. The document also shows that supplies did manage to arrive with regiments from *dépôt* in France to regiments in the midst of the Peninsular War. The regiment marched to Germany in July 1813. We have an eyewitness to the regiment wearing bearskins in the field in 1813. One of the regiment's officers, Captain d'Agoult, noted that:

> Four years in Spain had made neither the men nor the uniforms younger, and their appearance had something that of Robinson on his Island. Many were dressed not in green, but in brown cloth, which they called the curate's cloth, because the coat of more than one priest had become a soldier's garment. But what most bore the marks of the time and decay were the helmets and bearskins: the horsehair manes were no more, and the bearskins had only their leather left. All of this gave us an extraordinary look.[27]

Despite the regiment's bizarre appearance, it was apparently mounted on superb Andalusian horses. When the 4ᵉ *Dragons* charged the Russians, they quickly formed defensive squares. Fired at by small pockets of detached skirmishes, the dragoons hit the Russians as a compact formation. The Russians panicked and fled.[28]

## Regulations in Practice    51

Officer of the 4ᵉ *Dragons* by Martinet.

Trooper of the centre companies of the 4ᵉ *Dragons* by Martinet. The regiment retained its bearskins until 1814.

Disbanded in summer 1814 to become the *2ᵉ Dragons*, the regiment was wearing on 18 June:

| Item | Good condition | Needing repairs | Needing to be replaced | Items needed |
|---|---|---|---|---|
| *Habits* | 49 | 73 | 91 | 104 |
| *Gilets en drap blanc* | 53 | 41 | 86 | 107 |
| *Gilets d'écurie* | 6 | 18 | 62 | 231 |
| Stable trousers | | | | 317 |
| *Surculottes* | 6 | 2 | 11 | 298 |
| *Culottes de peau* | 104 | 25 | 68 | 120 |
| *Manteaux* | | | | 105 |
| *Bonnets de police* | 74 | | | |
| Helmets | 123 | 78 | 35 | 81 |
| Bearskins | 74 | | | |

Officers and trooper of the 4ᵉ *Dragons* from the Freybourg manuscript copied by LeBrun. The original, now lost, image was made in summer 1813. (*Collection KM*)

Musician and *sapeur* of the 4ᵉ *Dragons* drawn in summer 1813. The original image is lost, but thankfully a later copy exists. (*Collection KM*)

Trumpeter of the 4ᵉ *Dragons* from the Markholsheim manuscript copied by Rousselot. Presumably this uniform was in use until the end of the Empire. In 1814 the trumpeters were dressed in *bleu de ciel* habits with Royalist Livery. (*Collection KM*)

Tellingly, the elite company were in bearskins – clearly obtained post-1807 – and the men were wearing pre-Bardin clothing just as the Camp de Dresden manuscript tells us. The regiment was issued with 209 sabres in good condition, and 132 pairs of pistols in good condition and no other firearms. When we look at the items stowed in the men's *porte-manteaux*, we find the regiment was issued 494 shirts, 25 pairs of linen overalls, and just 100 regulation black stocks – clearly men used an improvised stock. Just 90 pairs of socks were issued, so boots were worn over bare feet; 178 pairs of shoes were also issued and 7 pairs of grey gaiters. Stores held 195m of white broadcloth, 117 *veste*s, 32 pairs of stable trousers, 56 brand-new *giberne* belts, 49 brand-new musket slings, 39 carbines needing repairs, 104 'knackered' sabres and 148 brand-new pistols, with 17 to be disposed of as beyond repair.[29]

A document written at the start of the 100 days tells us that the 4e *Dragons* had been re-christened the *Dragons du Reine*, and the regiment's *dépôt* contained the following items:[30]

| Item | New | Good condition | Needing Repairs | Total |
|---|---|---|---|---|
| *Habits-vestes* | 60 | | 20 | 80 |
| *Gilets en drap blanc* | 46 | | 41 | 87 |
| *Gilets d'écurie* | 149 | 12 | | 161 |
| *Pantalons en drap gris* | | 1 | | 1 |
| Stable trousers | 200 | | 19 | 219 |
| *Surculottes* | 52 | | | 52 |
| *Culottes de peau* | 52 | 76 | | 128 |
| *Manteaux* | 150 | | | 150 |
| *Bonnets de police* | 116 | 25 | | 141 |
| Helmets | 6 | | 136 | 142 |
| *Aigrettes* | 41 | | | 41 |
| Waistbelts | 239 | | | 239 |
| *Gibernes* | 432 | | | 432 |
| *Porte-gibernes* | 331 | | | 332 |
| Sword knots | 28 | | | 28 |
| Pair of boots | | 16 | | 16 |
| Gauntlets | 94 | | | 94 |

By spring 1815, the regiment had lost its bearskins and the process had begun to clothe the newly formed *Dragons du Reine* – in Bardin-regulation clothing. The elite company had scarlet *aigrettes*, and we assume epaulettes, which were counted with the *habits-vestes*. Armament wise, the regiment had 2 carbines in *dépôt*, 12 sabres in good condition and 67 needing repairs, and 80 pistols. Cloth in stores included 20m 56 *bleu de ciel* broadcloth, surely destined for trumpeters. We also note the regiment adopted crimson facings, stores holding 54m 58 crimson serge, according to the decree of 23 May 1814.[31]

Disbanded at the end of the 100 days, stores held 6 *habits*, 138 *gilets*, 10 *bonnets de police*, 38 pairs of *surculottes* as well as 74 pairs of grenadiers' epaulettes among other items. Cloth comprised 115m 31 green broadcloth, 159m white broadcloth, 29m 59 scarlet broadcloth, 122m 21 gris-beige broadcloth, 536m of green tricot, 44m of scarlet serge, buttons in two sizes for both the 2ᵉ and 4ᵉ *dragons*, 37m 06 silver lace, 126m 30 white worsted lace for rank stripes, 39m 90 red worsted lace for service chevrons and 198m 32 lace for the *porte-manteaux*. We also note the regiment was issued with 167 light cavalry carbines and 85 dragoon muskets.[32]

## 5ᵉ *Dragons*

Formed in 1668, the regiment was with the Grande Armée in 1805. Reviewed on 8 October 1804, the inspector notes plumes were in use, but we are ignorant of their colour. The elite company had 150 bearskins, 700 *habits* were in use and 381 *surtouts*.[33] In 10 November 1805 every man had a *habit* and a *surtout*, 806 of each being in use, and the elite company had 106 bearskins. We also note 518 *blanc picque de bleu manteaux* were in service accompanied by 413 pairs of green *pantalons à cheval* reinforced with leather. Some 504 *housses* were in service, with 549 *chaperons*. The inspector ordered 217 *habits* to be made, which required 440m 50 of green broadcloth, 49m of scarlet broadcloth and 7m 22 of white broadcloth. Sixty *manteaux* were to be made, lined in scarlet serge, and 433 *surtouts*, which were entirely green. The trumpeters were all armed with light cavalry *mousquetons*, as were 9

Elite company, reported of the 5ᵉ *Dragons*, in the centre of the image, if we believe the identification by Rousselot.

dragoons. We also note, fifty-six sets of tools were in use, each set comprised a shovel, pick axe, hatchet and sycle.[34] Where the white broadcloth was used on the *habits* we can only guess, other than piping to *revers* and collar. It also seems the tails of the *habits* were lined in green rather than the expected scarlet.

Reviewed by General Grouchy on 28 October 1807, the elite company bearskins were all missing, while every man had a *habit*, *surtout* and pair of *surculottes*. Some 585 pairs of black twill gaiters were in use, with stores reporting 588m of black twill being used to make them. The *manteaux* were still *blanc picque de bleu*, and the trumpeters were still armed with *mousquetons*. *Housses* and *chaperons* were still in service.[35]

Officer of the elite company of the 5ᵉ *Dragons*. In the first image by Berka we see the officer in full dress, in the second we see campaign dress from the Brunswick manuscript.

The regiment served in Spain from 1808 to 1813 and marched to France in winter 1813 to take part in the French campaign of 1814. It charged at Ligny. While in Spain, the regiment received from its *dépôt* in France the following items during September 1811:

123 *habits*, 123 *vestes blanche*, 258 *gilets d'écurie*, 308 *pairs culottes de peau*, 301 pairs of *pantalons du treillis* – stable trousers – 301 pairs of linen underwear, 114 pairs of boots, 250 pairs of shoes.[36]

This shows that even in the midst of the Peninsular War, kit did get sent from the *dépôt* in France to where it was needed in Spain. We note that the paper archive for the regiment is remarkable. It contains not only quarterly returns for the expense of the regiment's office in terms of paper, ink, pens etc, but also for horse feed, shoeing as well as the fines imposed on the men for losing or damaging their uniform and equipment. If one wants to study how a dragoon regiment operated, the 5ᵉ *Dragons* is a prime candidate for such a study.

The master tailor noted in July 1814 the regiment had just adopted *habits* of the new model, and we note the regiment had *contre-epaulettes*: these are noted to have been made from copper scales with copper crescents, backed on to leather which was lined in scarlet broadcloth. No doubt these were identical to those of the Marine de la Garde Imperiale. Such contre-epaulettes were used by the 27e and 30e dragons.[37] The tailor was also busy preparing trumpeters' *habits* in *bleu de ciel* with Royalist Livery.[38] We also note that trumpeters' *habits* that existed in summer 1814 were turned and re-made, which cost 2fr 45. Presumably these were in reversed colours. Indeed, we note 42 of the unit's existing clothing was dismantled and re-made into *habits-vestes*, and 7 trumpeters' garments and a minimum of 251 pairs of *contre-epaulettes* issued.[39] The tailor, M. Poulain, charged 78fr for making 13 new *habits de trompette*, 245fr for converting a further 100 *habits* and 481fr for making 131 new *habits*, *vestes*, and *manteaux-capote*.[40] We add, an M. Dupont charged 109fr for sewing 109 pairs of grey *surculottes*, the cloth provided by the regiment.[41]

Inspected in August 1814, the regiment had the following items of equipment and clothing in use:[42]

| Item | In service, but due to expire in the next year | In need of repair | To be replaced in the next year | To be replaced | Items short |
|---|---|---|---|---|---|
| *Habits* | 154 | 37 | 13 | 18 | |
| *Gilets en drap blanc* | 100 | 4 | 9 | 18 | |
| *Gilets d'écurie* | 19 | 11 | 4 | 5 | |
| Stable trousers | 77 | 1 | 21 | 9 | |
| *Surculottes* | 84 | 2 | 4 | 2 | |
| Helmets | 194 | 25 | 4 | 3 | |
| *Bonnets de police* | 50 | 12 | 15 | 13 | |
| *Culottes de peau* | 137 | 6 | 8 | 3 | |
| Bearskins | 110 | 1 | 2 | 8 | |

The huge number of bearskins comes as a complete shock as these items went out of use in February 1813 – in theory – and none had existed in 1807, so they were clearly obtained during 1808. A further 17 bearskins were held in the *dépôt* that were fit only for being disposed of. The *dépôt* also held 52 brand-new plumes. Of interest, the 24e *Dragons*, which were disbanded along with the 5e to form the new 3e *Dragons*, possessed 88 bearskins! We have to imagine elite companies clinging tenaciously to their elite status with bearskins. The *dépôt* held 0m 78 of blue broadcloth, 24m 26 of linen and 15m 30 of worsted lace, 8 *vestes*, 17 bearskins and 46 pairs of boots. The inspector noted the regiment had not acted fully upon the provisions of Bardin regulation: so, we must imagine *habit a revers* were still in use.[43] The blue broadcloth was surely destined for trumpeters.

Disbanded on 1 December 1815, the *dépôt* held 5m 70 of scarlet broadcloth, 114m 3 of white broadcloth for *vestes*, 67m 43 of scarlet serge, 20m 70 of green tricot, 632m 15 of *blanc picque de bleu* for *manteaux*, 301m 69 of linen for linings, 352m of *treillis*, 17m 30 of red wool lace for service chevrons, 30m 50 of white lace for corporals' stripes, 285m of

Elite company trooper of the 5ᵉ *Dragons* from an engraving made in 1814, when we know the regiment was indeed still wearing bearskins. From 1814 copper fish scale *contre-epaulettes* were issued, identical in form to those of the *Marine de la Garde*. Those of the elite company had white fringing.

We know of no contemporary depiction of the trumpeters of the 5ᵉ *Dragons*. In the rear left of this image is a trumpeter in scarlet-faced green, with white lace. It may be the 5ᵉ.

white worsted lace for *porte-manteaux* and 208m of trumpeters' livery. The *dépôt* held large quantities of brand-new clothing, namely 125 new white *vestes*, 9 *gilets d'écurie*, 69 pairs of *surculottes*, 76 pairs of *culottes de peau*, 16 pairs of stable trousers, 42 *porte-manteaux*, 163 helmets, 298 pompoms, 225 *gibernes*, 220 *porte-gibernes*, 230 waistbelts, 280 sword knots and 200 *banderole-porte-mousquetons*. Among the items in good condition, we find 20 bearskins and a further 60 needing repairs! Had they been kept in use, we wonder? Yet no *aigrettes* or epaulettes are listed for the elite company![44] Surely the latter were counted with the *habits*, as an unsophisticated portrait of a *fourrier* (quartermaster-corporal) of the elite company, kept at the Musée de l'Armée implies. He is wearing the *habits-vestes*, his epaulettes are white with fringes with the shoulder board covered with white metal scales, and his *porte-giberne* is decorated with a stamped brass grenade. He is wearing a helmet and not a bearskin, which is rather at odds with the regiment's paper archive. The image seemingly dates to the first Restoration period, into the 100 days, certainly no earlier.

Also in *dépôt* were 282 pairs of linen stockings, 24 pairs of black gaiters, 63 black stocks, 235 stock buckles, 27 pairs of knee guards and 618 rabats for the black stocks. The rabat is a piece of white linen, folded in half that was inserted into the top of the

Centre company officer of the 5ᵉ *Dragons* by Martinet.

Centre company trooper of the 5ᵉ *Dragons* by Martinet.

black stock to give a narrow white piping to the top edge of the stock. The rabat could be changed as needed to be washed. The *dépôt* also held 67 clothes brushes, 75 brushes for cleaning metal items, 87 shoe brushes, 5 grease boxes, 12 polishing tools for waxing the *gibernes*, 100 musket covers, 2 button sticks, 70 pairs of knee buckles and remarkably 64 linen *giberne* covers – the only reference we have ever found to these items existing in the cavalry. The *dépôt* also held 52 brand-new plumes.[45]

One unique aspect of the 5ᵉ for most of its history was the dress of the elite company. We know the 5ᵉ received white *aiguilettes* in 1802 and had kept them, it seems, up until 1812–13, with white-fringed epaulettes. The regiment had received them when under the command of Louis Bonaparte and one may consider this distinction as a discreet referral to the *aiguillettes* worn at the end of the monarchy by the dragoon regiment colonel-general; the origin of the 5ᵉ. The white *aiguillettes* were abandoned at the end of the Empire, as is proved by their absence in archive paperwork.[46]

## Officers' uniforms

Officers provided their own clothing and equipment at their expense. Sous-Lieutenant Galeaux's effects in his *porte-manteaux* were 'lost in action' and he submitted a claim for the following items:[47]

2 pairs of silk stockings. 6fr
A pair of knee breeches and *veste* in white broadcloth. Total 10fr 50
An old pair of knee breeches and *veste* in green broadcloth. Total 1fr 50
2 pairs of *pantalons* in nankeen. Total 21fr
2 pairs of *pantalons* in black silk. Total 44fr

Clearly in the summer when off duty the officers wore nankeen *pantalons*. Rather than wearing hot and cumbersome *culottes de peau*, officers used these items made from white broadcloth. In winter black silk *pantalons* were worn.

## 6<sup>e</sup> *Dragons*

Formed in 1673 as the *Dragons de la Reine*, unfortunately, the regiment's archive is particularly weak when it comes to the records of clothing and equipment. On 16 June 1803, every man was wearing a *surtout*. No *habits* existed whatsoever. We also note the elite company had 56 bearskins, and that the regiment was issued 342 *banderole-porte-mousquetons* and 472 light cavalry *mousquetons*.[48] Inspected on 7 December 1807, the elite company had no bearskins and just 90 plumes were in use, presumably for the elite company. We note 39 bearskins were in store needing repairs and 3 were issued to the trumpet major and the trumpet corporals. The 19 trumpeters were armed with light cavalry *mousquetons*, the men were now issued 854 *fusils de dragons*.[49] When reviewed in August 1814 the regiment's clothing was as follows:[50]

| Item | In service, but due to expire in the next year | In need of repair | To be replaced as life expired | To be replaced | Items short |
|---|---|---|---|---|---|
| *Habits* | 27 | 37 | 10 | 130 | 50 |
| *Gilets de drap blanc* | 50 | | 7 | 122 | 75 |
| *Gilets d'écurie* | 60 | 16 | 43 | 8 | 127 |
| *Surculottes* | 40 | 1 | | 6 | 207 |
| Stable trousers | 57 | | | | 197 |
| *Culottes de peau* | 30 | | | | 224 |
| *Manteaux* | 69 | 90 | | 57 | 38 |
| *Bonnets de police* | 82 | 1 | 1 | | 170 |
| Helmets | 73 | 110 | | 43 | 28 |
| *Crinieres* | The regiment has none | | | | |

The lack of *crinieres* is interesting – did helmets really lack these items? It seems so. In addition, the regiment was armed with 58 dragoon muskets in good condition and 12 more needing repairs, yet the regiment had 38 light cavalry style *banderole-porte-carabines* issued! Clearly these much longer and more cumbersome firearms had been carried off shoulder belts and attached to the carbine clip by the leather *boucleteaux* fastened around the stock! Only 58 sabres were in good condition, 149 needed repairs and 15 were to be written off. Fifty bayonets were issued, as were 161 pistols in good condition and 21 needing repairs.

*Dépôt* also held a lot of brand-new, unissued, clothing, notably 292 *habits-vestes*, 294 white *gilets*, 166 *gilets d'écurie*, 138 pairs of stable trousers, 118 pairs of *culottes de peau*, 300 *manteaux*, 264 *bonnets de police*, 237 helmets, 59 pairs of grey broadcloth *pantalons* with black leather reinforcement to the inner leg – totally non-regulation, but clearly used – 308 sabre belts, 273 *gibernes*, 417 *porte-gibernes*, 265 sword knots, 160 pairs of boots, 174 pairs of spurs, 140 pairs of gauntlets, 50 scarlet *aigrettes* and 3 pairs of trumpeters' epaulettes. W also remark upon 20m 56 *bleu de ciel* broadcloth destined for trumpeters' clothing. *Dépôt* also held 1 *habit* needing repairs and 25 to be written off. The return lists *surtouts* and *manteaux-capote* but none were held, likewise *crinieres* and epaulettes for adjutants.[51] It seems remarkable that the elite company were marked out only by their *aigrette* – unless the epaulettes were quite logically counted with the *habits*. Assuming this, then trumpeters' epaulettes, which are listed separately, were different to the, we suppose, scarlet ones in use, ergo were they white? The total absence of *crinieres* in use or in *dépôt* makes us thinks the helmets were devoid of these! The regiment was disbanded at the end of August to become the 4ᵉ *Dragons*.

A document written at the start of the 100 days tells us that the 4ᵉ *Dragons* had been re-christened the *Dragons du Monsieur*, and the regiment's *dépôt* contained the following items:[52]

| Item | New | Good condition | Needing Repairs | Total |
| --- | --- | --- | --- | --- |
| *Habits-vestes* | 60 | | 20 | 80 |
| *Gilets en drap blanc* | 46 | | 41 | 87 |
| *Gilets d'écurie* | 149 | 12 | | 161 |
| *Pantalons en drap gris* | | 1 | | 1 |
| Stable trousers | 200 | | 19 | 219 |
| *Surculottes* | 52 | | | 52 |
| *Culottes de peau* | 52 | 76 | | 128 |
| *Manteaux* | 150 | | | 150 |
| *Bonnets de police* | 116 | 25 | | 141 |
| Helmets | 6 | | 136 | 142 |
| *Aigrettes* | 41 | | | 41 |
| Waistbelts | 239 | | | 239 |
| *Gibernes* | 432 | | | 432 |
| *Porte-gibernes* | 331 | | | 332 |
| Sword knots | 28 | | | 28 |
| Pairs of boots | | 16 | | 16 |
| Gauntlets | 94 | | | 94 |

By spring 1815, the regiment had lost its bearskins and the process had begun to clothe the newly formed *Dragons du Monsieur* in Bardin-regulation clothing. The elite company had scarlet *aigrette*s, and we assume epaulettes, which were counted with the *habits-vestes*. Armament wise, the regiment had 2 carbines in *dépôt*, 12 sabres in good condition and 67 needing repairs and 80 pistols. Cloth in stores included 20m 56 *bleu de ciel* broadcloth, surely destined for trumpeters, accompanied by 167m 22 of Royalist Livery. We also note the regiment adopted crimson facings, stores holding 143m 35 crimson broadcloth and 407m 88 crimson serge, according to the decree of 23 May 1814. Also, in stores was 22m 89 Aurore broadcloth and 209m 19 of matching serge – inherited from the 27ᵉ *Dragons* – as well as 2 seal skins to make replacement turbans for the helmets and 48 black leather cow hides for the production of *pantalons à cheval* from gris-beige broadcloth. Just 1 pair was in use, perhaps on an experimental basis, but clearly more were to be produced.[53]

The regiment at the time of disbandment in 1815 held some stocks of cloth and materials in its store rooms, notably 340m 45 of green broadcloth, 112m 58 crimson broadcloth, 0m 25 beige broadcloth, 1,333m 50 of *blanc picque de bleu* broadcloth, 31m 25 white broadcloth, 99m 40 of crimson serge for lining, 4m 57 green tricot, and 684m 30 linen.

Also present in the *dépôt* was 12m white worsted lace, 40m 56 red worsted lace, 350m 62 linen lace for *porte-manteaux* and *housses* as well as 316m 70 of trumpeters' livery. The regiment had inherited 167m 22 of Imperial Livery in 1814 from the *dépôt* squadron of the 27ᵉ *Dragons*, so clearly lace in 1815 was either more of the same, both Royalist and Imperial Livery classed simply as 'trumpeters' lace', or simply entirely Royalist Livery. Sadly, we cannot say due to the lack of further archive sources. *Dépôt* held 33 pairs of *culottes de peau*, 100 *manteaux* and 223 helmets.[54] If the regiment had taken back its denomination as the 6ᵉ during the 100 days, without a shadow of a doubt the men were in crimson facings and had buttons bearing the number '4', as no new buttons were made or issued.

Tucked away at the back of the image by Major Jolly of the 6ᵉ *Lanciers*, we spot this trumpeter of the 6ᵉ *Dragons*, reaching up to a woman in a upper window. His *habit* is in reversed colours with white lace to the collar and long pockets. White grenades appear on the turnbacks. (*Collection KM*)

Officer of the 6ᵉ *Dragons* by Martinet.

Trooper of centre company of the 6ᵉ *Dragons* by Martinet. We know of no contemporary depiction of the elite company.

## 7ᵉ *Dragons*

Raised by the Marquis de Sauveboeuf at Tournai in 1673, it became the *Dragons de Dauphin* in 1675. Reviewed 6 August 1803, the elite company swaggered in 56 bearskins, with another 56 being authorised for purchase. We also note that of the 32m of blue broadcloth in stores, 18m 26 had been used, we assume on trumpeters' clothing. The men had all been recently issued a *habit* – something they had lacked since 1799.[55] Inspected on 10 January 1805, we report that 496 *habits* were in service, 630 *surtouts*, and 358 pairs of breeches made from white broadcloth in lieu of *culottes de peau*. We also note 452 sets of *chaperons* were used along with 352 sheepskin *schabraques*, which were all to be taken out of service. The biggest surprise from the review is that 13m 74 of blue broadcloth had been used to make, presumably, trumpeters' clothing.[56] We cannot say if the *habits* were blue faced in crimson, or crimson faced in blue. Inspected again on 10 September 1805, the elite company had 56 bearskins, clearly those authorised for purchase never arrived.[57]

Partial regimental accounts report that in December 1806, the following amounts of cloth had been purchased:[58]

Officer of the 7ᵉ *Dragons* by Martinet.   Centre company trooper of the 7ᵉ *Dragons* by Martinet.

47m 50 *Blanc picque de bleu*
176m 71 Green broadcloth
35m 08 Crimson broadcloth
1,040m 41 White broadcloth
2,056m 69 linen for lining

The amount of cloth for the *manteaux* suggests very few were made, or more likely the cloth was used for repairs; ditto the green broadcloth, when we look at the amount of cloth purchased in 1807:[59]

2,542m 11 Green broadcloth, 1,791m 82 used
85m 3 Crimson broadcloth, 75m 21 used
1,650m 78 Green tricot, 1,349m 36 used
268m 78 Black tricot for gaiters, none used
8,786m 63 Linen for lining, 4,197m 72 used

Of the cloth, 467m of green broadcloth was sent back to the manufacturer due to its poor quality. The black tricot was destined for the production of 284 pairs of black gaiters, the manufacture and buttons costing 496fr 99. The 7ᵉ *Dragons* were inspected on 4 January 1808. Clothing and equipment in use then was as follows:[60]

| Item | Good conduction | In need of repair | To be written off | Total | Number made since last review |
|---|---|---|---|---|---|
| *Habits* | 662 | | | 662 | 662 |
| *Surtouts* | 579 | 108 | 143 | 830 | 830 |
| *Manteaux* | 587 | 72 | | 659 | 587 |
| *Gilets* | 648 | | | 648 | 648 |
| *Gilets d'écurie* | 554 | 126 | 119 | 799 | 799 |
| *Culottes de Peau* | 835 | | 224 | 1,059 | 1,059 |
| *Caleçons* | 547 | | | | 547 |
| *Pantalons d'écurie* | 846 | | | 846 | 846 |
| *Casques* | 647 | 67 | | 714 | 631 |
| *Bonnets à poil* | 121 | | | 121 | 71 |
| *Bonnets de police* | 750 | | 101 | 851 | 851 |
| *Ceinturons* | 786 | | | 786 | 786 |
| *Gibernes* | 804 | | | 804 | 804 |
| *Porte-gibernes* | 804 | | | 804 | 804 |
| *Bretelles de fusil* | 518 | | | 518 | 518 |
| *Porte-manteaux* | 647 | | | 647 | 647 |
| *Bottes* | 603 | 130 | | 733 | 733 |
| *Selles completes* | 605 | 50 | | 655 | 655 |
| *Brides complete* | 655 | | | 655 | 655 |
| *Bridons d'abreuvoir* | 690 | | | 690 | 690 |
| *Licol et longe* | 694 | | | 694 | 694 |
| *Sangles* | 655 | | | 655 | 655 |
| *Housses* | 651 | | | 651 | 651 |
| *Chaperons* | 554 | 97 | | 651 | 651 |
| *Couvertures* | | | | | |

## Regulations in Practice

Elite company trooper of the 7ᵉ *Dragons* by Martinet. By 1808 the 9ᵉ company boasted *sapeurs*. We are ignorant of their dress other than a copy of naïve image from the epoch by Rousselot or Knoetel.

Trumpeter of the 7ᵉ *Dragons*, presumably in campaign dress, from the Markholsheim manuscript by Rousselot. Presumably the elite company wore the same garment. (*Collection KM*)

Of note, the elite company bearskins were all in good condition, so we assume were in use through to 1812 and beyond. Cloth used since 1805 and 4 January 1808 was as follows:[61]

| Item | In *Dépôt* 1805 | Purchased since 1805 | Total | Amount Used | Remaining in *Dépôt* |
|---|---|---|---|---|---|
| Green broadcloth | 745m 12 | 4,445m 71 | 5,190m 83 | 5,100m 52 | 90m 31 |
| White broadcloth | nil | 1,862m 86 | 1,862m 86 | 1,802m 90 | 59m 96 |
| Crimson broadcloth | 38m 85 | 209m 12 | 247m 97 | 199m | 48m 97 |
| *Blanc picque de bleu* | nil | 3,621m 95 | 3,621m 95 | 2,783m 45 | 838m 50 |
| Green tricot | nil | 2,345m 47 | 2,345m 47 | 1,650m 78 | 694m 59 |
| Crimson serge | nil | nil | nil | nil | nil |
| Black tricot | nil | 507m 30 | 507m 30 | 268m 52 | 238m 78 |
| White Serge | 777m 68 | 4,233m 02 | 5,010m 70 | 4,309m 54 | 701m 16 |
| *Treillis* | 1,129m 65 | 13,833m 63 | 14,963m 28 | 14,750m 39 | 212m 89 |

Clothing existing in 1805, made since and issued by 22 December 1807, was as follows:[62]

| Item | In *Dépôt* 1805 | Purchased since 1805 | Total | Number issued | Remaining in *Dépôt* | Repaired in *Dépôt* |
|---|---|---|---|---|---|---|
| *Habits* | nil | 670 | 670 | 670 | nil | nil |
| *Surtouts* | nil | 1,496 | 1,496 | 1,496 | nil | nil |
| *Manteaux* | 43 | 593 | 636 | 566 | 70 | 70 |
| *Gilets* | 192 | 464 | 656 | 656 | nil | nil |
| *Gilets d'écurie* | 150 | 971 | 1,121 | 1,084 | 37 | 37 |
| *Culottes de Peau* | 2 | 2,239 | 2,241 | 2,212 | 29 | 29 |
| *Caleçons* | nil | 988 | 988 | 959 | 29 | 29 |
| *Pantalons d'écurie* | 260 | 1,509 | 1,769 | 1,769 | nil | nil |
| *Casques* | nil | 827 | 827 | 827 | nil | nil |
| *Bonnets à poil* | nil | 111 | 111 | 111 | nil | nil |
| *Bonnets de police* | 73 | 1,418 | 1,491 | 1,421 | 70 | 70 |
| *Ceinturons* | nil | 640 | 640 | 585 | 55 | 55 |
| *Gibernes* | nil | 1,042 | 1,042 | 992 | 50 | 50 |
| *Porte-gibernes* | nil | 992 | 992 | 50 | 992 | 50 |
| *Bretelles de fusil* | 39 | 692 | 731 | 695 | 36 | 36 |
| *Porte-manteaux* | 70 | 452 | 522 | 507 | 15 | 15 |
| *Bottes* | 48 | 1,049 | 1,097 | 1,084 | 13 | 13 |
| *Selles completes* | 21 | 639 | 660 | 593 | 67 | 67 |
| *Brides complete* | 39 | 639 | 678 | 611 | 67 | 67 |
| *Licol et longe* | nil | 1,339 | 1,339 | 1,155 | 184 | 184 |
| *Sangles* | 21 | 851 | 872 | 805 | 67 | 67 |
| *Housses* | 39 | 828 | 867 | 774 | 93 | 93 |
| *Chaperons* | 110 | 633 | 743 | 723 | 20 | 20 |
| *Couvertures* | 25 | nil | 25 | nil | 25 | nil |
| Pairs of scissors and combs | nil | nil | nil | nil | nil | nil |
| Oat bags | 111 | 350 | 461 | 422 | 39 | 39 |
| Shirts | 191 | 345 | 536 | 446 | 90 | 90 |
| Black stock | 13 | 605 | 618 | 510 | 108 | 108 |
| Pairs of socks | 289 | 351 | 638 | 516 | 122 | 122 |
| Pairs of gaiters | 95 | 307 | 402 | 402 | nil | nil |

Clothing needed for new issue and replacement in the year 1808 was to be the following items:[63]

| Item | Total Items | Duration of issue | To be replaced |
|---|---|---|---|
| *Habits* | 858 | 4 yrs | 214 |
| *Surtouts* | 858 | 9 yrs | 429 |
| *Manteaux* | 858 | 9 yrs | 96 |
| *Gilets* | 858 | 4 yrs | 214 |
| *Gilets d'écurie* | 858 | 2 yrs | 429 |
| *Culottes de peau* | 858 | 1 yr | 214 |
| *Pantalons d'écurie* | 858 | 1 yr | 858 |
| *Casques* | 728 | 10 yrs | 72 |
| *Bonnets à poil* | 124 | 6 yrs | 21 |
| *Bonnets de police* | 858 | 2 yrs | 426 |
| *Ceinturons* | 852 | 20 yrs | 43 |
| *Gibernes* | 852 | 20 yrs | 43 |
| *Porte-gibernes* | 852 | 20 yrs | 43 |
| *Bretelles de fusil* | 852 | 20 yrs | 43 |
| *Porte-manteaux* | 852 | 9 yrs | 94 |
| *Bottes* | 852 | 3 yrs | 584 |

Of note, the elite company was to be issued with new bearskins. We assume the elite company epaulettes were counted with the *habits*. The *dépôt* also held 8 curb bits, 5 sabres, 495 pairs of shoes, 12 pairs of spurs, and 82 pairs of gaiters. We also note 9 sets of *sapeurs*' equipment was issued to the *sapeurs* in the war squadrons.[64]

We know nothing about the dress of the regiment until its disbandment in summer 1814:[65]

| Item | In service, but due to expire in the next year | In need of repair | To be replaced as life expired | To be replaced | Items short |
|---|---|---|---|---|---|
| *Habits* | 248 | 4 | | | 3 |
| *Gilets en drap blanc* | 247 | | | 2 | 6 |
| *Gilets d'écurie* | 251 | | | | 4 |
| *Culottes de peau* | 251 | | | | 4 |
| Helmets | 251 | | | | 4 |
| *Bonnets de police* | 250 | | | 2 | 3 |
| Stable trousers | 245 | | | | 10 |
| *Manteaux* | 180 | | | 5 | 70 |
| *Surculottes en drap gris* | 114 | 7 | 4 | 2 | 128 |

Of note, the men wore their boots over bare feet, as not a single pair of socks were in use. The men also had 452 pairs of shoes accompanied by 286 pairs of black tricot gaiters for dismounted duties. We note every man, 286, had a black stock, were issued between them 850 shirts and a further 13 black stocks were in stores accompanied by 40 stock buckles, 198 pairs of black gaiters, 211 boxes of grease, 121 brushes for cleaning copper, 47 *trousses* – soldier's 'housewife' containing needle and thread, cloth for repairs, razor etc – 104 grease brushes, 138 awls, 12 forage ropes, and 33 nose bags. Not a single pair of underwear existed either.

The inspector further noted that the regiment's clothing was not made according to the decrees of 19 January and 17 February 1812, nor had the regiment acted upon

Centre company trooper of the 7ᵉ *Dragons* painted in 1814 by a serving officer. Of interest to us are the copper fish scale *contre-epaulettes*. (*Collection KM*)

the decree of 23 April 1814 the inspector added, and had not removed Imperial symbols and dressed the trumpeters in blue. He ordered that this was to be carried out, and that all clothing and equipment was to be replaced, or altered, to exactly accord with the regulations of 1812.[66]

We know nothing more till disbandment in 1815. Clothing in use and in the *dépôt* on 30 September 1815 was as follows:[67]

| Item | In *dépôt* 1 September 1815 | Items in service | | Total |
|---|---|---|---|---|
| *Habits* | 0 | 159 | | 159 |
| *Vestes sans manche* | 0 | 121 | | 121 |
| *Gilets d'écurie* | 0 | Good | 19 | |
| | | In need of repair | 25 | |
| | | To be replaced | 70 | |
| *Bonnets de police* | 0 | 161 | | 161 |
| *Capotes manteaux* | 92 | 105 | | 97 |
| *Porte-manteaux* | 12 | Good | 137 | 149 |
| | | In need of repair | 41 | 41 |

| Item | In *dépôt* 1 September 1815 | Items in service | | Total |
|---|---|---|---|---|
| *Culottes de peau* | 146 | 156 | | 302 |
| Stable trousers | 0 | 19 | | 19 |
| Helmets | 155 | Good | 24 | 24 |
| | | In need of repair | 199 | 348 |
| Pairs of boots | 32 | Good | 23 | 23 |
| | | In need of repair | 39 | 71 |
| | | To be replaced | 58 | 58 |
| Waistbelts | 430 | 163 | | 593 |
| *Gibernes* | 545 | 212 | | 757 |
| *Porte-gibernes* | 545 | 212 | | 757 |
| Trumpets | 0 | Good | 4 | 4 |
| | | In need of repair | 3 | 3 |
| Pairs of gauntlets | 0 | Good | 66 | 66 |
| | | In need of repair | 15 | 15 |
| Sword knots | 517 | 122 | | 639 |
| Pompoms | 0 | 156 | | 156 |
| Sabres | 249 | Good | 20 | 269 |
| | | In need of repair | 115 | 68 |
| | | To be replaced | 3 | 3 |
| *Mousquetons* | 178 | Good | 32 | 210 |
| | | In need of repair | 81 | 81 |
| | | To be replaced | 2 | 2 |
| Bayonets | 306 | 35 | | 341 |
| Bayonet scabbards | 306 | 9 | | 315 |
| Pistols | 13 | Good | 13 | 26 |
| | | In need of repair | 30 | 30 |
| | | To be replaced | 10 | 10 |

Clearly, the unit had been armed with light cavalry firearms, but not a single belt to carry the weapon from. Men had these in the field, but how they were carried is a mystery. Cloth and materials included 180m 12 green broadcloth, 46m 91 crimson broadcloth, 67m 30 white broadcloth, 665m 25 *blanc picque de bleu* broadcloth for *manteaux* and 0m 25 of beige broadcloth for *surculottes*. No trumpeters' lace existed.

### 8e *Dragons*

Created on 1 March 1674, the unit was converted to *lanciers* in 1811. The regiment was reviewed on 30 September 1804. The men were issued a *habit, surtout, veste, blanc picque de bleu manteaux* as well as a pair of *culottes de peau* and stable trousers and stable coat. The elite company had 143 bearskins and scarlet plumes. The horses were equipped with

Officer of the 8ᵉ *Dragons* by Martinet.

Centre company trooper of the 8ᵉ *Dragons* by Martinet. We know of no contemporary images of the elite company or trumpeters.

*chaperons* and *housses*. Part of the regiment was dismounted, and these men were issued 260 *havresacs*, two pairs of shoes and a pair of black twill gaiters.⁶⁸

Reviewed again on 8 August 1805, the regiment had 8 trumpeters and 12 drummers, as well as drum major and a trumpet major. We note 503 men were mounted and 305 dismounted. Just 84 bearskins were in use, and we note 300 pairs of leather wrist gloves and 400 pairs of gauntlets were in service. As before, men had both a *habit* and *surtout*, and the *manteaux* were *blanc picque de bleu* rather than green. The drummers and trumpeters were issued 16 light cavalry *mousquetons*.⁶⁹

Inspected 10 March 1808, the elite company had lost their bearskins on campaign, 26 remained in stores, and every single *mousqueton* had likewise been lost in action. Everything was in appalling condition, the inspector noted, all except the 400 *habits* in use, which somehow had escaped the rigours of the campaign: just 200 *surtouts* remained from the 505 that had existed before the campaign began, and were all life expired. Indeed, 1,300 had been made and issued since 1805, representing a huge loss of clothing. Likewise, 794 *habits* had been made, 308 further examples remained unissued in stores, and 163 had been repaired.⁷⁰ We have commented upon the regiment's accounts from 1808 to 1811 earlier.

## 9ᵉ *Dragons*

This unit was created in the Franche-Comte in 1673. General Oudinot, the future Marshal, inspected the regiment on 2 March 1802. The inspection was far from thorough; he made no record on clothing and equipment other than '*bon*', which tells us virtually nothing. The *dépôt* had issued 496 plumes and 4 remained in stores along with 9 *habits*, 46 *manteaux*, 160 pairs of stable trousers, 18 waistbelts and 198 *porte-gibernes*.[71]

Oudinot did not have an eye for detail, that is certain, when we compare his with the next inspection, by General Canclaux, on 4 July 1803. He noted the regiment's clothing was well made and in good condition, but the master tailor, it was felt, should spend more time researching the regulation so that the clothing conformed better to the model. The inspector commented that the *Chef de Brigade*, i.e., the colonel, 'after certain circumstances in the last wars had made, rather than *culottes de peau*, tricot *pantalons* garnished with leather. The *pantalons* were worn in place of the *culottes*.' Canclaux ordered that *culottes de peau* were to made without delay to replace the 402 pairs of tricot *pantalons* in use. The elite company had not yet received any bearskins. Furthermore, the inspector noted that the leather breeches were in bad condition and 200 pairs of boots were shabby and needed repairs. Also, despite the regulations, the regiment had retained

Officer of centre company of the 9ᵉ *Dragons* by Martinet.

Centre company officer of the 9ᵉ *Dragons* by Martinet.

its sheepskin *schabraques* and old-pattern, round, *porte-manteaux*. Indeed, 26 old-pattern *porte-manteaux* had been made since 1802 and 56 sheepskin *schabraques*. In terms of armament, the regiment had not yet received its dragoon muskets or any new-model sabres. Since the previous inspection 70 *habits*, 92 *surtouts*, 50 *manteaux*, 76 *gilets*, 107 stable coats, 494 pairs of *culottes de peau*, 580 pairs of stable trousers, 70 helmets and 58 *bonnets de police* had been made and issued. Remarkably, the *sous-officiers* had 38 pairs of *culottes de daim* (doe hide breeches) issued – these are a pale ochre colour compared to the bright white of the sheepskin breeches of the other ranks and cost almost twice as much per pair! We also note that 500 brand-new pairs of underwear had been made and issued. Repaired in the same period were 200 *surtouts*, 180 *manteaux*, 200 stable coats and 65 helmets. Yet we find not a single pair of fringed epaulettes for the elite company.[72] In a subsequent letter to the war minister, Canclaux noted that perhaps for use in winter, *pantalons* with leather reinforcement should be officially sanctioned, and perhaps they should even remove from use the *culotte de peau*. From his observation all the regiments he had inspected had adopted this principle and replaced the *culotte de peau* with cheaper and more durable items of legwear. This was superior to wearing the stable trousers over the *culottes de peau*.[73]

Inspected on 4 October 1804, the inspector noted the regiment's clothing was well made and in good condition, but again, the master tailor, it was felt, should spend more time studying the regulation. Regimental accounts report 20,5140fr had been spent on shoes, smocks and *capotes* for the dismounted company, and 284fr 45 had been spent on lace for *sous-officiers* and other distinctions for the rank and file. Since 4 July 1803, 500 *capotes* had been made, 561 smocks, 60 bearskins – making 119 in use – and 551 *havresacs*. We also note the *dépôt* had produced for the foot companies 403 pairs of tricot *pantalons*, 388m 39 of linen had been used making grey gaiters and 204 pairs of black worsted gaiters had been made, with 203 pairs issued. *Dépôt* had also issued 590 plumes but we are ignorant of their colour.[74]

When reviewed on 29 July 1805 the inspector remarked that the regiment's clothing was generally good, and the materials used were of good quality. The regiment had a dismounted squadron. The regiment's account lists 371fr 25 had been spent on *capotes*, smocks and shoes and 284fr 45 had been spent on lace for *sous-officiers* and other distinctions. The regiment had a mix of legwear in use, 341 pairs of linen overalls had been issued to the foot company, some 1,007m 82 of linen being used for this purpose, alongside 652 pairs of stable trousers. Some 388m 39 of linen had been used to make gaiters for the foot companies – 606 pairs of grey linen gaiters were issued and 28 pairs of black tricot gaiters, yet just 107 pairs of shoes were issued and 114 pairs had been lodged in stores. No *chaperons* existed, but 453 *housses* and 453 *demi-schabraques* had been made and issued. Lace in *dépôt* included 18m 68 27mm wide white worsted lace for corporals' stripes, 309m 48 60mm wide lace for *housses*, 69m 20 35mm white worsted lace for *porte-manteaux*, 79m 60 10mm wide white worsted lace for numbers on the *housses* and *porte-manteaux*. In theory the numbers were to be cut from white cloth, but clearly the 9[e] used lace. For the foot company, two drums and carriages were

# Regulations in Practice 73

*Sapeur* of the 9ᵉ *Dragons* from the Markholsheim manuscript, copied by Rousselot. (*Collection KM*)

Trumpeter of the 9ᵉ *Dragons* c.1802. Presumably by 1805 the *aiguilette* had been removed from use, and we assume the dress of the elite company trumpeters was identical bar difference in headdress.

in use and 12 light cavalry carbines were issued to trumpeters along with 8 pairs of pistols and 20 sabres – clearly a mix of firearms were in use, but we assume trumpeters had *gibernes* and belts. Despite the 1801 regulation, the regiment marched to war retaining its sheepskin *demi-schabraques* – some 453 in use – along with 453 *housses* and 540 round *porte-manteaux*.[75]

About the regiments training, the inspector noted that most men could manoeuvre, and that the basics of equitation were understood – how competent the men actually were would soon be discovered, the inspector remarked! The regiment had been inspected by Prince Murat, who had been satisfied with the regiment, but the officers and *sous-officiers* needed to be on their guard to ensure the men carried out their duties, cared for their horses – a great number were being injured by the ignorance of the men and corporals – and overall the men needed more training in all duties.[76] Inspected in November 1807, the regiment was wearing:[77]

| Item | Good conduction | In need of repair | To be written off | Total | Number made since last review |
|---|---|---|---|---|---|
| *Habits* | 625 | 190 | 208 | 1,013 | 749 |
| *Surtouts* | 598 | 226 | 208 | 1,032 | 1,091 |
| *Manteaux* | 493 | 152 | 56 | 691 | 573 |
| *Gilets* | 730 | 163 | 130 | 1,023 | 794 |
| *Gilets d'écurie* | 548 | 157 | 261 | 966 | 297 |
| *Culottes de peau* | 648 | 250 | 134 | 1,032 | 939 |
| *Pantalons d'écurie* | 405 | 294 | 267 | 966 | 797 |
| *Casques* | 609 | 207 | 88 | 904 | 441 |
| *Bonnets à poil* | 40 | 58 | 21 | 119 | |
| *Bonnets de police* | 528 | 254 | 250 | 1,032 | 750 |
| *Ceinturons* | 670 | 233 | 120 | 1,023 | 490 |
| *Gibernes* | 545 | 221 | 200 | 966 | 278 |
| *Porte-gibernes* | 545 | 221 | 200 | 966 | 278 |
| *Bretelles de Fusil* | 624 | 204 | 138 | 966 | 462 |
| *Porte-Manteaux* | 627 | 199 | 197 | 1,023 | 627 |
| *Bottes* | 433 | 140 | 118 | 691 | 694 |

Furthermore, the regiment had 691 *housses* in use, 488 pairs of cloth *chaperons* and 203 brand-new sheepskin *demi-schabraques*. Cloth and materials which passed through the *dépôt* is remarkable for its details – Grouchy clearly was a thorough inspector:[78]

| Item | In *Dépôt* 1805 | Purchased since 1805 | Total | Amount Used | Remaining in *Dépôt* |
|---|---|---|---|---|---|
| Crimson broadcloth | 196m 75 | 134m 76 | 241m 51 | 161m | 80m 51 |
| Green broadcloth | 596m 21 | 4,191m 33 | 4,787m 54 | 4,444m 20 | 343m 34 |
| Blanc pique de bleu broadcloth | | 2,730m 62 | 2,730m 62 | 2,527m | 203m 62 |
| White broadcloth | 473m 15 | 693m 43 | 1,166m 58 | 1,023m 40 | 143m 18 |
| Crimson serge | 1,518m 08 | 2,548m 62 | 4,066m 70 | 3,069m 96 | 1,997m 34 |
| White serge | 1,027m 94 | 1,476m 84 | 2,504m 78 | 2,167m 20 | 337m 58 |
| Linen for lining | 448m 50 | 2,674m 48 | 3122m 98 | 3122m 98 | |
| Linen for *caleçons* | | 640m | 640m | 640m | |
| *Treillis* | | 2,773m 42 | 2,773m 42 | 2,723m 13 | 50m 29 |
| Lace for corporals | 18m 68 | | 18m 68 | 18m 68 | |
| Lace for *housses* and *chaperons* | 309m 48 | 3,079m 88 | 3,389m 96 | 3,389m 96 | |
| Lace for *porte-manteaux* | 69m 20 | 802m 20 | 871m 40 | 868m | 3m 40 |
| Lace for numerals | 79m 60 | 375m 20 | 454m 80 | 450m 80 | 4m |

| Item | In *Dépôt* 1805 | Purchased since 1805 | Total | Amount Used | Remaining in *Dépôt* |
|---|---|---|---|---|---|
| Silver lace for *sous-officiers* | | 12m 90 | 12m 90 | 6m 48 | 6m 42 |
| Large buttons | 657 dozen | 1,360 doz | 2,017 doz | 1,880 doz | 136 doz |
| Small buttons | 1,439 doz | 1,241 doz | 2,680 doz | 2,647 doz | 32 doz |
| Green tricot | | 266m | 266m | 266mm | |

The *dépôt* had also produced and issued 12 pairs of *culottes* made from broadcloth – for trumpeters or *sous-officiers*? In terms of armament, the regiment had been issued since 1805, 1,180 dragoon muskets but 355 of these had been lost in action. Some 1,192 bayonets had been issued, 274 being lost, 1,141 sabres had been issued and 244 had been lost. Likewise, 884 ½ pairs of pistols had been issued, 235 pairs being lost in action. The regiment had 12 light cavalry *mousquetons* issued to trumpeters, clearly discounting the trumpet major and trumpet corporals, as the regiment had 16 trumpeters yet weapons for just 12.

A letter of 17 November tells us that the men were generally well dressed, but needed boots 'as expected given the rigours of campaign'. The inspector, General Grouchy, pointed out 'there does not exist a model for the *habit* or *surtout*, nor for the other items of clothing in the 9<sup>e</sup> regiment'. He goes on to comment that the regiment was well dressed but was ignorant of the regulations, so was not able to check if the clothing matched the regulation. From this it is implied that the regiment deviated somewhat from the regulation. The regiment's armament was considered to be generally in good condition, but all the sabres were of the old model in the greater part and needed 127 dragoon muskets.[79] In 1811 the 9<sup>e</sup> was converted to a lancer regiment.

## 10<sup>e</sup> *Dragons*

Created in 1674, it became the 5<sup>e</sup> *Lanciers* in 1811. At the review of 19 July 1803, the inspector, Grouchy, commented that the unit had 56 bearskins with the elite company, and all the sheepskin *schabraques* had been removed from use. Stores held 19m 30 of blue broadcloth, which had been purchased in April 1802.[80] Reviewed on 19 October 1804, the regiment had 189 dismounted men with 8 drummers and 548 mounted with 4 trumpeters. The dismounted men had black twill gaiters, *havresacs* and *capotes*, which like the *manteaux* were made from *blanc picque de bleu* broadcloth. We note 701 *habits* were in use and 739 *surtouts*, 447 *manteaux* and 127 bearskins for the elite company. The horses were equipped with *chaperons* and *housses*. Regimental accounts report 19m 90 of blue broadcloth had been used to clothe the trumpeters and drummers.[81] By the time of the next review on 28 July 1805, the drummers and trumpeters were issued 16 light cavalry *mousquetons*.[82] Inspected again at Abbeville on 16 November 1807, not an inch of blue broadcloth is recorded, so presumably the trumpeters had changed their uniform by this

Centre company trooper of the 10ᵉ *Dragons* by Martinet. We know of no contemporary image of the elite company.

Centre company trooper copied by Rousselot from the Markholsheim manuscript. We assume the elite company trumpeters wore the same uniform, but different headdress. (*Collection KM*)

date. The elite company had 120 bearskins, and the men had both a *surtout* and a *habit*. The *manteaux* were still *blanc picque de bleu*, and 17 *mousquetons* were still in service. The inspector noted 'the cut of the *habits* does not accord to the regulations', but how they did not we cannot say.[83] We can say nothing else about the dress of the regiment.

## 11ᵉ *Dragons*

This unit was formed in 1674 and became the *Dragons d'Angouleme* in 1688. The regiment was with the Grande Armée in 1805, in Spain from 1805 and attached to the Grande Armée from July 1813.

The paper archive for the regiment is remarkable for its completeness and complexity. The regiment was reviewed on 1 February 1802 by General d'Hautpoul. He found little wrong with the clothing, but a lot wrong with the regiment's equitation, drill and

Regulations in Practice 77

Officer of centre company by Martinet.

Centre company trooper of the 11ᵉ *Dragons* by Martinet. We know of no contemporary representation of the elite company.

discipline. He referred the officers and *sous-officiers* to the 1788 cavalry regulations and the 1792 *police* regulations for the internal discipline of a regiment. He stressed that the regiment's tailors needed to study better the model items, and that the captain clothing officer needed to be more rigorous in quality control and checking the master tailor had exactly copied the model item and regulation. Many old *vestes* needed whitening, as did the buff work. From the inspection, d'Hautpoul comes across as a very thorough, well read and informed officer, very magnanimous in his approach to shortcomings – all in all an excellent officer. The elite company had not yet received any items to mark out their status. One oddity in the inspection is that the regiment was armed with light cavalry-style carbine worn from *banderole-porte-mousqueton*, and possessed not a single bayonet.[84]

More than a year passed until the next inspection on 29 July 1803, conducted by General de Bourmont. By this date the elite company were decked out in 56 brand-new bearskins. Since the last review 437 *habits* had been made, 402 *surtouts*, 437 *vestes*, 340 stable coats, 361 pairs of *culottes de peau*, 303 pairs of stable trousers and 427 *bonnets de police*. Dépôt held 66 brand-new *habits*, 54 brand-new *surtouts*, 80 *manteaux* needing repairs and 13 to be written off, while 76 *manteaux* in service needed repairs. Dépôt held

Trumpeter of the 11ᵉ *Dragons*, presumably in campaign dress, from the Markholsheim manuscript by Rousselot. Notes by Rousselot implies the elite company trumpeters wore white colpacks and had copper fish scale boards to their white-ringed epaulettes. (*Collection KM*)

*Sapeur* of the 11ᵉ *Dragons* by Otto, copied by Rousselot. (*Collection KM*)

7 helmets needing repairs and 230 to be written off. The regiment was still armed with carbines.[85]

When reviewed on 15 October 1804 the regiment's clothing was described as being in good condition and 'clean and tidy' thanks 'to the example set by the *sous-officiers* of the elite company'. Regimental accounts attest to 6,596fr being spent on buying new buff work for the regiment to enable the use of dragoon muskets, and 200fr on lace for *sous-officiers* and other distinctions since the last on review 20 June 1804, the report for which alas says nothing about clothing. The regiment now had 107 bearskins in service, 51 being obtained since July 1803. The regiment now wore *bottes à l'écuyère*, instead of *bottes forte*, some 425 pairs being in use and 169 being issues since 1803. Dépôt had used 32m 2 of crimson tricot – for trumpeters' *porte-manteaux* we wonder? Further, some 428 pairs of shoes were in use, with a further 445 pairs in *dépôt*, accompanied by 288 pairs of black worsted gaiters. The inspector officially reported that *bonnets de police* were to made from materials reclaimed from old clothing rather than new cloth being used for these, and were certainly not to have lace or worsted tassels, he remarked. The regiment had received 840 dragoon muskets and had retained 17 light cavalry carbines, 16 of which were issued to the trumpeters and drummers.[86]

Under a year passed until the regiment was next inspected on 18 August 1805. The biggest surprise in the inspection is the vast sum of 908fr 60 being spent on dressing the drum major! The mind boggles as to the extravagance of this uniform for such a large sum of money. Further, 516fr had been spent on lace for *sous-officiers* and other distinctions – presumably plumes and the epaulettes for the elite company. The regiment now had 540 linen smocks in use, 540 *capotes*, 540 pairs of black gaiters, the same number of linen overalls, 540 pairs of shoes and 304 infantry *havresacs*. The elite company had 116 bearskins, and 330 pairs of cloth *chaperons* were in service along with 405 sheepskin *demi-schabraques*. Of interest, the regiment's 22 drummers and trumpeters were armed with 16 light cavalry carbines, 22 sabres and 8 pairs of pistols.[87] The next review, at the end of 1807, cannot be located at the time of writing.

The next document is from August 1814 and reveals the following items the regiment had, and the shortfall.[88]

| Item | In service, but due to expire in the next year | In need of repair | To be replaced in the next year | To be replaced | Items short |
|---|---|---|---|---|---|
| *Habits* | 38 | 88 | 67 | 94 | 187 |
| *Gilets en drap blanc* | 59 | 40 | 40 | 95 | 234 |
| *Gilets d'écurie* | 59 | 69 | 77 | 100 | 158 |
| *Surculottes* | 16 | 6 | 4 | 29 | 413 |
| Stable trousers | 44 | | | 9 | 423 |
| *Culottes de peau* | 51 | | 4 | 21 | 398 |
| *Manteaux* | 143 | 66 | 17 | 69 | 165 |
| *Bonnets de police* | 95 | 5 | 34 | 81 | 259 |
| Helmets | 156 | 37 | 23 | 50 | 171 |
| Waistbelts | 256 | 20 | 3 | 31 | 150 |
| *Gibernes* and belts | 229 | 34 | 3 | 34 | 163 |
| Pairs of gauntlets | 34 | | | | 433 |
| Sword knots | 164 | 1 | | 40 | 264 |
| *Porte-manteaux* | 123 | 77 | 37 | 118 | 114 |
| *Banderole-porte-carabines* | 105 | 9 | 2 | 16 | |
| Pairs of boots and spurs | 42 | 59 | 50 | 85 | 238 |
| Pompoms | 316 | | | | 150 |

The regiment was armed rather unexpectedly with 81 An XI light cavalry *mousquetons* in good condition, 41 needing repairs and 2 to be written off. The men on parade that day had 917 shirts, 336 black stocks, 424 white stocks, 270 pairs of linen socks, 66 pairs of woollen socks, 363 pairs of shoes and 1,036 pairs of black tricot gaiters. Stores held no cloth nor materials beyond 24m 26 of linen and 387m 90 of *treillis*. Clothing in the *dépôt* consisted of 14 new *gilets d'écurie*, 207 pairs of stable trousers, 162 pairs of *culottes de peau*, 73 pairs of braces, 60 *giberne* belts and 137 pompoms!

When disbanded in November 1815, the *dépôt* held 0m 10 blue broadcloth, proof positive that the trumpeters were dressed in blue *habits* with Royalist Livery during the first Restoration and may well have been indeed worn during the 100 days.[89]

No lace of any kind was listed for *porte-manteaux*, silver for *sous-officiers*, for corporals, trumpeters or chevrons. The regimental *dépôt* held 36 new *habits-vestes* and 34 old-model *habits* to be disposed of, 34 *vestes*, 100 *gilets d'écurie*, 89 *bonnets de police*, 119 pairs of *pantalons à cheval*, 57 pairs of *culottes de peau*, 119 new *manteaux*, 33 needing repairs and 60 to be written off. Also listed were 182 pompoms, 100 pairs of grenadiers' epaulettes and 43 grenadiers' *aigrettes*. Clearly, the elite company had epaulettes and *aigrettes* as per the Bardin regulation and the regulation pompom was worn by the centre companies in the helmet. The *pantalons à cheval* were clearly ankle-length items made from beige broadcloth with black leather reinforcement to the inner leg. Armament wise, the *dépôt* held 38 *fusils de dragon* and 8 carbines Model An XI, 68 bayonets and 162 sabres. We also find in stores *effect de modèle habits* for trumpet major, trumpet and dragoon and both patterns of *manteau*. Alas, we cannot say if the trumpeters' items were green or blue: I suggest the latter.

A second report reveals the *dépôt* of 1ᵉ, 2ᵉ and 3ᵉ squadrons held 42 *habits-vestes* and *vestes*, 42 *bonnets de police*, 60 new *manteaux* and 64 needing repairs, 42 new pairs of *pantalons à cheval*, 106 new helmets, and 234 needing repairs, 25 new *gibernes*, 226 needing repairs and 164 to be disposed of, 216 new *porte-gibernes* and 111 needing repairs, 168 *banderole-porte-mousquetons* that were brand new and 88 needing repairs. Just 3 waistbelts in good condition were in *dépôt* along with 295 needing repairs and a further 46 that were scheduled to be disposed of or cannibalised for materials. The *dépôt* held 245 carbines of the model of An XI, 90 sabres and 330 pistols – clearly the regiment had been equipped with light cavalry firearms and belt.[90]

## 12ᵉ *Dragons*

Formed in Maastricht in 1675, General Kellermann, the future Marshal, inspected the regiment on 3 April 1802. The regiment's clothing was in appalling condition: out of 529 *habits*, 466 needed immediate replacement. Just 3 *surtouts* were in use. Out of 332 *manteaux*, 256 needed replacement, every single pair of *culottes de peau* were also listed for replacement, and of the 389 sheepskin *schabraques*, 297 were to be replaced. They were used side by side with 300 new pairs of *chaperons*, with 503 *housses*. Stores held no cloth to make any new clothing. Kellermann ordered 466 habits to be repaired and the regiment to purchase 1,678m of crimson serge for this purpose, and authorised 200fr be spent to repair 100 helmets. He also authorised the purchase of 581 plumes costing 871fr 10 and 581 cockades for the helmet costing 87fr 15.[91]

Kellermann again inspected the regiment on 30 June 1803. He noted 479 *habits* had been made, of which 461 were in service, along with 463 *surtouts* and 407 brand-new *manteaux*. We also note 468 brand-new *housses* and pairs of *chaperons* had been made and issued.[92]

Officer of the 11ᵉ *Dragons* by Martinet.

Centre company trooper of the 11ᵉ *Dragons* by Martinet. We know of no contemporary iconography of the elite company or trumpeters.

Reviewed once more 10 October 1804, regimental accounts report 20,250fr had been spent buying shoes, *capotes* and smocks for the foot company and a further 20,339fr 12 to clothe them. No bearskins existed for the elite company.[93]

The regiment was next reviewed on 23 August 1805. The first surprise is that 11m 08 of blue broadcloth had been used to make trumpeters' clothing and over 73m remained in stores. We note 611 *habits* were in use, 687 *surtouts* and just 398 *blanc picque de bleu manteaux*. No bearskins were reported for the elite company. The horse equipment included *housses* and *chaperons*. Trumpeters and drummers were armed with 14 light cavalry *mousquetons*, the dragoons with 705 dragoon muskets. Some 671 sabres, 719 bayonets and 993 pistols were in use.[94]

The regiment was with the Grande Armée from 1805 to 1807, and then served in Spain from 1808 to 1813, when it fought at Danzig and thence in the battle for Paris. The paper archive for the regiment 1808 to 1814 has no records whatsoever regarding clothing of the regiment.[95] Among the papers of the 15ᵉ *Dragons* at incorporation as the 10ᵉ *Dragons* in August 1814 we find an inspection return of the men taken into that new regiment from the 12ᵉ:[96]

| Item | In service, but due to expire in the next year | In need of repair | To be replaced as life expired | To be replaced | Items short |
|---|---|---|---|---|---|
| *Habits* | 30 | 7 | | | 25 |
| *Vestes* | 30 | 3 | | | 29 |
| *Gilets d'écurie* | 39 | | | | 23 |
| *Surculottes* | 30 | 5 | | | 27 |
| *Pantalons* | | | | | 62 |
| *Culottes de peau* | 30 | 5 | | | 27 |
| *Manteaux-capote* | 69 | | | | |
| *Bonnets de police* | | 62 | | | |
| *Helmets* | 49 | 10 | | | 3 |
| *Gauntlets* | | | | | 62 |

The men were armed with 62 sabres, 3 of which were to be written off, 62 An XI light cavalry carbines, of which 38 needed repairs, and no man had a bayonet. The 62 men were wearing in addition 124 shirts, 60 pairs of linen *pantalons*, 62 black stocks, 62 pairs of shoes – not a single pair of socks or gaiters were issued, ergo the men were barefoot and bare legged. Furthermore, not a single pair of underwear was in use. The bulk of the regiment became the *Dragons d'Orleans* in 1814. Not a single piece of paper has survived from the *Dragons d'Orleans* nor the 12[e] *Dragons* from the end of the Empire concerning its dress and equipment.

## 13[e] *Dragons*

Formed in the Languedoc in 1676, it became the *Conde Dragons* in 1724, and thence *Dragons de Monsieur* in 1774. As the 13[e] *Dragons*, from 1791 the regiment seemingly adopted the provisions of the 1798 dress regulation to wear *bleu de ciel* with yellow facings. The regimental archives show that between 13 February 1802 and 16 May 1803 stores had used of 188m 87 of blue broadcloth and not an inch of green, to make 61 *habits*, 87 *surtouts* and 158 *housses*. We also note the elite company had 56 bearskins. Other materials used included 77m 49 of white broadcloth and 231m 14 white serge.[97] Not an inch of yellow broadcloth existed, so we are left to wonder how the regiment was dressed. Presumably these *bleu de ciel habits* were 'more of the same' of those in already in use. Yet, at the time of the 1802 inspection, stores held 201m 10 of green broadcloth and 98m 22 of *rose* broadcloth.[98] The *habits* may well have been *bleu de ciel* with white facings and linings if we rely solely on the archive documents. By 18 October 1804, the regiment was wearing green *habits*, 500 being produced since 18 December 1803. On this date the elite company had 125 bearskins.[99] Inspected on 25 July 1805, the elite company and trumpeters had 158 sheepskin *schabraques*, all scheduled for replacement, so too 25 blue *habits* no doubt worn by trumpeters and drummers.[100] Reviewed on 12 December 1807, we note 77 bearskins were in use, and 480 plumes for 988 men: clearly these were restricted to the elite company and perhaps *sous-officiers*.[101]

Regulations in Practice 83

Officer of the 13ᵉ *Dragons* by Martinet.

Centre company trooper of the 13ᵉ *Dragons* by Martinet.

The regiment served in Spain from 1808, marched to Germany in summer 1813 and fought at Leipzig and thence in France in 1814. That summer the regiment possessed the following clothing:[102]

| Item | In service, but due to expire in the next year | In need of repair | To be replaced as life expired | To be replaced | Items short |
|---|---|---|---|---|---|
| *Habits* | 185 | 2 | | 50 | 27 |
| *Vestes en drap blanc* | 145 | 5 | | 81 | 33 |
| *Gilets d'écurie* | 157 | 1 | | 82 | 24 |
| Stable trousers | 211 | | | 2 | 51 |
| *Culottes de peau* | 221 | | 3 | 10 | 30 |
| *Manteaux* | 127 | 36 | | 39 | 62 |
| *Bonnets de police* | 181 | | | 59 | 24 |
| Gauntlets | 28 | | | | 236 |
| Helmets | 159 | 58 | | | 26 |
| Bearskins | 6 | 10 | 35 | | |

Elite company trooper of the 13e *Dragons* by Martinet. Interestingly, Martinet gives scarlet or white bearskins cords. Rousselot notes the *sapeurs* of the regiment wore the same uniform, but with the addition of a scarlet *aiguilette* to the left shoulder. They carried a lance with white over red pennant.

The stand out item from the inspection are 51 bearskins in service. Not every man had a *veste*, nor a *habit*. To make up for the lack of a *habit*, a *gilet d'écurie* must have been worn. This still left a shortfall in 3 garments! For the men lacking helmets we assume they only had their *bonnet de police*, yet insufficient numbers of these existed. No man had his regulation allocation of clothing. Other items in use included 465 shirts, 221 black stocks, 157 pairs of stockings, 195 pairs of shoes for stable duties, 136 pairs of black gaiters, 149 pairs of knee buckles as well as 181 *habit* brushes, 162 brushes for cleaning the helmet, 160 brushes for cleaning buttons and 126 polishing tools for the *giberne* in terms of stores.[103]

Stocks of clothing and equipment comprised 72 brand-new *gilets d'écurie*, 348 brand-new pairs of stable trousers, 10 pairs of *culottes de peau*, 70 *manteaux*, 169 *bonnets de police*, 50 pairs of boots, 269 plumes, 188 new helmets, 6 trumpets, 42 waistbelts, 35 *gibernes* with *porte-gibernes*, 2 musket slings, 110 sword knots, 15 *porte-manteaux*, and 205 pompoms for helmets; all brand-new and waiting to be issued. More plumes existed than could be used by the elite company, so we assume plumes were used by both this and centre companies, as suggested by Aaron Martinet in his plate of the regiment. In terms of armament, the regiment had 45 *fusils de dragon* in good condition and 26 needing repairs, 192 sabres in good condition and 43 needing to be repaired and 4 that were to be disposed of. There were 146 pistols in good condition and 26 needing repairs as well as 48 light cavalry carbines. The regiment used a mix of firearms – yet not a single shoulder belt for carbine or the sling to carry the dragoon musket existed! Presumably the firearms were carried over the rider's back on the musket sling. The carbines are likely to be for the elite company.

The inspector's comments are of huge interest to us. He reports that the regiment had not adopted the 1812 regulations, and ordered that *habits-vestes* and cut round *gilets* were to be made. The inspector also noted that the *gilets d'écurie* were cut like *habits-vestes* in that they were double breasted and reported that the trumpeters were to dispose of their green *habits* and adopt blue *habits* with the livery of the King! As an interim measure, the quarter-master was to ensure that the lining of the *habits* inherited from the 23[e] *Dragons* were to have new lining and distinctions sewn on to harmonise all ranks as the new *Dragons de Conde*.[104]

We know nothing else as no disbandment paperwork has survived for the regiment, but we can be sure that from 1811 to 1814 the trumpeters were in green with the Imperial Livery, and from 1814 to 1815 in blue *habits* faced in crimson with Royalist Livery![105]

## 14[e] *Dragons*

This unit was created on 3 March 1672 and named the 14[e] *Dragons* from 1791. Inspected on 2 April 1802, we note just 92 *habits* were in use, alongside 201 *surtouts*. General Grouchy, who conducted the inspection, ordered 271 *habits* made and the same number of *surtouts*.[106] When inspected on 9 June 1803, 381 *habits* were in use, 269 being made since the last review, as had 283 *vestes*, 339 *surtouts* and 152 *blanc picque de bleu manteaux*. The elite company had 56 bearskins and 505 plumes had been distributed.[107]

The regiment was with the Grande Armée and was reviewed 14 October 1804, by which time 101 bearskins were in use, and 399 additional *habits* had been made along with 768 *surtouts*. We also note 764 plumes were in service and the foot company had 307 *havresacs* and 8 drums and carriages had been issued. Worthy of comment, stores had held 33m 60 of blue broadcloth in 1803, a

Elite company trooper of the 14[e] *Dragons* in a print published in 1814 by Bassett. Rousselot notes the *sapeurs* of the regiment wore the same uniform, but with the addition of a lance with white over red pennant and yellow crossed axe badges to the upper arm.

Officer of the 14ᵉ *Dragons* by Martinet.

Centre company trooper of the 14ᵉ *Dragons* depicted by Martinet.

further 45m 70 had been purchased, of which 59m 64 had been used to make drummers' and trumpeters' clothing, leaving 19m 70 in stores. Rather than dragoon muskets, the regiment was armed with light cavalry *mousquetons*.[108]

When reviewed again on 19 August 1805, the men were wearing *habits*, *surtouts*, *blanc picque de bleu manteaux*, and the elite company had 107 bearskins. The horse harnesses included *chaperons* and *housses*. Over the preceding year more blue broadcloth had been bought, making a total of 37m 40 of blue broadcloth, of which 23m 80 had been used to make – we assume – trumpeters' clothing. These were armed with light cavalry *mousquetons*, the rank and file now being armed with dragoon muskets. We also report 53m 94 of scarlet broadcloth had been used, leaving 20m 25 in store: we guess this cloth was also used on the trumpeters' and drummers' clothing.[109]

Inspected on 26 December 1807, 86 bearskins were in use with the elite company, and 698 sets of *housses* and pairs of *chaperons* were in service. Since 1805 a further 77m 56 of blue broadcloth had been purchased, and 37m 50 being used, leaving 37m 46 in stores.[110] The quantities suggest the trumpeters' *habits* and *surtouts* were blue, as were their *chaperons* and *housses*. All the remaining scarlet broadcloth had been used. Did the 14ᵉ keep its trumpeters in blue? We guess so. By disbandment the trumpeters seem to have been in reversed colours.

From 1808 the regiment served in Spain and fought at Leipzig, Dennewitz and Danzig in 1813. The regiment took part in the campaign in France in 1814 and that summer, at the end of the campaign, the regiment possessed the following clothing:[111]

| Item | In service, but due to expire in the next year | In need of repair | To be replaced in the next year | To be replaced | Items short |
|---|---|---|---|---|---|
| *Habits* | 179 | 7 | | 39 | |
| *Vestes* | 142 | 4 | | 63 | |
| *Gilets d'écurie* | 163 | | 23 | 7 | |
| *Culottes de peau* | 122 | | 74 | 33 | |
| Gauntlets | 146 | 4 | 49 | 28 | |
| Pairs of boots | 173 | 10 | 6 | 39 | |
| Helmets | 154 | 18 | | 4 | |
| Plumes | 136 | 3 | 51 | 48 | |
| Grenadiers' epaulettes | 20 | | 36 | | |
| *Pantalons à cheval* | 3 | | 154 | | |
| *Surculottes* | 98 | 3 | | 3 | |
| *Bonnets de police* | 167 | | 35 | | |
| Bearskins | 56 | | | 17 | |

The regiment's elite company swaggered with scarlet grenadiers' epaulettes, bearskins and plumes. We also note the totally non-regulation issue of *pantalons à cheval*, an item worn by light cavalry regiments, in addition to the regulation *surculotte* and *culotte de peau*.

In addition, the men had 177 *manteaux* in good condition, 8 needing repairs and 38 men lacked one. The 217 men were armed with 39 dragoon muskets in good condition with a further 25 needing repairs, 187 sabres in good condition, and 42 needing repairs. Sixty-one pistols in good condition were in use alongside 17 needing repairs, 1 that was beyond repair and 2 bayonets! Furthermore, the men had issued to them 554 shirts, 3 pairs of *pantalons de toile*, 214 black stocks, and 153 white examples, 223 pairs of linen socks, 229 pairs of shoes, 223 pairs of black gaiters, and 291 handkerchiefs.

The *dépôt* held little in the way of materials, just 30m of beige broadcloth for *surculottes*, 25m of white broadcloth for *gilets*, 629m 20 linen for lining, and 233m 50 *treillis* for stable trousers. Clothing in the *dépôt* included 59 new pairs of *culottes de peau*, 120 pairs of *pantalons* and 120 worn-out helmets. The inspector ordered the trumpeters into blue with Royalist Livery and the regiment to adopt all the provisions of the Bardin regulation.[112]

We know nothing more as the regiment's disbandment paperwork has not been located by the author.

## 15ᵉ *Dragons*

The regiment was created on 20 December 1688 by the Duc de Noailles, and became a dragoon regiment in 1776. It was named 15ᵉ *Dragons* in 1791, and was with the Grande Armée until 1808.

Reviewed on 14 July 1803, the elite company had 57 bearskins and we note also that the trumpeters' clothing was blue: 15m of blue broadcloth had been used since 1802 for this purpose.[113] The regiment was organised on 10 November 1803, which witnessed the formal creation of the elite company.[114] When next reviewed on 7 October 1804 the regiment was in cantonments at Versailles. The regiment musted 553 other ranks with 427 troop horses: it needed a further 132 mounts. Stores had issued 250 pairs of shoes, 269 *havresacs*, 256 pairs of gaiters and 256 *sacs a distribution* to the foot company.[115]

Inspected on 8 August 1805, the unit was based at Laon. The men's dress was remarked as being particularly good, and we further note the elite company had 106 bearskins, the men had both a *habit* and a *surtout*, and the *manteaux* were made from *blanc picque de bleu* broadcloth. Also in service were 587 plumes for 592 helmets, every single one of which needed repairs, and 72 men had no headdress beyond their *bonnets de police*. The horses were equipped with *housses* and *chaperons*. We note 1,078 *porte-crosses* were in use. The dismounted company were provided with 678 *havresacs*.[116]

Reviewed again on 30 October 1807, the elite company had 128 bearskins, all the plumes had been lost on campaign, and we note *housses* and *chaperons* were used alongside *blanc picque de bleu manteaux*. A huge amount of clothing needed replacing: of 975 *habits*, just 100 were in good condition, 344 needed repairs and the remaining 531 were destined to be thrown away. Since August 1805, 532 *habits* had been made and 1,247 *surtouts*, of which just 975 remained in service, 272 being lost in action. Of those remaining, just 348 were in good condition. Not a single pair of *culottes de peau* were in use; *pantalons à cheval* were in use instead.[117]

More of these were ordered in 1809, being made from beige broadcloth with black cow hide reinforcement to the inner leg, some 48 pairs being ordered in the last quarter of the year accompanied by the same number of *bonnets de police*, 108 pairs of boots, and 48 pairs of grenadiers' epaulettes for the elite company. In new year 1812 16 new trumpets with cords were purchased for 379fr, and some 120fr 15 was spent repairing clothing: for the men taken into the regiment's *dépôt* from the general cavalry *dépôt* at Saintes, the regiment's major reported that the men's *habits* needed new collars, *revers*, cuffs, piping and buttons to bring them into the regulation of the 15ᵉ *Dragons*. Some 371fr was spent in spring 1813 buying 495 pairs of *manchettes du botte*. The inspector noted that the expense was regrettable because of failings by the regiment's master boot maker and breeches makers. The inspector noted, because the men's boots were cut too low to cover the knee of the breeches, and the breeches were cut so tight that they barely fastened around the knee, the regiment had no option but to issue *manchettes du botte*. He lamented that the *manchettes* were easily soiled and difficult to whiten.[118]

Officer of the 15ᵉ *Dragons* as depicted by Martinet.

Centre company trooper of the 15ᵉ *Dragons* depicted by Martinet. We know of no contemporary iconography of the elite company.

In new year 1813 the 3ᵉ and 4ᵉ squadrons were brought up to strength with an influx of new conscripts, some 367 troopers, 3 sergeant majors, 15 sergeants, 4 *fourriers*, 8 corporals and 8 trumpeters. The inspector, in his review dated 16 March 1813, reported that all the clothing was a stockpile of old regulation clothing that had been held in stores since 1812, but despite this was in good condition. Cloth had been ordered to make 150 *habits* for 7ᵉ company, and that cloth was needed to complete the clothing of 251 men in the 3ᵉ squadron. Rather than *surculottes* the men were wearing grey *pantalons à cheval* reinforced with basane.[119] In the last quarter of the year, the regiment spent 77fr 75 on additional pairs of *manchettes du botte* and again the inspector noted the *culottes de peau* were badly made, far too short, and exposed the men's knees.[120] Either the regiment had an influx of unreasonably tall men, or the regimental workmen, in order to maximise the number of items made from each leather hide, had made the items literally too small for use.

At the close of the First Empire, the regiment was inspected in summer 1814 before being reformed as the 10ᵉ *Dragons*. The regiment's clothing was in tatters or missing:[121]

| Item | In service, but due to expire in the next year | In need of repair | To be replaced as life expired | To be replaced | Items short |
|---|---|---|---|---|---|
| *Habits* | 131 | 19 | 198 | | 37 |
| *Vestes en drap blanc* | 113 | 1 | 8 | | 263 |
| *Gilets d'écurie* | 259 | 5 | 18 | | 103 |
| *Surculottes* | 12 | | | | 373 |
| *Pantalons* | 9 | | | | 376 |
| *Culottes de peau* | 82 | 4 | 5 | | 294 |
| *Manteaux* | 187 | 72 | 74 | | 52 |
| *Bonnets de police* | 186 | 1 | 80 | | 118 |
| Helmets | 244 | 34 | 5 | | 33 |
| Gauntlets | 17 | | | | 368 |
| Bearskins | 48 | 16 | | | 5 |

As with the clothing, the regiment was missing 39 waistbelts, 36 *gibernes* and belts, 93 sword knots, 28 *porte-manteaux*, and a staggering 140 pairs of cavalry boots. In terms of armament the regiment had 305 sabres in good condition along with 203 pistols, 76 light cavalry carbines and 53 bayonets, but of these only 34 had scabbards! The carbines were presumably issued to the elite company. New, unissued clothing in the *dépôt* included 44 *habits*, 3 *vestes*, 75 *gilets d'écurie*, 101 *bonnets de police*, 19 pairs of *culottes de peau*, 92 helmets with *criniere*, 55 pompoms for helmets, 61 waistbelts, 171 *gibernes*, 88 porte-*gibernes*, 100 *bottes de fusil*, i.e., the strap to carry the dragoon musket from the saddle, of which the regiment had none, 60 *porte-manteaux* and 3 pairs of boots. Cloth in the *dépôt* included 22m 54 of blue broadcloth, suggesting that trumpeters were wearing some shade of blue, 170m 98 of white broadcloth, 15m 66 of scarlet – *rose*? – broadcloth, 498m of white serge, 26m of *rose* serge, 73m of lace for the *housses*, 96m of lace for the *porte-manteaux*.[122]

Concerning the dress of the trumpeters, the regiment's archive notes that 36fr was spent on a new trumpet at the end of 1813 and that in the second quarter of 1814 170fr 25 was

Trumpeter of the 15e *Dragons* c.1803 copied from the Markholsheim manuscript by Rousselot. We know of no contemporary iconography of a trumpeter from the regiment. (*Collection KM*)

spent on making 6 trumpeters' *habits* for the war squadrons, and at the same time 7 new trumpets costing 191fr 20 were purchased. A further 100 *giberne* belts were ordered at the same time. The inspector noted that the *habits* did not respect the latest regulation of 23 April 1814 and that in consequence the request for government funds to pay for these garments was rejected as they had 'the wrong lace, were made from the wrong colour broadcloth and had the wrong buttons'.[123] Potentially these garments were Imperial Livery, and the blue broadcloth seems to have been all that was left from making new blue Royalist Livery *habits*.

When disbanded in November 1815, the *dépôt* of the regiment contained 15m 66 of *rose* broadcloth, 305m of white serge, 76m of *rose* serge, 30m 49 of *treillis*, 24m of silver lace for *sous-officiers*, 56m 70 of lace for corporals' stripes and 7m 56 of lace for *porte-manteaux*. Clothing comprised 27 *habits* fit only for the rubbish bin, 121 *gilets d'écurie* for disposal and 34 needing repairs as well as 8 new garments. Also in stores were 33 new pairs of linen overalls, 132 new pairs of *culottes de peau* and a further 13 pairs only fit for cannibalisation for materials, 316 new *gibernes*, 250 *gibernes* needing repairs and 103 needing to be disposed of, along with 512 new *porte-gibernes*, 58 needing repairs and 38 needed to be disposed of or used for parts and materials. Stores also held 439 waistbelts, 173 of which were new, 236 needed repairs and the rest were worn out. *Dépôt* also held 209 carbines in need of repair along with 349 *banderole-porte-carabines*, 162 bayonets, 229 sabres and 80 pistols all needing to be repaired. We also find 202 *porte-crosses*, which are the leather items to carry the dragoon pattern musket from the saddle, 116 carbine boots, 185 brand-new *housses*, 20 brand-new sheepskin *schabraques*, 57 shirts, 40 black stocks, 51 pairs of *manchettes du botte*, and 34 pairs of black gaiters.[124] Alas, we can say nothing on trumpeters or the elite company.

## 16ᵉ *Dragons*

Created as the 16ᵉ *Dragons* in 1791 from various 'free corps', the regiment was with the Grande Armée in 1805, and again in 1814 after service in Spain. The regiment was inspected at Soissons in October 1803. Regimental accounts reported 37,250fr had been spent making *capotes*, and we note the elite company had 101 bearskins. The horses were equipped with 354 sheepskin *schabraques*, and just 12 pairs of *chaperons* potentially for the trumpeters. The *manteaux* were made from regulation *blanc picque de bleu* broadcloth.[125]

Reviewed on 1 August 1805, 680 *habits* were in use as well as 720 *surtouts*, 177 bearskins, 16 sets of *chaperons* and 338 sheepskin *schabraques*. The 362 *manteaux* in use were all *blanc picque de bleu*. The trumpeters were armed with light cavalry *mousquetons*.[126] Reviewed again on 16 December 1807, 89 bearskins were in service, along with 502 *habits* and *vestes*, 920 *surtouts* and 537 *manteaux*. We also note 390 smocks were in use with a further 104 in stores. The trumpeters were still armed with 13 *mousquetons*.[127] Regimental accounts report that on 16 October 1809 96 bearskins were purchased, and in early 1812 we note a pair of *pantalons de nankeen* were obtained.[128]

Trooper of the 16ᵉ *Dragons* as they appeared in 1798–1802 when, for experimental purposes, a single company was dressed in regulation *bleu de ciel*-faced *rose*. Green clothing was in uniform use by 1805. The trumpeters retained this colour scheme for some time beyond 1802.

Officer of the 16ᵉ *Dragons* in the middle years of the Empire by Martinet.

At the end of the 1814 campaign, when the sick, the lame, the injured and old had left the regiment, it mustered just 176 rank and file. The clothing was mostly good, but a lot was missing:[129]

| Item | In service, but due to expire in the next year | In need of repair | To be replaced in the next year | To be replaced | Items short | Observations |
|---|---|---|---|---|---|---|
| *Habits* | 108 | 19 | 6 | 10 | 33 | This does not include the men who have been placed on leave and have been allowed to take their uniform with them. |
| *Vestes or gilets* | 40 | 5 | | 15 | 116 | |
| *Culottes de peau* | 107 | 5 | 28 | 8 | 28 | |
| Stable trousers | 37 | | 25 | 5 | 109 | |
| Braces | 37 | | | | 134 | |
| *Manteaux* | 71 | 21 | | 22 | 62 | |
| *Bonnets de police* | 74 | 6 | 11 | 65 | 20 | |
| *Gilets d'écurie* | 18 | 28 | 25 | 37 | 68 | |
| *Surculottes* | 14 | 4 | 8 | 14 | 136 | *Sous-officers* and soldiers yet to return from prison number 174 men. Two men are proposed to be sent to the Gendarmerie. |
| Helmets | 113 | 14 | | 14 | 35 | |

## Regulations in Practice 93

Centre company trooper of the 16ᵉ *Dragons* in the middle years of the Empire by Martinet. We are not aware of any contemporary imagery of the elite company.

Copied by Rousselot from the Markholsheim manuscript is this trumpeter in *rose*-faced *bleu de ciel*, harking back to the later 1790s. (*Collection KM*)

We note that 48 men had no *giberne* and belt, 29 no sabre belt, 55 men need a pair of boots, 71 men had no gloves and 29 men no sabre knot. The regiment was armed with 123 sabres in good condition, 17 needed repairs and 2 needed to be replaced. It had 65 pistols in good condition and not a single dragoon musket or other firearm in use, although 48 dragoon muskets were in stores. For the 176 men on parade, they had 467 shirts between them, 99 black stocks, 66 pairs of linen stockings, 153 pairs of shoes, and 101 pairs of black tricot gaiters. Many men did not have a complete allocation of kit and equipment. Interestingly, the regiment used a mix of cloth *chaperons* and sheepskin *schabraques*.

Given how desperate the men were for clothing and equipment, it is remarkable that the *dépôt* was overflowing with brand-new, unissued clothing comprising: 224 *habits* and *gilets*, 347 pairs of *culottes de peau*, 185 pairs of stable trousers, 96 sets of braces, 66 *bonnets de police*, 42 pairs of boots, 124 pairs of gauntlets, and 107 sword knots. Kit needing repairs to enable it to be made serviceable included 30 helmets, 30 *gibernes*, 23 *porte-gibernes*, and 16 waistbelts. In terms of cloth, the *dépôt* held 89m 21 of *rose* broadcloth, 178m 63 of green broadcloth, 3m 80 *blanc picque de bleu* broadcloth for *manteaux*, 265m

Copied by Rousselot from the Markholsheim manuscript is this elite company trumpeter in rose, faced green. No archive documents support the existence of white bearskins in the regiment. (*Collection KM*)

Copied by Rousselot from the Markholsheim manuscript is this trumpeter in rose, faced green. (*Collection KM*)

91 of white and *rose* serge, 1m 02 of green tricot, 423m 05 linen, 31m 14 of Imperial Livery for the trumpeters, 41m 85 of wool lace for chevrons, 137m 93 of linen lace for the *housse*, 223m 34 of *treillis*, and 0m 30 of silver lace for *sous-officiers*.

Of great interest, the inspecting officer noted that the regiment had not strictly adhered to the regulations of 19 January and 7 February 1812 concerning the dimensions and cut of clothing and equipment. He further commented that the instruction of 23 April 1814 concerning substitution of the *Lys* for Imperial symbols and the change in the dress of trumpeters and musicians had not been carried out in the regiment. Henceforth the existing clothing was to be replaced with Bardin-regulation *habits* and the trumpeters were to receive new *habits* cut from *bleu de roi* cloth, adorned with Royalist Livery.[130]

We know nothing more as disbandment paperwork has not survived, or at least the author has been unable to locate it.

In the early years of the Empire the 16e *Dragons* seemingly had mounted drummers. At the inspection of the regiment in August 1803 (a month after receipt of the order of *1 Vendémiaire An XII*), there remained four drummers with the regiment who were used for dismounted manoeuvres and were also used mounted. General Canclaux, who carried out the inspection, reported 'as an old Dragoon, knowing their use did not suppress them'.¹³¹

## 17ᵉ *Dragons*

Formed in 1743 by the Comte de Saxe, as the 17ᵉ *Dragons* from 1791, the regiment was with the Grande Armée from 1805.

Inspected at Laon in October 1803, the regiment mustered 730 other ranks, of which 155 were dismounted and 549 allocated to the mounted contingent, for whom 442 horses existed. The men were well dressed, but the inspector noted the shade of *rose* – pink – used for the regiment's facings did not match the government's sample in terms of colour, quality of material and cost. This is borne out by a period portrait of the regimental colonel, who is distinctly not wearing 'hot pink' as decreed by the regulations, but a more sombre orange hue of pink. The elite company was issued with 147 bearskins, one remained in stores and the unit's *manteaux* were made from *blanc picque de bleu* broadcloth.¹³²

Officer of the 17ᵉ *Dragons* by Martinet.

Reviewed again on 8 August 1805, the barracks were in poor condition and needed repairs, so too the beds and blankets. For that reason, the inspector tells us, the townsfolk had been asked to supply these. We note the dismounted contingent had 500 *capotes* and 439 *havresacs*, and wore black gaiters and shoes. The mounted contingent had 456 *blanc picque de bleu manteaux* and the elite company had 107 bearskins. The trumpeters were armed with light cavalry *mousquetons*, as were the drummers, who were also issued *gibernes*.¹³³

When reviewed on 2 January 1808, 116 *habits* were in use alongside 965 *surtouts*. The elite company had just 59 bearskins, with 22 in stores needing repairs. *Housses* and *chaperons* were used on the horses, and the *manteaux* were *blanc picque de bleu*.¹³⁴ One unique aspect of the regiment's clothing was that contrary to the regulations, the *bonnets de police* had lace on the turban – 14m of lace were purchased in 1807 for this purpose for 160fr – and had worsted fringe tassels – 650 being purchased for 147fr in 1807 – with more lace and tassels obtained in 1808.¹³⁵ The regiment marched to Spain in 1808, and was divided during the spring of 1813. The three squadrons in Spain were consolidated with the disbandment of the 3e squadron into the first two on 23 February 1813. In France, two squadrons were raised for service in Germany.136

On 13 March 1813 General Latour-Maubourg reported that the *dépôt* at Haguenau, a company of 79 dragoons, was ready to march on 25 March to join the Grande Armée. He remarked that if the helmets and tack that the major had ordered in February arrived on time, that number could be raised to 100 men. This company, he reported, would be placed under the command of a lieutenant. The sergeant major and the four sergeants were all, bar one, volunteers or 1813 conscripts. The men and horses were of a good quality but, tellingly, the men destined for the 10e, 11e and 12e companies were far from ideal. The general reported that these men 'who have only just arrived, are of a very bad quality. Moreover, on the two hundred men that the 57e *de Ligne* had transferred to the regiment, 105 did not even reach the 5-foot height mark.' The report concludes by stating that 'nothing is organised, be it for clothing, equipping, tacking or mounting these two companies. There is only a single crippled second-lieutenant left in the *dépôt*.'137 One month later, the *dépôt* workshops were still unable to produce any clothing or equipment in the number required due to 'chronic lack of materials and workmen', complained the major.138

*Sapeur* of the 17e *Dragons* c.1810. We note he has no arm badges, and that his axe case belt is fastened over his *giberne* belt with a copper stud. We assume the elite company wore the same uniform but lacked the axe case and beard. In the background we see a trumpeter wearing reversed colours, sporting a colpack as headdress.

Despite these difficulties, on 30 April 1813 at Haguenau three new squadrons were formally mobilised and added to the army in Germany, some 646 other ranks with 604 horses. The new 3e squadron was not yet ready to take to the field and needed 99 horses, the 4e squadron had been formed in Danzig, where it had been armed and equipped and needed 51 men and 72 horses to be brought up to full strength. The 5e squadron *bis* – the supplementary *dépôt* squadron that became the new 7e squadron – had been clothed, equipped and armed by the 'efforts of the regiments Council of Administration' but still needed 164 horses and 160 sets of harness and saddles. 'The *dépôt* is totally empty,' reported the major, and admitted clothing and equipment that was to 'be written off' had been pressed into use.[139]

At the end of the year, the 2ᵉ squadron, then serving in Spain, was disbanded and the cadre sent back to France. The remaining men were distributed between the 1ᵉ, 5ᵉ and 6ᵉ, which were serving in Spain. The 3ᵉ, 4ᵉ and 7ᵉ were on campaign in Germany.[140]

Despite copious documents surviving that refer to the constant shuffling of men and horses between Spain and Germany, precious little archive material exists for the dress of the regiment. Regiment accounts concluded on 20 July reports unpaid debts existed for 217m 47 green broadcloth, 6m 56 white broadcloth, 10m of white lace, 30m of Imperial Livery, 30 musket slings, 30 waistbelts, 30 *giberne* belts, 1m 15 *rose* broadcloth; a sum of 3,139fr 19. We also note 975fr was paid out buying bearskins and epaulettes for the elite company.[141] Clearly at last two trumpeters had Imperial Livery adorning their *habits*. The clothing of the regiment was in good condition in summer 1814:[142]

| Item | In service, but due to expire in the next year | In need of repair | To be replaced in the next year | To be replaced | Items short |
|---|---|---|---|---|---|
| *Habits* | 218 | 53 | | 23 | |
| *Vestes* | 209 | 40 | | 3 | |
| *Gilets d'écurie* | 98 | 55 | | 51 | |
| *Bonnets de police* | 189 | 26 | | 38 | |
| *Culottes de peau* | 242 | 3 | | | |
| *Surculottes* | 120 | 10 | | 9 | |
| Stable trousers | 35 | 3 | | 18 | |
| Bearskins | 40 | | | 1 | |
| Helmets | 285 | 27 | | 3 | |
| Pompoms | 101 | | | | |
| Plumes | 24 | | | | |
| Gauntlets | 248 | 6 | | 1 | |
| Pairs of boots | 118 | 61 | | 23 | |

The standout items in the inspection are the 41 bearskins in use – clearly the elite company had clung on to these. The 24 plumes were for the trumpeters perhaps, everyone else wore a pompom in the helmet as per the Bardin regulation. The regiment's equipment was also almost entirely new, possessing 292 good-condition waistbelts, 355 *gibernes*, of which 325 were in good condition, 355 *porte-gibernes*, of which 6 needed repairs, 275 sword knots, 15 *banderole-porte-carabines* for the 35 allocated weapons [!], and 9 trumpets with banners. Indeed, the regiment was armed with 36 An XI light cavalry carbines and 35 dragoon muskets! The *dépôt* held 723 brand-new shirts, 79 pairs of *pantalons de toile*, 253 black stocks, 108 white stocks, 225 pairs of socks, 230 pairs of shoes, 156 pairs of black gaiters, and 422 pairs of *manchettes du botte*. The inspector noted that the regiment had not acted on the Bardin regulations. Also held in stores were 248 *porte-crosses*; these were the leather straps to suspend the dragoon musket from the

Centre company trooper of the 17ᵉ *Dragons* by Martinet.

Elite company officer, possibly of the 17ᵉ, in summer 1813. We know the regiment still had bearskins for the elite company in summer 1814, so this may well represent the regiment as it appeared a year earlier. (*Collection KM*)

saddle, of which the regiment had none. We note the regiment was issued 32 dragoons' muskets, 7 needed repairs and 36 light cavalry carbines: the latter presumably issued to the elite company, but only 15 *porte-carabines* were issued! Arguably they were worn across the man's shoulders? Stores held no clothing, as it had all been issued.

Cloth held included 583m 80 of beige broadcloth, 169m 57 of blue broadcloth, 17m 68 of scarlet broadcloth, and 130m white serge, which was all used to clothe the men transferred to the 105ᵉ *Régiment de la Ligne*. To be retained by the regiment was 16m 13 of *rose* broadcloth. Not an inch of Imperial Livery existed, but it had done earlier in the year.[143] We guess the regiment had worn infantry clothing due to shortages of green broadcloth, or more realistically dye.

At disbandment in 1815, stores held one brand-new *habit-veste*, 207 in good condition and 62 to be disposed of, alongside 205 *vestes*, 258 *bonnets de police*, 267 helmets all in good condition, as well as 97 pompoms and 25 red plumes. The regiment was armed with 39 dragoon muskets, 171 light cavalry carbines, 117 pistols and had 198 sabres in good condition and 332 needing repairs.[144]

## 18ᵉ *Dragons*

Formed in Metz in 1744, the regiment became the 18ᵉ *Dragons* in 1791 and was with the Grande Armée from 1805. Inspected on 26 September 1804, 67 bearskins were in service,[145] with 133 in use by 5 August 1805. The foot company had 500 *capotes*, 449 pairs of *pantalons de toile*, and only 225 *sacs à peau*. Notably, the men's waistcoats were green, some 292m 74 of green broadcloth being used for this purpose.[146] Reviewed on 4 January 1808, the elite company had 115 bearskins, and the 15 trumpeters were armed with the light cavalry *mousquetons*.[147]

The *dépôt* of 5ᵉ squadron in France was reviewed on 20 March 1813. It mustered 2 officers, 2 sergeant majors, 7 sergeants, 6 corporals, 3 trumpeters and 218 troopers with 87 horses. The inspector noted that for the 252 conscripts in the *dépôt*, 160 *habits*, 181 *vestes*, 219 *bonnets de police*, 74 *gilets d'écurie*, 216 *manteaux*, 241 helmets were needed: the men had the clothes they had arrived at the *dépôt* in and virtually nothing else. Likewise, the squadron needed 242 dragoon muskets and bayonets, 127 pairs of pistols, 252 sabres, 242 sabre belts, 242 *gibernes* and belts, 227 sabre knots, 242 musket slings, 318 *portemanteaux*, 225 pairs of boots and 160 sets of harness and saddlery. The men were all

Officer of the 18ᵉ *Dragons* by Martinet.

Centre company trooper of the 18ᵉ *Dragons* by Martinet. We know of no contemporary iconographic depiction of the elite company.

mediocre, weak and malnourished, and more importantly, the inspector noted, none of them could ride. The *dépôt* had only sufficient materials to make just 30 *habits*.[148]

We know nothing more about the dress of the regiment until summer 1814, when it possessed the following clothing:[149]

| Item | In service, but due to expire in the next year | In need of repair | To be replaced in the next year | To be replaced | Items short |
|---|---|---|---|---|---|
| *Habits* | 20 | 67 | 34 | 11 | 98 |
| *Vestes sans manche* | 44 | 5 | 31 | 4 | 146 |
| *Gilets d'écurie* | 19 | 22 | 65 | 10 | 114 |
| *Culottes de peau* | 35 | | 40 | | 155 |
| Helmets | 45 | 157 | 20 | | |
| *Bonnets de police* | 41 | 12 | 88 | 5 | 88 |
| Stable trousers | | | | | 230 |
| *Manteaux* | 31 | 72 | 42 | 9 | 73 |
| *Surculottes en drap* | 31 | | | | 179 |
| Gauntlets | 21 | | | | 206 |

The regiment's clothing was in shreds and hugely incomplete. In addition, the men were wearing or had been issued 651 shirts, 92 black stocks – most men wore a black neck cloth, the inspector noted – 130 pairs of socks – again some men wore boots or shoes over bare feet – 239 pairs of shoes, 25 pairs of black tricot gaiters, and 16 pairs of grey linen gaiters. The regiment must have presented a very diverse appearance on parade with men wearing *habits* and *gilets d'écurie*. As insufficient of each existed for a man to have both, it was either or. We assume a mix of old- and new-pattern *habits* were in use – the men without a *veste* we assume had *habits-vestes* to conceal the shirt and the top of the *culotte*. Every man had a helmet. For legwear a mix of *surculottes* and *culottes de peau* were used, as again not enough existed to give every man a pair of both. The *dépôt* held no new clothing at all. It had 20 *habits* to be disposed of, along with 14 *manteaux*, 16 helmets and 20 *gibernes*, all to be disposed of or cannibalised for materials and usable parts. In addition, 29 *gibernes* and 36 *porte-gibernes* needed repairs and not an inch of cloth existed to make new items. The regiment

Copied by Rousselot from the Markholsheim manuscript is this trumpeter in rose, faced green. (Collection KM)

was armed with 74 An XI light cavalry musketoons, 37 dragoon muskets, 157 sabres in good condition with 62 needing repairs and 11 to be written off. There were 134 pistols and 11 needing repairs, with 1 to be written off. A further 21 carbines were in store; yet not a single cross belt was issued to carry these weapons, which must have been slung across the dragoon's back on the musket sling. The regiment's saddlery was totally 'life expired' and the men were riding in sheepskin *schabraques* that were passed to the 4[e] *Hussard* as they were light cavalry pattern.[150] We note during the 100 days the trumpeters were re-dressed in blue and 150 scarlet plumes were obtained for the elite company.[151]

## 19[e] *Dragons*

The regiment was created with the decree of 27 February 1793. Inspected in October 1804, we note 502 *habits* were in service, 625 *surtouts* and 164 linen smocks along with 105 bearskins and 600 plumes. A total of 707 buff leather sword knots were in use and 150 *gibernes* and belts were needed. The foot company had 500 broadcloth *capotes*.[152] By August 1805, the 16 trumpeters were issued light cavalry *mousquetons*. Since the last review 121 *habits* had been made and issued, along with 226 *vestes*, 72 smocks and 217 *manteaux*.[153]

Officer of the 19[e] *Dragons* by Martinet.

Centre company trooper of the 19[e] *Dragons* by Martinet. We know of no contemporary iconographic depiction of a trumpeter or member of the elite company.

When reviewed on 17 December 1807, 338 smocks had been lost on campaign, and just one bearskin was in service with the trumpet major, while 88 were in stores needed repairing. The inspector noted he was totally ignorant of the dress of the war squadrons, but reported that 483 *habits*, 715 *vestes* and 1,342 *surtouts* had been made and issued since August 1805. Stores held 274 *habits*, 399 *vestes*, and 104 *surtouts* ready to be issued. The trumpeters alone had *chaperons*, 25 pairs being in use, while every other member of the regiment had a sheepskin *schabraque*. In terms of armament, the regiment acknowledged 1,045 *fusils de dragon*, 1,348 *mousquetons* and 986 sabres. Some 544 *mousquetons* and 21 sabres had been lost on campaign.[154]

When reviewed on 14 March 1810 the 1st and 2nd squadrons had 312 men and 192 horses. The horses were all issued *chaperons*.[155] At the time of the amalgam in summer 1814 the regiment was wearing the following clothing and equipment:[156]

| Item | In service, but due to expire in the next year | In need of repair | To be replaced in the next year | To be replaced | Items short | Observations |
|---|---|---|---|---|---|---|
| *Habits* or *habits–vestes* | 118 | 77 | | 18 | 17 | Not including the items taken away by the men on leave: 72 *habits*, 72 *vestes*, 72 pairs of *culottes de peau*, 72 *bonnets de police*. |
| *Gilets sans manche* | 96 | 8 | 3 | 25 | 98 | |
| *Gilets d'écurie* | 10 | 20 | 18 | 34 | 148 | |
| *Bonnets de police* | 96 | 1 | 20 | 25 | 88 | |
| *Surculottes* | | 10 | 15 | | 205 | |
| *Culottes de peau* | 181 | 4 | 11 | 19 | 15 | |
| Stable trousers | 50 | 5 | 79 | | 96 | |
| *Capotes* or *manteaux* | 152 | 36 | 10 | 32 | | |
| Helmets or bearskins | 184 | 40 | | 6 | | |
| *Porte-manteaux* | 108 | 64 | 4 | 24 | 30 | |
| Pairs of gloves | 141 | 20 | | | 69 | |
| Pairs of boots | 48 | 20 | 14 | 79 | 69 | |
| *Gibernes* | 172 | 45 | | | | |
| *Porte-gibernes* | 172 | 45 | | | | |
| *Banderole-porte-carabines* | | | | | 217 | |
| Waistbelts | 212 | 9 | | | | |
| Musket slings | | | | | | |
| Sabre knots | 213 | 2 | | | | |
| Trumpets and cords | 12 | | | | | |
| Dragoon muskets | 25 | | | | | |
| Sabres | 124 | 87 | | 10 | | |
| Pistols | 245 | 23 | | 2 | | |
| Carbines | 161 | 17 | | 1 | | |
| Bayonets | 134 | 10 | | | | |

Clearly the regiment was in the process of converting to Bardin regulation: the elite company still had bearskins and no doubt the same men had *habits a revers* and the *manteau*! The inspector noted the regiment had not acted on the decree of February 1812 nor that of 1814 to dress the trumpeters in blue and remove Imperial Livery and other iconography from use, but noted the major had begun the process.

We also note a single *banderole-porte-carabine* existed for 179 carbines: presumably the carbine was carried off the saddle – 169 sets of *botte de carabine* existed – or the soldier's back. Just 25 *fusils de dragon* were issued. The men also had issued 609 shirts, 212 black stocks, 411 white stocks, 380 pairs of woollen stockings, 206 pairs of shoes, 42 pairs of grey linen gaiters, and 390 pairs *of manchettes du botte*.

We note at the time of amalgamation, the trumpeters were decked out in Imperial Livery as stores held 16m 92, as well as 29m 86 of lace for corporals, and 20m 6 lace for chevrons. Stores held 13m 91 of yellow serge, 3m of *blanc picque de bleu* for *manteaux*, 252m 2 of green broadcloth, 0m 15 of green tricot and 22m 43 of *treillis*. Of note, trumpeters had *chaperons* and everyone else had a sheepskin *schabraque*. In addition, the *dépôt* held 14 brand-new *gilets*, 365 brand-new pairs of stable trousers, 242 new pairs of *culottes de peau*, 188 sets of braces and 242 pompoms for centre company helmets, 400 pairs of shoe buckles, and 30 helmet peaks. The *dépôt* mostly held items that were no longer fit for service, which included 14 *habits*, 5 *gilets d'écurie*, 29 *capotes*, 30 helmets, 31 *porte-manteaux*, 27 *gibernes* and belts, 6 *banderole-porte-carabines*, 22 waistbelts and 2 trumpets.[157]

The regiment was with the Armée du Rhin in 1815, and after fighting two actions at Ober-Hausbergen and Mittle-Hausbergen it was disbanded that summer. The *dépôt* held the following materials:[158]

155m 65 green broadcloth
23m blue broadcloth
168m 75 *blanc picque de bleu* broadcloth for *manteaux*
57m 10 aurore broadcloth
0m 74 beige broadcloth for *surculottes*
108m 70 green tricot
119m 70 aurore serge
13m 91 yellow serge
1036m 62 linen for lining
1138m 22 *treillis*
44m 22 white worsted lace for *porte-manteaux*
11m 25 silver lace for *sous-officiers*
18m white lace for corporals' stripes
590m trumpeters' lace
11m 10 red wool lace for chevrons
78m 75 black twill for gaiters

The amount of trumpeters' livery suggests it was a single purchase that was never used, of we assume more Imperial Livery delivered during the 100 days. The blue broadcloth tells us that the trumpeters had blue *habits* with Royalist Livery. The *dépôt* held in addition:[159]

| Item | New | In need of repair | To be written off |
| --- | --- | --- | --- |
| *Habits vestes* | 2 | 10 | 185 of the old model |
| *Gilets sans manche* |  | 6 | 12 |
| *Gilets d'écurie* |  | 11 | 17 |
| *Bonnets de police* |  |  | 105 |
| Stable trousers | 34 |  | 4 |
| *Culottes de peau* | 50 | 36 | 75 |
| *Surculottes* |  |  | 5 |
| *Manteau* | 160 | 90 | 64 |
| *Porte-manteaux* | 22 | 91 | 118 |
| Helmets | 94 | 130 | 170 |
| Infantry greatcoats | 8 |  |  |
| Pairs of gloves |  | 31 | 28 |
| Sabre belts | 278 | 48 | 98 |
| *Gibernes* | 260 | 130 | 78 |
| *Porte-gibernes* | 276 | 98 | 220 |
| Sword knots | 140 | 55 |  |
| *Banderole-porte-carabines* | 48 | 5 |  |
| Musket slings | 585 | 33 |  |
| Pairs of boots |  | 28 | 60 |
| Pairs of spurs |  | 9 | 66 |
| Pompoms | 246 |  |  |
| Trumpets |  |  | 8 |

The infantry greatcoats come as something of a surprise, unless of course the 29 *capotes* in store a year earlier were infantry *capotes* and not *manteaux-capote*! Also held were 53 brand-new shirts, 137 pairs of grey gaiters, 12 pairs of black gaiters, 3 pairs of *manchettes du botte*, 12 pairs of knee buckles, 36 shoe brushes, 365 pairs of shoe buckles and 78m 75 of black tricot to make gaiters. *Dépôt* also held 5 *habits de modèle*, which included items for the trumpet major and trumpeter, 2 patterns of *vestes*, 2 pattern of stable coat, 2 *bonnets de police* – one for a dragoon the other for a trumpeter we assume – a pair of stable trousers, 2 types of *surculottes* and a *manteau-capote*.[160]

## 20ᵉ *Dragons*

Created in July 1793, the regiment was with the Grande Armée in 1805, and again from summer 1813, having served in Spain since 1808. Reviewed on 27 July 1805, we note the elite company had no bearskins, 22 light cavalry *mousquetons* were in use with the trumpeters and the men had *habits, surtouts* and *blanc picque de bleu manteaux*.[161] When reviewed on 28 December 1807 the inspector noted that the regiment mustered 1,019 *sous-officiers*, trumpeters and men, noting the elite company had 106 bearskins, 993 *habits* were in use, with 30% needing to be replaced, and 1,096 *surtouts*, with 50% to replaced urgently. A total of 978 helmets were in use, with 25% life expired, and again 50% of the *culottes de peau* needed to be replaced immediately, 463 examples. For over 1,000 men, just 613 horses were with the regiment, equipped with *housses* and *chaperons*. The dismounted men were issued 678 pairs of black gaiters and shoes, while the mounted men had 418 pairs of grey linen gaiters, and also a pair of shoes. Each man had a pair of underwear, a pair of socks, a shirt and a black regulation stock. The trumpeters were armed with An XI light cavalry *mousqueton*.[162]

Officer of the 20ᵉ *Dragons* by Martinet.

Centre company trooper of the 20ᵉ *Dragons* by Martinet. We know of no contemporary iconographic depiction of a trumpeter or member of the elite company.

In summer 1814, having fought at Saint-Dizier, Brienne, La Rothière, Mormant, Montereau and Troyes, the regiment had the following clothing and equipment in use:[163]

| Item | In service, but due to expire in the next year | In need of repair | To be replaced in the next year | To be replaced | Items short |
|---|---|---|---|---|---|
| *Habits* | 155 | 11 | 3 | 1 | 13 |
| *Vestes* | 160 | 3 | 2 | 1 | 17 |
| *Culottes de peau* | 169 | | | | 14 |
| *Surculottes* | 94 | 6 | 7 | | 76 |
| *Manteaux* | 136 | 42 | 1 | | 4 |
| *Gilets d'écurie* | 140 | 16 | 3 | | 24 |
| Stable trousers | 133 | | 1 | 2 | 47 |
| *Bonnets de police* | 132 | 41 | | | 10 |
| Helmets | 116 | 47 | 1 | 3 | 16 |
| Trumpets | 8 | | | | 2 |

The men were wearing a mix of *habits* and *gilets d'écurie*, and a mix of *surculottes* and *culottes de peau*, but overall the clothing was in good condition. The *habits* were all old pattern, the inspector noted, and remarked that the *surculottes* were *pantalons* made from grey broadcloth with black leather reinforcement. Equipment in use comprised:[164]

| Item | In service, but due to expire in the next year | In need of repair | To be replaced in the next year | To be replaced | Items short | Observations |
|---|---|---|---|---|---|---|
| *Gibernes* | 125 | 41 | | | 17 | The 9 sabres listed as to be replaced are not of the dragoon model. |
| *Porte-gibernes* | 125 | 41 | | | 17 | |
| Waistbelts | 141 | 41 | | | 1 | |
| Sword knots | 182 | | | 1 | | |
| Pairs of boots | 59 | 39 | 1 | 29 | 55 | |
| *Porte-manteaux* | 109 | 44 | 13 | 1 | 17 | |
| Gauntlets | 173 | | | | 10 | |
| Pompoms | 44 | | | | 139 | |
| Musket slings | 126 | | | | 57 | |
| Saddles | 127 | 49 | | | 38 | |
| Bridles | 120 | 56 | | | 38 | |
| *Housses* | 105 | 70 | | | 39 | |
| *Schabraques* | 96 | 79 | | | 39 | |
| *Fusils de dragon* | 105 | 9 | | | | |
| Sabres | 136 | 43 | | 9 | | |
| Pistols | 135 | 5 | | | | |
| Carbines | 21 | | | | | |

One oddity we see from the table is that the regiment was armed with both dragoon muskets and light cavalry carbines. Presumably, based on numbers issues, only the elite company had *culottes de peau* and carbines. The men on parade were issued 445 shirts, 170 black stocks, 285 white stocks, 161 pairs of linen socks – sufficient for nearly every man to have a pair – 166 pairs of shoes, 96 pairs of black gaiters and 117 pairs of *manchettes du botte*. The *dépôt* held virtually no materials, merely 247m 02 of serge and 29m 29 of lace for corporals' stripes. New clothing, ready to issue, included 58 *habits*, 122 *vestes*, 47 *gilets d'écurie*, 52 *bonnets de police*, 325 pairs of *culottes de peau*, 1 pair of stable trousers, 68 pairs of gauntlets, 116 helmets and 40 needing repairs, 54 *manteaux de capote*, 50 pompoms, 215 waistbelts, 287 *gibernes*, 175 *bottes de fusil*, 28 *porte-gibernes*, 42 *housses* and 30 *schabraques* only fit to be discarded.

*Sapeur* of the 20ᵉ *Dragons* by Ernest Fort based on a supposedly contemporary image.

Also, in stores for the *sous-officiers* were 14 black silk '*mouchoires*', i.e., kerchiefs, that were used in replace of the regulation stock. The reviewing officer noted that items of clothing had not yet been replaced to accord with the instruction of 25 May 1814, and more importantly noted that the 20ᵉ had not adopted the provisions of the decree of 7 February 1812 introducing the Bardin regulation. Further, the decree of 23 April 1814 concerning modifications to the dress of trumpeters and removal of Imperial symbols had not been carried out. The inspector ordered that *fleur-de-lys* were to be worn on the tails of the *habits* as well as on the *gibernes*, and that henceforth the trumpeters were to wear *bleu de roi* and the King's Livery. The inspector initiated a "scrap and replace" policy: the regiment was to be dressed in new clothing made to the Bardin regulation.[165]

Disbanded on 24 November 1815, we know beyond any shadow of a doubt that the regiment's trumpeters had Imperial Livery during the 100 days as the inspecting general ordered all 306m of trumpeters' livery to be burnt on 2 December 1815. Had any been used? Hard to say. Possibly not.

Other materials in the *dépôt* included 248m 63 of green broadcloth, 0m 25 of *blanc picque de bleu* broadcloth, 16m 91 of aurore broadcloth, 120m 60 of green tricot, 202m 46 of aurore serge, 100m 65 yellow serge, 1,708m 87 linen for linings, 411m 74 *treillis* to line *porte-manteaux* and make stable trousers from, 77m white lace for corporals' stripes, and 2m 5 red worsted lace for chevrons. Brand-new unissued clothing included 127 *gilets d'écurie*, 32 pairs *culottes de peau*, 468 pairs of stable trousers, 7 *bonnets de police* and

11 helmets, 30 *porte-manteaux*, 225 *gibernes*, and 104 *porte-gibernes*. Also in stores were 41 black stocks, 20 pairs of linen socks, 91 pairs of black tricot gaiters, 24 pairs of linen gaiters, 26 complete *trousses* – i.e., soldier's housewife – 10 handkerchiefs, and 63 pairs of *manchettes du botte*. Old clothing in stores included 7 *gilets*, 2 *gilets d'écurie*, 8 pairs of *culottes de peau*, 7 *manteaux*, 100 helmets, 35 *porte-manteaux*, 137 *gibernes* with belts, 90 sabre belts, 29 sword knots, 58 light cavalry carbines, 5 pistols, 58 bayonets and 10 *sapeurs'* axes.[166]

Cloth purchased in 1815 comprised 0m 27 green broadcloth and 0m 33 yellow serge for the sum of 3fr 53, but other standout items from the accounts are the purchase of 477 pairs of black gaiters, costing 1,439fr 25, 100 pairs of shoes costing 600fr, and 50 pompoms costing 50 centimes.[167] We note not a single *aigrette* or pair of epaulettes are listed for the elite company: were the epaulettes counted with the *habits*? Possibly.

During the 100 days, 180fr was spent on equipping the 9 *sapeurs* of the regiment.[168] *Dépôt* held 10 *sapeurs'* axes: proof positive that the 20ᵉ *Dragons* had *sapeurs* in 1815, the only regiment – except possibly the 2ᵉ – that we can be 100% certain had *sapeurs* post-Bardin.

## 21ᵉ *Dragons*

Formed in April 1801 from Piedmontese dragoons, the paper archive for the regiment is very weak when it comes to records relating to dress and equipment. It served with the Grande Armée in 1805–07, Spain in 1808–13, and fought at Leipzig and the campaign of France. The regiment was inspected on 20 February 1802 and it is quite remarkable that of 441 *habits* in service for 447 men, 122 needed repairs and 98 were to be written off! Every *habit* was blue, so too the *surtouts*. The regiment's clothing was either life expired or totally missing. Yet despite the acute shortages, the regiment had 163 newly issued bearskins in use. Despite 441 *habits* being in use, just 156 *manteaux* were issued and a mere 200 pairs of *culottes de peau*. No helmets had been issued, and the men had to make do with 109 *bonnets de police* as headdress. The *dépôt* had literally nothing – no cloth, no materials, no clothing or equipment. The inspector, General Canclaux, remarked that the officers were totally negligent in their dress and it was far from uniform, and for the other ranks everything needed replacing. To this end he ordered 617 *habits* and *surtouts* were to be made, 462 *manteaux* and 617 *gilets*, stable coats, pairs of stable trousers and *culottes de peau*, helmets, *bonnets de police* and sets of buff equipment. Every single piece of equipment, harness and saddlery was condemned. Weapons wise, the regiment had no dragoon muskets and had old-pattern carbines and sabres in use. Those firearms that existed were in bad condition.[169]

In a letter of 16 March 1802, General Canclaux wrote to the War Ministry informing them that the elite company had not yet been formed in the regiment. He informed the ministry of his appointments for the officers of the company, as well as the *sous-officiers* and other ranks, including the transfer of horses to the company. The company needed bearskins, 42 *habits*, 180 pairs of boots, 30 *porte-manteaux*, 100 *gibernes* and belts.[170]

The future Marshal, General Oudinot, inspected the regiment on 28 June 1803. The regiment's account reveals that 1,159fr 61 had been spent on lace for *sous-officiers*

Officer of the 21ᵉ *Dragons* by Martinet.

Centre company trooper of the 21ᵉ *Dragons* by Martinet.

and other distinctions – presumably epaulettes for the elite company, plumes, bearskin cords etc and we wonder what else – since 1 September 1802, along with 2,355fr 36 on repairing clothing as well as 2,750fr 25 on cloth and 9,678fr 5 on making new clothing. The inspector noted that the regiment was impeccably dressed, the elite company being noted for its imposing demeanour. They were wearing 56 brand-new bearskins.[171]

Oudinot commented that 400 blue *habits* had existed at the previous review. Of these, 133 had been 'carried away' with deserters, 110 were in use, the rest had been converted into *surtouts* or had been cut up to make *bonnets de police*. Some 442 *surtouts* were in use, just 201 *manteaux*, 339 *gilets*, 359 stable coats, 411 pairs of *culottes de peau* and 344 helmets. We note 409 *bonnets de police* were in use. It is clear that the regiment was still in the process of harmonising its uniform with the French model from that of Piedmont. For the horses, 200 saddles and sets of bridles existed, 200 *housses* and oddly 253 pairs of *chaperons*! Dépôt held 79 brand-new, unissued *habits*, 18 *surtouts* that were likewise brand new and 41 needing repairs, 138 new *manteaux* and 91 old Piedmontese ones needing repairs, 49 new *gilets* and 61 needing repairs, 101 new stable coats and 8 needing repair, 7 new pairs of *culottes de peau*, 74 helmets and 91 *bonnets de police*. Oudinot authorised 149 *habits* to be made for new arrivals to the regiment, along with 597 pairs of *culottes de peau* and stable trousers, 597 *bonnets de police* and 199 pairs of dragoon boots to replace the Piedmontese-issue boots then in service. Since the previous inspection the regiment had received 698 dragoon muskets, 253 pairs of pistols and 716 sabres.[172]

When reviewed on 9 February 1803 the regiment mustered 427 rank and file and had 339 new *habits* in service. The regiment had no *habits* in use, and was wearing 424 *surtouts*, all brand new, with 36 more in *dépôt* accompanied by 60 *manteaux*. Some 391 pairs of stable trousers were in use, with 27 more in the *dépôt*, 369 brand-new helmets with 109 more in *dépôt*, and 59 bearskins with 16 in *dépôt*. The *dépôt* also held 1,254 leather hides to make *culottes de peau*, 1,227m 40 *blanc picque de bleu* broadcloth to make *manteaux*, 848m 33 green broadcloth, had used 95m 10 of yellow broadcloth, and held 495m 74 green tricot, 858m 22 white serge, 1,588m 36 yellow serge, 762m 82 linen, 1,492m 35 *treillis*, 689 dozen large buttons and 34m 18 of yellow tricot. Tricot was used either for legwear or *porte-manteaux* – so did trumpeters have yellow *porte-manteaux*? The elite company had 59 bearskins in use and a mix of *culottes de peau* were in use: 363 brand-new pairs in *dépôt* from sheepskin and 391 pairs made from doe hide – given their ochre colour and the fact they cost twice that of sheepskin breeches, were these for the elite company and *sous-officiers*? Arguably so. Needed for An 11 were 135 *habits*, 170 *surtouts*, 54 *manteaux*, 105 *veste*s, 270 stable coats, 540 pairs each of *culottes de peau* and stable trousers, 48 helmets and 14 bearskins. Materials authorised for purchase were 37m 80 yellow serge to make *manteaux*, 7m 20 white serge for *gilets*, 199m 80 *treillis* to make stable trousers, 15m 40 *treillis* to line the *porte-manteaux*, 5m 40 *treillis* to line 18 repaired *housses* and 2m 55 *treillis* to line 17 pairs of *chaperons*.[173]

Inspected on 23 September 1804, the 866 *sous-officiers* and men under arms had a full allocation of clothing and equipment. We are ignorant as to the effects issued to the dismounted company, which mustered over 140 men. We note 107 bearskins for the elite company were in service.[174] When reviewed on 31 July 1805, the 697 men under arms were issued 691 *habits*, 697 *surtouts*, 410 *manteaux* for the mounted companies and 691 helmets. We also note 410 sets of horse equipment, which included cloth *chaperons*, were in use. No bearskins existed for the elite company.[175] Inspected on 5 February 1808, we

Possibly a centre company trooper of the 21ᵉ *Dragons* by Berka.

Elite company trooper of the 21e *Dragons* by Martinet.

Copied by Rousselot from the Markholsheim manuscript is this elite company trumpeter. (*Collection KM*)

note just 31 *habits* had been made since 1805, and 372 *habits* were in use alongside 1,114 surtouts for 1,119 men: *habits* being issued to *sous-officiers*, trumpeters and also the elite company, 127 of whom now wore bearskins.[176]

When disbanded in summer 1814, we are sure that the regiment had some of its trumpeters decked out in Imperial Livery as the *dépôt* of the 1e and 2e squadrons held 103m 21 of trumpeters' lace. The elite company, when it was taken into the newly raised *Dragons du Monsieur*, had 104 *aigrettes,* all brand new and unissued. For the centre companies some 44 new pompoms were in *dépôt.* The elite company clearly had scarlet epaulettes as 50 new pairs of *epaulettes de grenadiers* were in store, accompanied by the same number of plumes. In addition, the two squadrons had in service at the time of disbandment 32 bearskins that were in bad condition, and along with 87 helmets were 57 brand-new pairs of *culottes de peau*, 7 pairs of *pantalons*, 2 helmets, 2 *bonnets de police*, and 1 *manteau* needing repairs. The *dépôt* held 1m 70 of *blanc picque de bleu* broadcloth for manteaux, 0m 11 of yellow broadcloth, 139m of yellow serge, 0m 35 of silver lace for *sous-*

*officiers* and 5m 50 of red worsted lace.[177] Therefore, the elite company had epaulettes, plumes and bearskins.

The 3ᵉ and 4ᵉ squadrons were taken into the newly raised *Dragons de Berry* and possessed:[178]

| Item | In service, but due to expire in the next year | In need of repair | To be replaced in the next year | To be replaced | Items short |
|---|---|---|---|---|---|
| *Habits* | 52 | 17 |  | 9 | 27 |
| *Gilets en drap blanc* | 26 | 15 | 4 | 9 | 51 |
| *Gilets d'écurie* | 15 | 14 | 15 | 5 | 50 |
| *Culottes de peau* | 34 | 4 |  | 1 | 66 |
| Stable trousers |  |  |  |  | 105 |
| *Surculottes* |  |  | 4 |  | 101 |
| *Manteaux* | 48 | 17 |  | 5 | 35 |
| *Bonnets de police* | 51 | 24 | 8 | 3 | 19 |
| Helmets | 62 | 25 |  | 3 | 15 |

The men were armed with 71 sabres in good condition, 13 needing repairs and 3 to be written off. Likewise, 40 pistols were in use and a further 12 needed repairs. In addition, the men were wearing 184 shirts, had just 6 white stocks – most men used improvised neck cloths – 27 pairs of linen socks, and 12 pairs of shoes. The inspector noted the regiment's clothing did not 'conform to the model', i.e., it was not Bardin regulation.

## 22ᵉ *Dragons*

Raised in Piedmont in 1635, the regiment became the 13ᵉ *Cavalerie* in 1791 and the 22ᵉ *Dragons* in September 1803. The regiment was with the Grande Armée from 1805 to 1807, thence in Spain and took part in the Saxon campaign of 1813 and the campaign of France.

The 13ᵉ *Cavalerie* were reviewed in Strasbourg for the last time on 24 September 1803. The regiment had 333 *habits* in service, of which 119 had been delivered just prior to the review. Some 294 *chapeaux* were in use and the elite company had 59 bearskins. The *dépôt* held stocks of cloth and materials:[179]

507m 33 blue broadcloth
35m 18 crimson broadcloth
294m 31 white broadcloth for *vestes*
905m 38 white serge
583m 68 crimson serge
24m 07 linen
232m 66 *treillis*
105m 69 lace for *housses*
38 leather hides for breeches.

Officer of the 22ᵉ *Dragons* by Martinet.

Centre company trooper of the 22ᵉ *Dragons* by Martinet. We know of no depiction of the elite company or of trumpeters of the regiment created during the Empire period.

The *dépôt* held clothing, notably 82 *habits* to be written off accompanied by 6 *veste*s, 68 *surtouts* and 54 stable coats in the same worn-out state. New items included 5 *surtouts*, 96 stable coats and 71 pairs of *culottes de peau*. Some 333 *manteaux* were in use and a further 49 worn-out *manteaux* were in *dépôt*. *Dépôt* also lists *pantalons* made from broadcloth and also knee breeches made from broadcloth, 64 pairs of stable trousers, 134 *chapeaux* and 5 bearskins: all brand new. Also lodged in *dépôt* were 38 *housses* to be disposed of, 16 new pairs of *chaperons*, 26 brand-new *schabraques* and 189 needing repairs, 114 black stocks, 58 white stocks, 60 stock buckles, 42 pairs of shoe buckles, 42 pairs knee buckles, 372 pairs of stockings, 14 pairs of shoes, 131 pairs of linen gaiters, 127 red plumes and 302 *chapeaux* cockades. Of the men under arms, 333 sheepskin *schabraques* and *housses* were in use – clearly the regiment had just started to adopt cloth *chaperons* as per the 1801 decree. The regiment was armed with 'old-pattern' sabres, while 63 pairs of pistols were in *dépôt* accompanied by 29 carabines, but none were in service.[180] Quite clearly the regiment had formed its elite company, who were issued 59 bearskins and had fringed epaulettes that we assume were scarlet.

General Bourcier informed the War Ministry in a letter of 27 September 1804 that the 13ᵉ provided two squadrons to the new regiment, totalling 300 men. The 20ᵉ *Cavalerie* were disbanded into the 22ᵉ *Dragons* to bring it up to strength, once all the men seeking their discharge had left the 20ᵉ or had been sent to other corps; the 22ᵉ *Dragons* got the stragglers that the *cuirassiers* and *carabiniers* did not need or perhaps want.[181]

Reviewed on 8 October 1804, the inspector noted that the clothing and equipment was well made and followed very closely the model examples sent from the War Ministry. Repairs were needed to items of headdress and buff work. The helmets we are told were *cavalerie* model and not dragon model – therefore the 13ᵉ *Cavalerie* had started the process to convert to *cuirassiers* before disbandment, or did their use by the 22ᵉ *Dragons* presage Napoléon's January instructions for clothing dragoons as *cuirassiers*? Both are reasonable hypothesis. The inspector further commented that the regiment was not wearing dragoon clothing or equipment i.e., it was wearing the blue *habit-longue* of the *cavalerie* regiments. He remarked that some green broadcloth had arrived in the *dépôt* so 'construction' of dragoon uniforms could begin. Out of a matter of economy, it was to decided what old *cavalerie* items could be retained and what had to be changed in addition to the blue *habits*, blue *surtouts*, blue *bonnets de police* and blue stable coats. Clothing and equipment was as follows:[182]

| Item | Good conduction | In need of repair | To be written off | Total | Number made since last review |
|---|---|---|---|---|---|
| *Habits* | 280 | 98 | 104 | 482 | 274 |
| *Surtouts* | 225 | 89 | 46 | 360 | 370 |
| *Manteaux* | 308 | 78 | 80 | 466 | 150 |
| *Gilets* | 336 | 84 | 62 | 482 | 491 |
| *Gilets d'écurie* | 406 | 77 | | 483 | 844 |
| *Culottes de peau* | 472 | 12 | | 484 | 971 |
| *Pantalons d'écurie* | 108 | 227 | | 335 | 438 |
| *Casques* | 392 | | | 392 | 392 |
| Bearskins | 67 | | | 67 | 67 |
| *Bonnets de police* | 467 | 19 | | 486 | 467 |
| *Ceinturons* | 300 | 107 | 51 | 458 | 331 |
| *Gibernes* | 300 | | 116 | 416 | 314 |
| *Porte-gibernes* | 300 | | 116 | 416 | 314 |
| *Bretelles de Fusil* | 440 | | | 440 | 441 |
| *Porte-manteaux* | 307 | 25 | 89 | 421 | 197 |
| *Bottes* | 369 | 54 | 18 | 441 | 421 |

The clothing was a mix of old *cavalerie* items or new *cuirassier* items issued since 12 May 1803! The *dépôt* reported that since the last inspection 1,089m 61 of blue broadcloth had been used, 659m 40 green broadcloth, 513m 96 white broadcloth had been used to make 513 *vestes*, 70m 78 crimson broadcloth, 1,103m 59 *blanc picque de bleu* broadcloth to produce 150 *manteaux*, and 1,171m of white and crimson serge. It seems that 274 *habits* and 370 *surtouts* made since the last review had crimson facings and were likely to be blue. The dismounted company had 438 *chapeaux* issued. Stores held 507m 33 blue broadcloth, 1,076m green broadcloth and 75m 67 yellow broadcloth.

Also in *dépôt* were 208 *habits* needing repairs, 39 brand-new pairs of *culottes de peau*, 157 pairs of stable trousers, 9 *cavalerie*-model *chapeaux*, 111 *cuirassier* helmets, 36 *bonnets de police* that were brand new and 36 to be disposed of, 110 new *cuirassier* waistbelts and 108 old *cavalerie* model to be disposed of, accompanied by 267 brand-new *gibernes* with 210 belts. Some 258 *housses* were in use accompanied by 300 pairs of *chaperons* – clearly some men simply had the saddle blanket on show with *chaperons* and no *housses*! The inspector authorised the regiment to have 107 bearskins for the elite company, and gave permission for 17 to be made. The regiment as *cavalerie* had carried carbines and they had been replaced with 440 dragoon muskets on 24 December 1803, yet 483 *cavalerie* sabres were in use and 457 pairs of pistols.

Inspected on 21 July 1805, the inspector remarked that the regiment's dress was 'very good and very uniform' for all ranks and the 'same regularity and uniformity could be found for the officers and men in undress'. The inspector found fault with the regiment's *surtouts*, which he said were cut too long in front and the tails were too long as well. The process of converting from heavy cavalry regiment to dragoons had been costly: some 11,529fr 34 was spent on raw materials, 21,261fr 30½ on making new clothing and equipment, 9,892fr 35 on repairs. Just 99fr 38 was spent on distinctions for *sous-officiers* or the elite company. Clothing and equipment was as follows:[183]

| Item | Good conduction | In need of repair | To be written off | Total | Number made since last review |
|---|---|---|---|---|---|
| *Habits* | 442 | | 58 | 500 | 442 |
| *Surtouts* | 455 | 38 | | 493 | 410 |
| *Manteaux* | 308 | 33 | 168 | 509 | 58 |
| *Gilets* | 454 | 37 | | 491 | 442 |
| *Gilets d'écurie* | 348 | 80 | 39 | 467 | 235 |
| *Culottes de peau* | 368 | 134 | 25 | 527 | 210 |
| *Pantalons d'écurie* | 377 | | 150 | 527 | 269 |
| *Casques* | 413 | | | 413 | 21 |
| *Bonnets à poil* | None | | | | |
| *Bonnets de police* | 327 | 78 | 122 | 527 | 91 |
| *Ceinturons* | 476 | | | 476 | 110 |
| *Gibernes* | 450 | | | 450 | 141 |
| *Porte-gibernes* | 450 | | | 450 | 141 |
| *Bretelles de fusil* | 440 | | | 440 | |
| *Porte-manteaux* | 499 | | | 499 | 499 |
| *Bottes* | 400 | 90 | 11 | 501 | 250 |

The regiment was now dressed in green *habits* and *surtouts* – only some of the *manteaux* had been changed and men still mostly wore blue stable coats and *bonnets de police*. The helmets were still overall *cuirassier* pattern. Leather work was a mix of *cavalerie* and dragoon model – just 110 dragoon sabre belts were in use, yet all the round blue tricot *portemanteaux* had been swapped out for rectangular green examples. For the horses, 447 *housses* were in use accompanied by 447 pairs of *chaperons* – the vast majority of which were blue! With *cuirassier* helmets, blue saddle furniture, dragoon *habits* and *cavalerie* leather work the regiment was highly distinctive! We note 58 men had *cavalerie* habits: had some been retained for trumpeters? Blue faced in crimson would make them distinctive.[184] Going forward in time, could some of the blue broadcloth have been used to face up yellow trumpeters' *habits*? Not impossible, and highly plausible.

Dismounted trooper of the 22ᵉ and 6ᵉ *Dragons* copied from the Otto manuscript by Rousselot. (*Collection KM*)

*Dépôt* held 505 leather hides to make *culottes de peau* and 27m 40 crimson broadcloth – much less than the 35m 18 remaining in 1804, which we suppose suggests repairs were made to garments with crimson facings, or was this 7m 48 of crimson cloth used to make crimson garments? The *dépôt* reported that it had used 13 ounces of silver lace for *sous-officiers*, 43m of worsted lace, and 897m 84 of linen lace for *housses* and *chaperons*, 1,678m yellow serge, 2,023m green broadcloth, 492m white broadcloth, 133m *blanc picque de bleu* broadcloth for *manteaux*, and 110m yellow broadcloth. Other items in *dépôt* included 61 brand-new pairs of *culottes de peau*, 150 plumes, 253 brand-new stable coats, 9 *manteaux*, 134 *gilets*, 36 bearskins for the elite company – all the regiment had of these – 12 *bonnets de police*, 60 waistbelts, 186 *gibernes*, and 129 *porte-gibernes* among other items. Every inch of blue broadcloth and crimson serge that had existed in 1804 had been used prior to the review making new clothing: the ratio of green to blue clothing is not known. The regiment was armed with 440 dragoon muskets, 457 pairs of pistols and 476 sabres. The inspector noted that several pistols were not regulation issue – some 90 examples being too large to fit into the *fontes* (pistol holsters) – and many lacked ram rods – making them totally useless.[185]

Sadly, the winter 1807 inspection is missing from the regiment's papers, but regimental orders tell us on 17 September 1810, the colonel ordered 200 *habits*, 200 *vestes*, 200 *porte-manteaux*, 50 *manteaux*, 200 pairs of boots, 200 pairs of *culottes de peau* and 200 pairs of shoes to be sent to the regiment at Valladolid.

We know nothing else about the regiment's dress until it was disbanded in 1814, when clothing for 1ᵉ squadron was excellent. Of 111 *habits*, all were new to the recent regulation, the inspector remarked. Further, the regiment had 84 *vestes*, only 3 of which were needed to be replaced, and of 73 *gilets d'écurie*, 6 were marked down for replacement. Some 110 pairs of stable trousers were in good condition, 83 pairs of *surculottes* were listed as being in good condition, 9 needed repairs and 18 had to be replaced. Additionally, 103 helmets were in good condition, and 16 needed repairs, and lastly 106 *bonnets de police* were all in good condition, as were 92 pairs of *culottes de peau*. The squadron was well dressed in Bardin-regulation kit.[186] The trumpeters wore Imperial Livery.[187]

Copied by Rousselot from the Markholsheim manuscript is this centre company trumpeter. (*Collection KM*)

However, the clothing of 2ᵉ squadron was in shreds. Of the squadron's 142 *habits*, just 3 were in good condition, 98 needed repairs and 42 were fit only for disposal. Shockingly, 39 men had no *habit* at all. Indeed, all the clothing was reported as being of the old pattern. Of the *vestes*, 48 were good, 5 needed repairs, 29 needed to be replaced and 99 were needed to give every man a *veste*. Of the 122 *gilets d'écurie*, no doubt worn by some men to make up for the lack of *habits*, 90 were fit only for the bin. Just 2 were in good condition and 59 were needed to give each man one. The regiment needed 181 pairs of stable trousers, 127 pairs of *culottes de peau*, and 62 pairs of *surculottes*: insufficient for each man to have a pair. The helmets were also falling to bits. Of the 180 helmets, 101 needed repairing and 20 were fit only for spares or scrap! The equipment was also falling to bits. Of the 171 *gibernes*, 110 needed repairs, the waistbelts and *giberne* belts were in good condition, and no plumes or pompoms were issued. The *porte-manteaux* were in bad condition, 59 were good, 50 needed repairs, 63 were fit only for disposal and 9 new ones were needed to enable every man to have one. The boots were likewise falling to bits, with 46 new pairs needed to give every man a pair, 29 pairs needed to be repaired, and 81 pairs were beyond hope and were to be disposed of, leaving just 25 pairs in good condition. The saddles were mostly damaged or worn out, 35 were in good condition, 139 needed repairs and 14 were to be disposed of. The *housses* were mostly to be replaced: 82 were good, 41 needed repairs and 65 were fit only for the rubbish pile. Of the *schabraques*, 82 were in good condition, 30 needed repairs, and 76 were again destined for the rubbish heap.

The regiment's weapons were a mixed assortment, having 37 *fusils de dragon*, 157 sabres in good condition, 62 sabres needing repair and 11 to be disposed of, 134 pistols in good condition, 12 pistols needing repair or replacement and 74 light cavalry carbines. Yet the regiment had not a single carbine sling or *botte de fusil* with which to carry the firearms in the field. The *dépôt* had no materials whatsoever and what it did hold was either in need of repair (42 *gibernes*, 44 *porte-gibernes*, 10 waistbelts) or was to be disposed of, namely 10 *habits*, 28 *manteaux*, 30 helmets and 9 waistbelts.[188] Partial regimental accounts record that in 1812–14 27,413fr 60 had been spent on clothing the regiment, and that 11m 30 of trumpeters' lace had been purchased in the third quarter of 1813 accompanied by 100m of lace for *porte-manteaux* for 50fr.[189]

## 23ᵉ *Dragons*

Created on 23 September 1803 from the 15ᵉ *Régiment de Cavalerie*, the regiment was inspected on 7 October 1804, when 296 *habits* were in use, all being made since 1803 and dark green, and were used alongside 460 *surtouts*, of which 335 were blue, which were to be re-cut as stable coats. Again, they were all brand new, being made since

Officer of the 23ᵉ *Dragons* by Martinet.

Elite company trooper by Martinet.

Regulations in Practice 119

Elite company trooper in a print by Bassett printed in 1814, yet officially the regiment never had a single bearskin!

Centre company trooper by Martinet.

September 1803. The elite company had 72 bearskins. Stores reported that 1,052m 55 of blue broadcloth had been used since 1803 and 1,349m 53 of green. Interestingly, some 7m 85 of yellow broadcloth had been used – sufficient for just 34 garments, which given 296 *habits* were made suggests these garments were without *revers*, and therefore *surtouts* or perhaps *habits de cuirass* – and 547m 60 of yellow serge, while 154m 77 of crimson broadcloth and 1,342m 45 of crimson serge had been used. This seems a huge amount of crimson, considering *surtouts* needed very little facing cloth.[190] We wonder if all the clothing produced was actually blue?

Inspected again on 23 November 1805, the regiment was now dressed totally in green with 367 *habits* in use, all being made since October 1804, and 629 *surtouts*, of which 538 had been made since October 1804. Clearly whatever garments had been made up to October 1804 were considered to be non-regulation to require their complete replacement after less than a year in service. We note the elite company had 107 bearskins. Stores had used 1,349m 64 of yellow serge, 1,491m 94 green broadcloth, 93m 22 of yellow broadcloth – sufficient for 405 *habits*, the inference being some *habits* were yellow – and 705m 11 of crimson serge had been used. We are ignorant of its use. The *manteaux* were a mix of 298 *blanc picque de bleu* examples and 72 green. We also note 137m of black worsted had been used to make gaiters. Every man in the mounted squadrons had *housses* and *chaperons*. We note 51 sheepskin *schabraques* were in stores awaiting disposal.[191]

By the time of the 1808 inspection all the bearskins had been lost on campaign. Every man in the mounted squadrons had *housses* and *chaperons*.[192]

When disbanded in summer 1814, the regiment's clothing was in relatively good condition:[193]

| Item | In service, but due to expire in the next year | In need of repair | To be replaced in the next year | To be replaced | Items short |
|---|---|---|---|---|---|
| *Habits* | 102 | 15 | | | 26 |
| *Vestes* | 65 | 5 | 3 | | 70 |
| *Gilets d'écurie* | 68 | 8 | 6 | | 65 |
| *Surculottes* | 33 | 4 | 6 | 3 | 97 |
| *Pantalons* | 89 | | | | 54 |
| *Culottes de peau* | 110 | 3 | 1 | | 29 |
| *Manteaux-capote* | 92 | 7 | 2 | | 42 |
| *Bonnets de police* | 117 | | 14 | | 12 |
| Helmets | 83 | 26 | | | 34 |
| Pairs of gloves | 69 | | | | 68 |

Also in use were 363 shirts, 131 black stocks, 92 pairs of shoes – which were worn over bare feet like the boots – 104 pairs of black gaiters, 21 pairs of grey linen gaiters and 99 pairs of *manchettes du botte*. Ironically, given the shortages of clothing, the stores were literally bursting at the seams with new clothing. Unissued, brand-new clothing included 264 *habits-vestes*, 104 *vestes*, 284 *bonnets de police*, 35 pairs of stable trousers, 99 *manteaux-capote*, 674 pompoms for helmets, 234 waistbelts, 309 *gibernes*, 315 *porte-gibernes*, 347 *bottes de fusil*, 422 sword knots, 145 *porte-manteaux*. Dépôt also held 230 helmets needing repairs, 16 *habits* needed to be disposed of, along with 6 sabre belts, 6 *gibernes* with belt and 13 *porte-manteaux*. Not an inch of Imperial Livery was in the store, but 85m of silver lace for *sous-officiers* was, along with 12m 50 of red wool lace for chevrons. The *surculottes* were made from beige broadcloth as some 34m 50 of this fabric was held, along with 77m 35 of presumably *blanc picque de bleu* broadcloth for the *manteaux-capote*. Also in stores were 16 black stocks, 3 pairs of shoes, 5 *sacs a*

Copied by Rousselot from the Markholsheim manuscript is this elite company trumpeter. No documents from the period confirms the use of white bearskins. (*Collection KM*)

*distribution*, and 21 pairs of *manchettes du botte*. We note that not a single pair of socks or underwear were issued: ergo the men wore their boots and shoes for stable duties, of which 92 pairs were issued, over bare feet. We note 363 shirts were issued, 111 black stocks, 104 pairs of black tricot gaiters, 21 pairs of grey linen gaiters and 99 pairs of *manchettes du botte*. The regiment had a mix of firearms, 26 dragoon muskets and 98 An XI light cavalry musketoons in service, and just 26 bayonets and 137 sabres. The inspector noted the regiment had not fully adopted the Bardin regulation, but the major had overseen the production of new clothing, which was waiting to be issued, hence all the new items in stores.[194]

## 24e *Dragons*

Created on 24 September 1803 from the *15e Régiment de Cavalerie*, the regiment was with the Army of Italy and thence Naples until 1808, when it served in Spain, with some elements taking part in the campaign of France. In summer 1814, the regiment was dismembered among three dragoon regiments.

The earliest inspection return we can locate is dated 21 October 1805 and tells us the men were all clothed as dragoons, with the elite company having no bearskins.[195] Inspected again on 26 November 1807, the elite company now had 123 bearskins, the men had both a *habit* and a *surtout*, and the horses had *chaperons* and *housses*. The *manteaux* were regulation *blanc picque de bleu* and 51 men still had old *cavalerie chapeaux*. We also note some 34m 11 of crimson broadcloth had been used, sufficient for 13 *habits* – did trumpeters therefore have crimson *habits* or at least crimson somewhere on their uniforms? It would seem the case.[196]

We know nothing more about how the regiment was dressed until its disbandment in summer 1814. The 1e squadron was passed to the 13e *Dragons*. The standout item in the inspection return is the presence of 92 bearskins, of which 4 were in need of replacement. The squadron had 130 *habits* and *vestes* in good condition, 135 *gilets d'écurie*, of which 97 were in need of replacement, and all 138 pairs of stable trousers were fit only for the rubbish bin. In addition, the regiment had 49 helmets, 1 of which needed repairs, 55 *bonnets de police* in good condition and 78 in need of replacement and 130 new *culottes de peau*. The stores held no cloth, no materials, no clothing, and no equipment. Of great interest, the inspecting officer noted that the regiment had not strictly adhered to the regulations of 19 January and 7 February 1812 concerning the dimensions and cut of clothing and equipment. Not a single pair of *surculottes* were in use, and the elite company alone had sheepskin *schabraques*. No firearms were carried except saddle pistols.[197]

The 4e squadron was taken into the 16e *Dragons*, a mere 31 men, whose only clothing in good condition was 6 *habits* – everything was either in need of repair or scrapping.[198]

Officer of the 24ᵉ *Dragons* by Martinet.

Centre company trooper of the 24ᵉ *Dragons* by Martinet.

The 5ᵉ squadron was taken into the 17ᵉ Dragons, who possessed:[199]

| Item | In service, but due to expire in the next year | In need of repair | To be replaced in the next year | To be replaced | Items short |
|---|---|---|---|---|---|
| *Habits* | 55 | | | 1 | |
| *Gilets sans manche* | 47 | | | | |
| *Gilets d'écurie* | 38 | 4 | | 4 | |
| *Bonnets de police* | 60 | | | | |
| *Culottes de peau* | 50 | 4 | | 2 | |
| *Surculottes* | 16 | | | | |
| Stable trousers | 5 | 8 | 4 | | |
| Pairs of boots | 6 | 14 | | 3 | |
| Helmets | 52 | 4 | | 2 | |
| Pompoms | 6 | | | | |
| Gauntlets | 1 | | | | |

Regulations in Practice 123

Possibly a centre company trooper of the 24ᵉ *Dragons* drawn in summer 1813. (*Collection KM*)

Copied by Rousselot from the Markholsheim manuscript is this centre company trumpeter. (*Collection KM*)

This return is one of the few that show dragoons did actually use pompoms in their helmets! The 60 men were also issued 78 shirts, 29 black stocks, 25 pairs of shoes, 27 pairs of gaiters – these are impossible to wear without shoes! – and 56 pairs of *manchettes du botte*. The *surculottes* were noted as being non-regulation, and we suppose from contemporary iconography to have been *pantalons à cheval*.

From the various reports it seems clear that the regiment had not taken steps to introduce the Bardin regulation beyond the adoption of pompoms!

## 25ᵉ *Dragons*

Created on 23 September 1803 from the *16ᵉ Régiment de Cavalerie*, the regiment was with the Grande Armée from 1805, in Spain from 1808, and fought at Dresden with the Grande Armée in 1813 and in the campaign of France. Reviewed on 16 October 1804, the elite company had 73 bearskins – just 15 being made since 1803 – and the process had begun to reclothe the regiment as dragoons. We note 130 new *habits* had been made since September 1803, 329 *surtouts*, 3 *manteaux*, 186 *vestes*, 193 stable coats and 687 pairs of *culottes de peau*. The inspector noted 'everything is good, the blue *habits* are to be dyed green'. As could be expected from these comments, all the new clothing was green, as 1,185m 08 green broadcloth, 25m 10 aurore broadcloth, 507m 87 aurore serge and 538m 83 green tricot had been used. The green broadcloth seems to have been dyed to colour as 695fr had been spent dyeing broadcloth and serge green. Presumably the trumpeters had worn *rose habits* faced in blue, which were replaced – we assume – with aurore faced in green.

The men's footwear was still the heavy cavalry *botte forte*. We also must note 415 men were still dressed in their blue *cavalerie* habits, likewise 44 blue *surtouts* were in use. Of 412 *housses*, 323 were blue, of the 409 pairs of *chaperons*, 328 were blue. Trumpeters we guess were wearing crimson faced in blue. Of the leather work in service, 300 out of 522 sabre belts were dragoon model, and of the 428 *gibernes* and belts, 201 were dragoon model. The sabres were all *cavalerie* model.[200]

When inspected again on 15 August 1805, 544 *habits* were in use, every single one being made since October 1804 to the dragoon model, and just 138 *surtouts* – presumably for *sous-officiers* and trumpeters. All the old *cavalerie* clothing had, presumably, been eliminated from use. Also in use were 79 bearskins and the foot company had 205 *havresacs* issued, 212 pairs of shoes and 218 pairs of black gaiters. Both mounted and dismounted men had *blanc picque de bleu manteaux*. We note 45 old *cavalerie gibernes* and belts were still in service, and all the sabres were dragoon pattern.[201]

A document from 1811 tells us officers wore white broadcloth *vestes* and breeches on parade and grey *pantalons* on campaign with a *surtout* replacing the *habit*. In addition, officers had nankeen breaches for town dress.[202]

We know nothing else until the 1e and 2e squadrons were disbanded in summer 1814, when they were wearing:[203]

| Item | In service, but due to expire in the next year | In need of repair | To be replaced in the next year | To be replaced | Items short | Observations |
|---|---|---|---|---|---|---|
| *Habits* | 65 | 21 | 13 | 10 | 33 | Not including the items taken by the men on leave, namely, 40 *habits*, 40 *vestes*, 23 pairs of *culottes de peau* and 40 *bonnets de police*. |
| *Vestes* | 44 | 2 | 11 | 13 | 72 | |
| *Gilets d'écurie* | 19 | 32 | 65 | | 26 | |
| *Bonnets de police* | 66 | 11 | 44 | | 21 | |
| *Culottes de peau* | | | | | 142 | |
| *Surculottes* | | 1 | 12 | | 129 | |
| *Pantalons* | | | | | 142 | |
| *Manteaux* | 129 | | 13 | | | |
| Helmets and bearskins | 115 | 26 | | 1 | | |

Officer of the 25ᵉ *Dragons* by Martinet.

Centre company trooper of the 25ᵉ *Dragons* by Martinet.

The men were wearing non-regulation *pantalons à cheval*, the inspector noted, and of the 142 men, 114 carried a *banderole-porte-carabine* yet only 100 carbines were in use, 9 needed repairs and 1 was fit only for spares! Every man had a sabre, 97 men had a pistol and just 28 men had a bayonet. In addition, 125 men had no gauntlets, and 2 were missing their *porte-manteaux*. The men were also issued 398 shirts between them, 9 pairs of linen *pantalons*, 121 black stocks, 118 white stocks, 18 pairs of woollen stockings, 22 pairs of linen ankle socks – some men had no socks and not a single pair of underwear was in use – 34 pairs of shoes, 8 pairs of black gaiters, 42 red plumes, 42 pairs of red grenadiers' epaulettes and 42 sets of bearskin cords. The stores for the two squadrons held 3 stable coats to be disposed of, 17 brand-new *manteaux-capote*, and 39 *manteaux* needing repairs or 'to be binned', 57 helmets needing repairs or disposal, 37 worn-out *porte-manteaux*, 2 worn-out pairs of boots as well as 16 bearskins needing repairs.[204]

In comparison, when the 3ᵉ, 4ᵉ and 5ᵉ squadrons were wound up, the review informs us that the trumpeters were wearing Imperial Livery. The *dépôt* held 47m 84 of Imperial Livery, along with 7m 45 of wool lace and 67m 22 of linen lace, as well as 0m 85 beige broadcloth for *surculottes*, 282m 76 white broadcloth for *gilets*, 99m of green broadcloth,

Elite company trooper of the 25ᵉ *Dragons* by Martinet.

Elite (?) company trooper of the 25ᵉ *Dragons* by Martinet. Of interest are the copper fish scale boards to the scarlet-fringed epaulettes.

20m 5 of aurore broadcloth for facings, 200m 70 of aurore serge, 13m 10 of green tricot for *porte-manteaux* and 247m 83 of linen. Stores held unissued 49 new *gilets*, 77 pairs of *culottes de peau*, 8 pairs of gauntlets, 25 helmets, 236 musket slings, 1 waistbelt, 12 *gibernes* and 1,312 *porte-gibernes*. In addition, there were 9 *habits* that needed repair and a further that 35 needed to be disposed of or cut up to make *bonnets de police*. Also in stores were 70 stock buckles and 60 pairs of knee buckles for the *culottes de peau*. The reviewing officer noted that items of clothing had not yet been replaced to accord with the instruction of 25 May 1814 and more importantly recorded that the 26ᵉ had not adopted the provisions of the decree of 7 February 1812 introducing the Bardin regulation. Further, the decree of 23 April 1814 concerning modifications to the dress of trumpeters and removal of Imperial symbols had not been carried out.[205]

## 26ᵉ *Dragons*

Formed in September 1803 from the 17ᵉ *Cavalerie,* the paper trail for this conversion is remarkably complete. A letter of 29 October 1803 states that General Roussel d'Hurbal was in charge of forming the new 26ᵉ *Dragons*. A portion of the old 17ᵉ *Cavalerie* were to be dismounted, and in consequence 32 sergeants and 64 corporals were needed, as were 8 drummers and a corporal-drummer. These were all to be drawn from the infantry regiments in Verdun, where the new 26ᵉ was garrisoned. New trumpeters were to be drawn from the *enfant de troupe*. All the men in the 17ᵉ *cavalerie* deemed above regulation height for dragoons were to be sent to the *cuirassiers*, while the old soldiers and those wishing to be discharged were given their ticket of leave. The ranks were filled with infantrymen. The elite company was to be re-formed by men chosen from the ranks of the remaining *cavalerie* troopers. The regiment was not ordered to change its uniform immediately and was 'to retain the foundation colour of the clothing', i.e., blue for the time being, while the cost of the change to green had been formulated. All the items that were still serviceable were to be retained – indeed the regiment had literally a month earlier been issued with new pistols and carbines with bayonets destined for the 17ᵉ *Cavalerie*.[206]

Inspected on 4 October 1804, the inspecting officer noted the men were very well drilled in the school of the infantry, could fire very well in three ranks and noted the colonel was working the men very hard in perfecting infantry drill and the school of the battalion. The mounted contingent had excellent positions on horseback, and with time and more training the men would gain expertise at riding. Clearly the regiment's training time was spent learning to be infantry and not horsemen! The regiment's discipline was described as 'exact, firm and when needed very severe'. Uniform wise, the 'the regiment was working hard to complete the dragoon uniform'. Regiment accounts reveals that while camped at Strasbourg, remarkably under canvas, the following expenses had been made on tentage and other items:[207]

8-man tents repaired, 2,141fr
16-man tents, 3,309fr
Artillery tent, 441fr
Cavalry tent, 399fr
Officers' *pavillons*, 2,580fr
*Marmites*, 3,420fr
*Gamelles*, 10,842fr
*Grand-bidons*, 4,137fr
Canteens, 55,319fr

Regiment accounts furthermore tell us that since 5 June 1803 some 660 new dragoon *habits* had been made from green broadcloth with aurore facings. Of these, 648 had been issued and 12 remained in *dépôt*. In the same period, workers in the regimental *dépôt* had repaired 100 old *cavalerie habits* and stores held 37, of which 25 needed repairs. We note 77 men were dressed in blue *cavalerie habits*, and just 143 green *surtouts* existed out of 456 in use, so clearly the vast majority were blue. In addition, 451 *cavalerie manteaux* were in use and just 65 new of the dragoon type had been issued. Furthermore, 118 *cavalerie* white *veste*s were in use and 420 new dragoon *gilet*s had been made. Some 511 new green stable coats had been made and 425 issued, with 90 being lodged in *dépôt*, accompanied by 90 *bonnets de police*, of which 700 were made new. Clearly, the regiment had dragoon *habits* and stable clothing, but still wore in undress blue *surtouts*. The elite company had 80 bearskins, some 517 helmets had been issued and 583 plumes had been distributed, along with 583 sabre knots. Also in use were 413 *chapeaux*. The foot company had 150 *havresacs* and 346 pairs of shoes and black gaiters. The 8 drummers in the foot companies were armed with *sabre briquet* carried from infantry-pattern *baudrier*. Cloth and materials in the *dépôt* included 0m 60 *blanc picque de bleu*, 1,626m 29 green broadcloth, 36m 22 white broadcloth, 26m 92 aurore broadcloth, 959m 12 *treillis*, 16m 22 silver lace, 90m 95 worsted lace, 44m 02 lace for *housse* and *chaperons*, 142m 27 of green tricot had been used to make *porte-manteaux*, 35m 82 aurore serge was in store, as was 405m 34 white serge, 568m 42 linen and 42 sheepskin hides. Not an inch of blue broadcloth existed or had been used, so the concerns over the colour of the uniform had been addressed. For *bonnets de police* 700 tassels had been purchased and 1,544m 30 of worsted cording. We also find that 400 pairs of gauntlets had been issued, 422 sword knots, 486 lock covers, and 415 pistol lanyards – a non-regulation item but a very sensible one to attach the pistol to the saddle.[208]

When reviewed on 29 July 1805 the regiment's cloth was described as newly delivered and matched the samples provided by the war ministry.[209] Since October 1804, 8 *habits* had been made – for the trumpeters? – and a paltry 10 new *gilets*, accompanied by 392 brand-new green *surtouts* and 88 *manteaux*. Further, 29 new plumes had been issued, 18 helmets, 392 pairs of *culottes de peau* and 90 *bonnets de police*. All the old *cavalerie habits* had been taken from use, but the majority of *surtouts* and stable coats were blue. The *manteaux* were clearly green, as no *blanc picque de bleu* broadcloth had been purchased at all in the intervening months. We do note 600 *capuchons* were made and 522 issued. Presumably these were items of apparel, arguably sleeved cloaks for the foot company.[210]

Reviewed in January 1808, the regiment had been clothed as new since 1805, with 522 *habits*, 545 *veste*s, 574 *surtouts* and 432 *manteaux* being made new and issued accompanied by 402 pairs of *culottes de peau*, 92 plumes, 436 helmets, 33 bearskins – all the regiment had – and 453 *bonnets de police*. Literally every item of clothing and equipment in use was new! We note that the *manteaux* were now no longer green and some 2,204m of *blanc picque de* bleu broadcloth had been used to make new *manteaux*. A total of 1,115 'garmiures de bonnet de police' had been used – we assume this is the cording and tassels. The *dépôt* reveals that during the campaigns of 1805–07, 786 *habits* had been made, 1,098 white *veste*s, 1,558 *surtouts*, 682 stable coats, 1,335 pairs of stable trousers – which had been worn in lieu of the *culotte de peau*. Also, 850 plumes had been used as well as 150 pairs of grey linen gaiters, 78 *capuchons* and 148 *capotes*. The huge wastage of *surtouts* demonstrates this was worn as the primary garment on these campaigns.[211]

Officer of the 26ᵉ *Dragons* by Martinet.

Centre company trooper of the 26ᵉ *Dragons* by Martinet. We know of no contemporary iconography of the elite company or trumpeters.

A report of 24 July 1820 reveals that between 1 January 1812 and 26 August 1814, 533fr 10 had been spent on the purchase of 747 pairs of *manchettes du botte*, 54m 14 of beige broadcloth was purchased along with 162m 75 of bleached white broadcloth and 141m 75 green tricot. The report also details the purchase of 675 copper grenades to ornament the *gibernes*. Twelve *surtouts* were made costing 4fr 70 each, in lieu of the regulation 1fr 60 to make – we wonder if the cost was due to lace adornment? In the fourth quarter of 1807, 85 new bearskins costing 26fr 80 had been purchased and a further 38 bearskins costing 28fr 61 were purchased in 1808. Also obtained in 1808 were 14 sets of trumpet cords 125 grenadier plumes costing 6fr 19 rather than the established price of 3fr 70, and 2 pairs of adjutants' epaulettes and lace were purchased in 1810 for 44fr.[212]

Disbanded in summer 1814, the 1ᵉ squadron possessed the following items of clothing and equipment:²¹³

| Item | In service, but due to expire in the next year | In need of repair | To be replaced in the next year | To be replaced | Items short | Observations |
|---|---|---|---|---|---|---|
| *Habits* | 68 | 15 | | 1 | 4 | The men have been entirely dressed from the contents of the *dépôt*. |
| *Gilets en drap blanc* | 60 | 8 | 1 | 2 | 2 | |
| *Gilets d'écurie* | 8 | 18 | 1 | 9 | | |
| *Bonnets de police* | 27 | 3 | | 4 | | |
| *Culottes de peau* | 91 | | | | | |
| *Surculottes* | 1 | | | | | |
| Stable trousers | 83 | 1 | | 1 | | |
| Bearskins | 35 | | | | | |
| Helmets | 38 | 33 | 1 | 1 | | |
| Pompoms | The men have none ||||| |
| Plumes | ||||| |
| Gauntlets | 15 | 2 | | | | |
| Pairs of boots | 7 | 20 | | 19 | | |

The standout items in the inspection are the 35 bearskins in use – clearly by the elite company. Indeed, we note that in the fourth quarter of 1807, 85 new bearskins costing 26fr 80 had been purchased and a further 38 bearskins costing 28fr 61 were purchased in 1808. Bearskins had a regulation lifespan of 20 years, ergo no colonel would set their bearskins aside if they were still in good condition after spending 'serious money' to buy them and decrees from the war ministry could 'go to hell' it seems. The squadron had 102 good waistbelts, 7 needed repairs and 2 replaced; 66 good *gibernes*, 35 needing repairs and 5 replacing; 101 good *porte-gibernes* and 5 more needing repairs, and lastly 91 sword knots. The *dépôt* had no materials or clothing whatsoever.²¹⁴

We are sadly totally ignorant about the dress of the trumpeters, but the regiment was in pre-Bardin clothing.

## 27ᵉ *Dragons*

Created in 1674, it was named the 18ᵉ *Régiment de Cavalerie* in 1791 and became the 27ᵉ *Dragons* in September 1803. When reviewed on 21 September 1804, General Grouchy noted that the formation of the regiment had been entrusted to him by General Augereau. The regiment was to muster at time of war 1,138 men and 779 horses, or 906 men and 593 horses in peacetime, with a staff of 18 officers and 111 *sous-officiers* formed into 8 companies. On 24 September 1803, the 18ᵉ *Cavalerie* had mustered 30 officers and 392 *sous-officiers* and men taken into the war squadrons of the 27ᵉ *Dragons*, with 18 officers and 257 *sous-officiers* and men under arms. Of the 462 troop horses, only 221 were present. The regiment needed 145 men to complete the peacetime establishment. The elite company needed to be completed, some 111 men and 4 officers. The old elite company of the 18e *Cavalerie*, it seems, had been passed back to 1e and 2e *carabiniers*. Of the men then serving in the regiment, only 62 could be found that were suitable for service in the elite company and just 5 horses! Grouchy reported that of the 356 men on parade, 250 men were wearing *habits* in good condition and 106 needed repairs, and just 3 had been made since 24 June 1803 – the men were all clad in *cavalerie habits*! Just 341 men had a *surtout*, 135 needed repairs and 122 were new, while 352 men had *manteaux*, every single one being *cavalerie* pattern, as were all 365 white *gilet*s. Remarkably, 367 new green tricot stable coats were in use. Some 44 bearskins had been made new since 1803 and 86 were in use along with 523 helmets of the dragoon type. The *cavalerie* sheepskin *schabraque* had all been replaced by brand-new green broadcloth *chaperons* and *housses*, 280 of each existing, yet 424 *cavalerie porte-manteaux* were in use. Materials used by the *dépôt* included 560m 98 broadcloth, 654m of blue broadcloth, 646m 21 white broadcloth, 2m 2 crimson broadcloth, and 75m 58 *treillis*. Some 19m 78 crimson tricot had been used, and 158m 24 white tricot from making knee breeches. Also, 1,656m 53 white serge

Officer of the 27e *Dragons* by Martinet.

Centre company trooper of the 28e *Dragons* by Martinet. We know of no contemporary iconography of the elite company or trumpeters.

had been used, with 516m 40 remaining in *dépôt*, and 818m 42 crimson serge. Clearly the regiment had not changed to new aurore facings. The crimson tricot – trumpeters' stable coats? Or perhaps *porte-manteaux*? Both are plausible. The *dépôt* reported the production of 2 new *habits* and 121 *surtouts*, and held 14 new *cavalerie habits*, 2 *cavalerie surtouts*, 287 brand-new white *gilets*, 8 green stable coats, 352 pairs of *culottes de peau*, 277 pairs of stable trousers, 159 *chapeaux* with 39 in use, 1 bearskin and 2 *bonnets de police* – some 341 green examples being made and issued. The regiment was clearly a hybrid of dragoon and *cavalerie* in appearance. Interestingly, the mounted squadrons were issued 365 light cavalry *mousquetons*, and the foot companies 625 dragoon muskets and 9 infantry sabres for the drummers.[215]

As part of the decree of *1 Vendemiaire An XII* (24 September 1803), dragoons were to be clothed in *bleu de ciel*. However, nothing definite was agreed. On 27 February 1805 the Emperor gave orders that dragoons were to be dressed and armed identically as *cuirassiers*, but not armoured. He furthermore ordered the 27ᵉ *Dragons* were to be the test bed for the new uniforms.[216] Did this idea ever make it to reality? At the time of the 1803 inspection stores held 658m of blue broadcloth, by July 1805 it had been entirely used and not replaced. In the same period 2748m 96 of green broadcloth had been used. In that period 533 *habits* and 603 *surtouts* had been made, and 214 sets of saddle furniture, all needing green broadcloth. The amount of blue broadcloth would make 328 *habits*. Was a single squadron decked out? It is hard to say but seems reasonable.

Inspected on 24 July 1805, regimental accounts report that since 1804 39,976fr 62 had been spent making new clothing, 4,077fr 61 was spent on materials, and 3,487fr 15 on repairing clothing and equipment in use that could be adapted for continued service. In addition, 3,745fr 45 had been spent equipping new entrants, 3,800fr on gratuity for *sous-officiers* promoted to officers, and 325fr 20 was spent on lace and other distinctions for the elite company. Estimated expenses for 1805 came to just over 51,000fr!

Likewise, 402 *manteaux* were in use, 102 were new – the remainder were all old *cavalerie* pattern. Of the *gilets*, 461 were new, and 587 were in use, 636 pairs of *culottes de peau* were in use, 555 pairs being brand new. The elite company had 88 bearskins, 10 were new, the remainder coming from the 18ᵉ *Cavalerie* elite company! Some 544 helmets were in use, 54 being new. The regiment had changed its footwear from *bottes forte* to *bottes à l'écuyère*, 506 pairs being in use. We also note 9 new trumpets had been issued and the foot company had 8 drums, yet we find no specific clothing for the foot companies in use! The old *cavalerie* regiment sheepskin *schabraques* had been entirely replaced with cloth *chaperons*. *Dépôt* held 120 brand-new unissued *habits*, 134 *surtouts*, 120 *manteaux*, 121 *gilets*, 400 pairs of *culottes de peau*, 531 pairs of stable trousers, 14 *chapeaux*, with a further 145 in use, 24 helmets and 1 bearskin. Cloth in the magazine comprised 1,169m 61 green broadcloth, 727m 82 white broadcloth, 351m 11 *blanc picque de bleu* broadcloth, 49m 43 aurore broadcloth, 1,931m 50 white serge, 340m 74 aurore serge, 1,058m 22 *treillis* and 244m 77 of linen. Rather than dragoon muskets, the men were issued 406 light cavalry *mousquetons*.[217] From the return, it seems some men were still wearing the old *cavalerie chapeaux* and 10 old *habits* and *surtouts* remained in service: had these been retained for trumpeters? Were they crimson faced in blue?

Having been a cavalry regiment, the men in theory that remained in ranks were good riders and swordsmen and were not the 'jack of all trades' soldiers that true dragoons were. This excellence in equitation is reflected in the inspection of July 1805, whereby the equitation is described as good and well executed. We suppose all bar a hardcore cadre of old cavalry troopers remained. Yet the men were all 'a little small for dragoons' and the regiment's discipline was 'good, just and severe.'[218]

When inspected on 6 January 1808, 504 *habits* were in use, 1028 *surtouts* and white *vestes*, 130 bearskins and 715 sets of *housses* and *chaperons*. We also note 758 *blanc picque de bleu manteaux* were used alongside 150 infantry *capotes*, 120 pairs of white broadcloth breeches and the same number in green broadcloth. We also note 120 sheepskin *schabraques* were in service, 570 pairs of black gaiters, 600 pairs of grey gaiters.[219]

The regiment fought in Spain until 1813, when it formed part of the 3rd Cavalry Corps of the Grande Armée, and served in the campaign of France. During service in Spain 140m of green broadcloth, 162m aurore broadcloth, 162m of linen and 522m 36 of aurore serge had been employed in repairing clothing.[220] The clothing of the four war squadrons at time of disbandment in summer 1814 was mostly good, but a lot was missing:[221]

| Item | In service, but due to expire in the next year | In need of repair | To be replaced in the next year | To be replaced | Items short | Observations |
|---|---|---|---|---|---|---|
| *Habits* | 74 | 13 | 10 | 25 | 50 | Total men under arms 172. |
| *Vestes* or *gilets* | 59 | 8 | 8 | 13 | 84 | |
| *Culottes de peau* | 44 | 1 | 30 | 17 | 80 | |
| Stable trousers | | | 1 | 8 | 163 | |
| Braces | | | | | 172 | |
| *Manteaux* | 92 | 25 | 2 | 18 | 35 | |
| *Bonnets de police* | 81 | 3 | 21 | 24 | 43 | |
| *Gilets d'écurie* | 21 | 6 | 29 | 34 | 82 | |
| *Surculottes* | 2 | 1 | 9 | 10 | 150 | |
| Helmets | 84 | 49 | 4 | 1 | 11 | |
| Bearskins | 10 | 1 | 6 | 5 | | |

Clearly the elite company swaggered in its towering bearskins, contrary to Bardin regulations, and again had retained its old-pattern cloaks. Many men, the inspector noted, were wearing broadcloth *pantalons* reinforced with leather. In addition, there were 361 shirts, 115 black stocks, 168 white stocks, 59 pairs of linen stockings, 20 pairs of woollen stockings, 114 pairs of shoes and 26 pairs of black gaiters. Not enough pairs of socks existed for every man to have a pair. The *dépôt* of the war squadrons held 113 brand-new *gilets d'écurie*, 9 *gibernes*, 14 *porte-gibernes*, and 16 sabre belts.

When disbanded in summer 1814, clothing in the 5ᵉ squadron was as follows:²²²

| Item | In service, but due to expire in the next year | In need of repair | To be replaced in the next year | To be replaced | Items short |
|---|---|---|---|---|---|
| *Habits* | 21 | | | 6 | 39 |
| *Vestes* | 16 | 1 | | 5 | 44 |
| *Gilets d'écurie* | | | | 32 | 44 |
| *Surculotte* | 1 | | | 3 | 62 |
| Stable trousers | | | | 3 | 63 |
| *Culottes de peau* | 16 | 1 | | 11 | 38 |
| *Manteaux* | 16 | 2 | | 16 | 32 |
| *Bonnets de police* | 20 | | | 17 | 29 |
| Helmets | 23 | 16 | | | 27 |
| *Crinieres* | 23 | 16 | | | 27 |

The regiment mustered barely 80 men including officers, 66 other ranks and 12 officers. Despite this, the stores were literally bursting at the seams with new clothing, which included 66 brand-new *habits*, 16 *gilets*, 72 pairs of stable trousers, 229 pairs of *culottes de peau*, 1 *manteaux de modèle*, 1 helmet *de modèle*, 1 *criniere de modèle*, 11 sabre belts, 35 *gibernes*, 31 *porte-gibernes*, and 7 musket slings. Clothing needing repairs included 20 *habits*, 41 *gilets*, 267 pairs of stable trousers, 76 pairs of *culottes de peau*, 25 helmets and *crinieres*, 30 waistbelts, 15 *gibernes* with belts and 5 *porte-manteaux*. Clothing and equipment to be disposed of included 10 *habits*, 20 *gilets*, 5 pairs of *surculottes*, and 44 pairs of stable trousers of the old model.²²³ It seems the 5ᵉ squadron was decked out in Bardin kit and the war squadrons were wearing whatever came to hand.

## 28ᵉ *Dragons*

Raised in Saint-Germain in 1792 as the *Hussards de Liberté*, it became the 7ᵉ *bis Hussard* in 1794 and thence the 28ᵉ *Dragons* in September 1803. Reviewed on 9 April 1805, the regiment was still dressed mostly as *hussards*. The inspecting officer commented:

> Equipment. Gibernes, giberne belts, waistbelts, are all of the hussar model.
>
> Harness and Saddlery. Out of 861 there are 113 dragoon saddles and bridles. The rest are hussar model and are in bad condition. The porte-manteaux are dark blue with yellow lace of the hussar model. The housse is sheepskin schabraque of hussar model with red edging.
>
> Clothing. 240 new surtouts are in use, 260 pairs of culottes de peau are in service and are new, 40 new dragoon manteaux – the rest of the clothing is hussar model.

Officer of the 28ᵉ *Dragons* by Martinet.  Elite company trooper of the 28ᵉ *Dragons* by Martinet.

> Footwear. Not a single pair of dragoon boots exist in the regiment,
>
> Headdress. For 599 men there are 172 helmets, the rest wear shakos. The shako have a yellow ganse and cockade. The shako plates have been withdrawn from service.
>
> Weapons. The men have the dragoon sabre.[224]

When reviewed on 23 July 1805, 444 *dolmans* and *pelisses* were in use, 318 *surtouts*, 170 dragoon helmets, 435 *schakos* and colpacks, 170 pairs of *culottes de peau* and 544 pairs of *culottes hongroise*. For immediate needs 216 *habits* were ordered and 433 *surtouts*.[225] There are no archive records to inform us how and when the regiment became dressed as dragoons.

The regiment served in the Army of Italy from 1805 to 1811 and charged at Wagram. Regimental accounts report the *bonnets de police* had worsted lace to the turban and worsted fringed tassels, and seemingly every man had a copper grenades on their *giberne* as 375 were purchased in 1808.[226]

The regiment took part in the Russian campaign and served with the Grande Arméein 1813–14.

Centre company trooper of the 28ᵉ *Dragons* by Martinet.

Possibly an officer of the 28ᵉ in summer 1813, somewhere near Dresden. (*Collection KM*)

The regiment was disbanded in summer 1814. The elite company was taken into the new *Dragons de Berry* and possessed:[227]

| Item | In service, but due to expire in the next year | In need of repair | To be replaced in the next year | To be replaced | Items short |
|---|---|---|---|---|---|
| *Habits* | 87 | 4 | 3 | 3 | |
| *Gilets en drap blanc* | 78 | | 1 | | 18 |
| *Gilets d'écurie* | 66 | 2 | | 9 | 20 |
| *Culottes de peau* | 85 | 1 | | | 11 |
| Stable trousers | 80 | 1 | | 2 | 14 |
| *Surculottes* | 75 | | | 5 | 17 |
| *Manteaux* | 81 | | | | 16 |
| *Bonnets de police* | 77 | | | 15 | 4 |
| Helmets | 81 | 7 | | | 9 |

Of the 97 men on parade, 38 lacked a pair of boots, and only 87 men had a sabre and 28 men a pistol, and despite no *banderole-porte-carabines* being issued, 25 carbines were in use, which were presumably carried over the men's shoulders. Every man had two shirts and the *sous-officiers* three, just 73 black stocks were in use and 7 white. Also in use were 19 pairs of linen socks, and 7 pairs of woollen stockings -used by the men with white stocks and were likely to be *sous-officiers*? Yes- 72 pairs of shoes, 74 pairs of black gaiters and 30 pairs of linen gaiters. None of the clothing was, the inspector noted, made to the Bardin regulation. Clearly the elite company wore helmets, and we assume if they had epaulettes, they were counted with the *habits*.

The 2ᵉ, 3ᵉ, 4ᵉ and 5ᵉ squadrons of the regiment were taken into the *Dragons d'Angouleme* and were wearing:²²⁸

Centre company trooper of the 29ᵉ *Dragons* by Jolly. (*Musee de l'Armée*)

| Item | In service, but due to expire in the next year | In need of repair | To be replaced in the next year | To be replaced | Items short |
|---|---|---|---|---|---|
| *Habits* | 125 | | | | 13 |
| *Gilets en drap blanc* | 123 | | | | 15 |
| *Gilets d'écurie* | 129 | 4 | | | 5 |
| *Culottes de peau* | 123 | | | | 15 |
| Helmets | 123 | 2 | | | 13 |
| *Bonnets de police* | 130 | | | | 8 |
| Stable trousers | 121 | 1 | | | 16 |
| *Manteaux* | 124 | | | | 14 |
| *Surculottes en drap* | 117 | 2 | | | 19 |

In addition, the men were wearing between them 414 shirts, 138 black stocks – one for every man – and the same number of pairs of shoes and black gaiters. Equipment in use with the 28ᵉ *Dragons* was as follows:²²⁹

| Item | In service, but due to expire in the next year | In need of repair | To be replaced in the next year | To be replaced | Items short |
|---|---|---|---|---|---|
| *Waistbelts* | 125 | | | | 13 |
| *Gibernes* | 118 | | | | 20 |
| *Porte-gibernes* | 118 | | | | 20 |
| Sword knots | 125 | | | | 13 |
| *Porte-manteaux* | 124 | | | | 14 |
| Pairs of boots | 124 | | | | 14 |
| Pairs of spurs | 111 | | | | 27 |
| Pairs of gauntlets | 104 | | | | 34 |
| *Fusils de dragon* | | 24 | | | |
| Sabres | 117 | 18 | | | |
| Pistols | 62 | 16 | | | |

The regimental *dépôt* contained 160m Imperial Livery and 216 brand-new *habits-vestes*: the inspector noted the regiment had only recently adopted the provisions of the regulation of 1812. A further 88 stocks were in stores with a single pair of shoes and 5 pairs of black gaiters. The inspector further noted that the regiment's clothing was not made according to the decrees of 19 January and 17 February 1812, nor had the regiment acted upon the decree of 23 April 1814 in removing Imperial symbols and dressing the trumpeters in blue. To this end, we note some 160m of Imperial Livery was burned and that the inspector commented that the major had attended to reclothing the regiment since the return of the King.[230]

## 29ᵉ *Dragons*

Created in September 1803 from the 11ᵉ *Hussard*, it became the 6ᵉ *Lanciers* in 1811. When reviewed on 17 September 1804, 1 *habit* was in use, 20 *dolmans*, 497 *pelisses* and 490 *surtouts*. Headdress was 455 *schakos* and 95 helmets. Stores held 47m 04 aurore broadcloth, 2,427m 68 green broadcloth, 295m white broadcloth, 436m 50 *blanc picque de bleu* broadcloth, and had used 589m 57 scarlet broadcloth and 2,283m 72 *gris de fer* broadcloth. Stores held 30 brand-new *habits*, 79 helmets, as well as 175 *schakos*. The men's equipment and that of the horses was all *hussard* pattern. The unit must have presented a very unique look of men wearing *hussard* dress with dragoon helmets![231]

When inspected on 29 September 1805, 620 *pelisses* and *dolmans* had been taken from service, with 390 *habits* in use, all produced over the past year, with a further 216 in production to complete the transition to dragoon uniform. No bearskins existed for the elite company and all leather work had changed to dragoon pattern, as had the unit's weaponry. We also note 399 helmets were issued and fort rather than sabre belts, 458 *baudriers* – shoulder belts – were issued to carry sabres.[232]

A letter dated 6 January 1808 reports that the Colonel General of Dragoons had raised with the Emperor the issue that the regiment's clothing was not yet fully that

Officer of the 29ᵉ *Dragons* by Martinet.

Centre company trooper of the 29ᵉ *Dragons* by Martinet.

of dragoons: the *habits-vestes* in use were to be converted to stable coats by cutting off the tails, the *pantalons*, boots and other light cavalry items were to be sold to regiments of *chasseurs* or *hussards*.[233] Indeed, the review carried out the same day notes 504 *habits* were in use, of which 269 were life expired, 1,078 *surtouts*, 758 *manteaux* and 150 *capotes*, 579 pairs of black worsted gaiters, 600 pairs of grey linen gaiters and 802 black stocks. The infantry company had 120 wool knee breaches in green broadcloth and 120 pairs in white broadcloth. We also note 130 bearskins were in service and 838 helmets. The question of how the regiment was to be dressed was again raised in February and noted 'it is three years since the Colonel General ordered the adoption of dragoon clothing'.[234]

Elite company trooper of the 29ᵉ *Dragons* by Martinet.

Clearly whatever garments the unit was wearing, they were not yet dragoon model; we guess the habits were *habit-kinski* or something similar. When reviewed on 15 July 1808, 752 *habits* and 960 *surtouts* were in use. The elite company had no bearskins.[235] We know nothing else, but assume that by 1809 the regiment had taken on traditional dragoon uniforms.

## 30ᵉ *Dragons*

Created at Moulins from the 12ᵉ *Hussard* in September 1803, the regiment was with the Army of Italy from 1805 to 1811.

When reviewed on 19 September 1803, every man was dressed as a *hussard* with 553 *dolmans* in use and 4 *pelisses*. The elite company had 56 colpacks. We also note, 314m 35 of *bleu de ciel* broadcloth had been used, 461m 37 of chestnut brown broadcloth to make 200 capotes, 1,115m 83 of green broadcloth for *manteaux*, 31m 84 madder red broadcloth, and 828m *bleu de ciel* serge. A stockpile of cloth had been obtained to begin the process of converting to dragoons: 2,462m 74 green broadcloth, 126m 73 aurore broadcloth, 675m white broadcloth and 911m 70 *blanc picque de bleu* broadcloth.[236]

In January 1805 the regiment was dressed as a hybrid dragoon and *hussard* regiment. The men were all wearing *hussard* boots, and green *culottes hongroise* laced in white; red *hussard veste*s laced in white, and *surtouts* with the aurore collars. Every man rode on *hussard* saddles with the large sheepskin *schabraques*. The elite company was decked out in colpacks, some men had red *schakos* and others dragoon helmets. All ranks were armed as *hussards*. One would scarcely recognise the regiment as dragoons![237]

On 18 July 1805, 357 *habits* were in use and 495 *dolmans:* clothing and equipment was still a mix of patterns with 207 dragoon saddles and 179 hussar type in use. Stores reported 4 pairs of epaulettes were in use, 45m of *bleu de ciel* broadcloth had been used, and 15m 57 of madder red broadcloth.[238]

When inspected on 8 January 1808, 770 *habits*, *surtouts* and white *veste*s were in use, and the elite company had 106 bearskins and the same number of pairs of scarlet epaulettes. Stores held 736m of cording for *bonnets de police*, accompanied by 368m of white lace and 1,320 tassels, and uniquely 300 pairs of cotton *pantalons*. Stores also held stocks of materials to make *dolmans* and *pelisses*. Every man in the regiment had their *giberne* decorated with a copper grenade, 555 being issued. We also note 16 *sapeurs*' axes with cases. The foot company had worn chestnut-brown capotes as stores reported 194m 13 of *brun-marron* broadcloth being used to make 401 *capotes*. We also note 35m 40 of madder red broadcloth had been used, 41m 70 *bleu de ciel* broadcloth and 66m 30 *bleu de ciel* serge. Stores also reports 23m 76 of drummers' lace had been used and 1,413m 95 lace for *bonnets de police*. Again, we note 32 *hussard gibernes* and belts were in use as well as 543 plumes and 6 black sheepskin *schabraques* for trumpeters.[239]

The regiment took part in the Russian campaign and was with the Grande Armée at Bautzen, Dresden and Leipzig as well as in the campaign of France. The regiment

Officer of the 30ᵉ *Dragons* by Martinet.

Centre company trooper of the 30ᵉ *Dragons* by Martinet. We know of no contemporary iconography for trumpeters or the elite company of this regiment.

was refitted in spring 1813, and was one of the few regiments to actually receive Bardin clothing: the total expenditure was 2,722fr, which can only have been a partial reclothing of the unit. We note 379fr 50 was spent on 258 pairs of linen gaiters and 76 pairs of shoes.[240]

Disbanded in summer 1814, the regiment's stores held 39m 70 of beige broadcloth, 80m of *blanc picque de bleu* broadcloth for *manteaux*, 13m of white broadcloth, 12m 96 of aurore broadcloth for facings, 37m 44 of green broadcloth, 140m 42 of green tricot, 26m 10 of aurore serge and 140m 70 of lace for the *porte-manteaux*.[241] We know that the 5ᵉ or *dépôt* squadron was wearing *habit-vestes* as 24 were in use in good condition, 24 needed repairs and 2 were to be written off, along with 29 good *gilets*, 20 *gilets* needing repairs and 1 to be disposed of. The *dépôt* held a huge quantity of clothing and attests to the fact the regiment had been in the process of adopting Bardin regulation in the closing weeks of the Empire.[242]

| Item | New | In need of repair | To be disposed of | Total |
|---|---|---|---|---|
| *Habits-vestes* | 255 | 52 | 148 | 455 |
| *Gilets sans manche* | 307 | | | 307 |
| *Gilets d'écurie* | 170 | 12 | | 182 |
| *Bonnets de police* | 112 | 5 | | 117 |
| *Surculottes* | 181 | 20 | | 201 |
| *Culottes de peau* | 159 | 25 | | 182 |
| *Manteaux* | 450 | 30 | 40 | 520 |
| Helmets | 221 | 100 | 90 | 411 |
| Braces | 60 | | | 60 |
| *Porte-manteaux* | 231 | 90 | | 321 |

Here we have proof positive the regiment wore *habits-vestes* and were dressed as per Bardin. We have no idea as to the dress of the trumpeters as not an inch of lace existed for them.[243] The reviewing officer of the war squadrons taken into the new 15ᵉ *Dragons* noted that items of clothing had not yet been replaced to accord with the instruction of 25 May 1814. More importantly, he noted the regiment had not fully adopted the provisions of the decree of 7 February 1812 introducing the Bardin regulation, and that

Trooper of the 1ᵉ *Dragons* drawn *c.*1812 by Weiland. (*Collection KM*)

Trooper of centre company 26ᵉ *Dragons c.*1806. Of interest, he has a round *porte-manteau*.

the decree of 23 April 1814 concerning modifications to the dress of trumpeters and removal of Imperial symbols had not been carried out. We also note the regiment had copper fishcale contre-epaulettes, which were "tolerated" by the inspecting officer.[244]

### 1ᵉ *Régiment Provisoire de Dragons*

The unit was formed in Hanover on 1 March 1812 on the orders of General Bourcier. The man power for the new regiment was drawn from dragoon squadrons that had been intended to reinforce regiments in Spain, but had been re-directed to support the 1812 campaign.

Inspector of Review Nicolas Le Brun gave the regiment a root and branch shakedown inspection on 26 July 1812 when he noted the unit was to be called the 1ᵉ *Régiment de Dragons*. The unit had had been formed from the available cadres in the remount depot at Hanover from the 2ᵉ, 5ᵉ, 12ᵉ, 13ᵉ, 17ᵉ, 19ᵉ and 20ᵉ regiments of dragoons stationed in Hanover. The inspection tells us exactly what these various detachments were wearing in July 1812:

### 2ᵉ *Dragons*

Clothing and equipment in use was as follows:[245]

|  | *Habits* | *Vestes* | *Surtouts* | *Culottes de peau* | *Bonnets de police* | *Gilets d'écurie* | Helmets | Black twill gaiters | Gauntlets | Stable trousers | Black stocks | *Manteaux* | *Gibernes* | *Banderolles* |
|---|---|---|---|---|---|---|---|---|---|---|---|---|---|---|
| 4ᵉ Company | 121 | 121 | 5 | 121 | 121 | 116 | 121 | 116 | 60 | 116 | 121 | 60 | 116 | 116 |
| 8ᵉ Company | 114 | 114 | 5 | 114 | 114 | 109 | 114 | 109 | 174 | 108 | 112 | 114 | 110 | 110 |
| Total | 235 | 235 | 10 | 235 | 235 | 225 | 235 | 226 | 174 | 224 | 233 | 174 | 226 | 226 |

The inspector noted that the *sous-officiers* (sergeants and sergeant majors) and trumpeters wore both a *surtout* and a *habit*, and that the *sous-officiers* were not issued *gibernes*. Arguably the trumpeters' *habit* was in *revers*ed colours with white lace, and the *surtouts* was much more sombre and workmanlike, again perhaps reversed colours. Not a single plume existed. The squadron had 150 horses allocated to it; yet only 125 saddles and *schabraques* were issued along with 159 *porte-crosses*, i.e., the bucket and straps to carry the dragoon musket. The squadron had no linen *caleçons* in use.

## 5ᵉ *Dragons*

Clothing and equipment in use was as follows:[246]

| | Habits | Vestes | Culottes de peau | Bonnets de police | Gilets d'écurie | Helmets | Plumes | Black twill gaiters | Gauntlets | Stable trousers | Black stocks | Manteaux | Gibernes | Banderolles |
|---|---|---|---|---|---|---|---|---|---|---|---|---|---|---|
| 4ᵉ Company | 58 | 58 | 58 | 58 | 58 | 58 | 58 | 43 | 44 | 58 | 58 | 46 | 51 | 51 |
| 8ᵉ Company | 54 | 54 | 54 | 54 | 54 | 54 | 54 | 36 | 54 | 54 | 54 | 48 | 48 | 48 |
| Total | 112 | 112 | 112 | 112 | 112 | 112 | 112 | 79 | 98 | 112 | 112 | 94 | 99 | 99 |

Of comment, all ranks in both companies had plumes. The *sous-officiers* and trumpets did not have *giberne*s. Many men lacked gaiters, a *manteau* and gauntlets. The squadron had 150 horses allocated, yet only had 93 saddles, which were fully equipped with *housses* and sheepskin schabraques. The squadron also had 126 pairs of linen *caleçons* in service.

## 12ᵉ *Dragons*

Clothing and equipment in use was as follows:[247]

| | Habits | Vestes | Culottes de peau | Bonnets de police | Gilets d'écurie | Helmets | Plumes | Black twill gaiters | Gauntlets | Stable trousers | Black stocks | Manteaux | Gibernes | Banderolles |
|---|---|---|---|---|---|---|---|---|---|---|---|---|---|---|
| 4ᵉ Company | 67 | 67 | 134 | 67 | 67 | 67 | 67 | 67 | 67 | 67 | 67 | 67 | 59 | 59 |
| 8ᵉ Company | 65 | 65 | 130 | 65 | 65 | 65 | 65 | 65 | 65 | 65 | 65 | 65 | 58 | 58 |
| Total | 132 | 132 | 264 | 132 | 132 | 132 | 132 | 132 | 132 | 132 | 132 | 132 | 117 | 117 |

Every man was fully equipped and sufficient *culottes de peau* existed to equip each company if it ever became full strength. The squadron had 85 horses allocated. In lieu of the sheepskin *schabraque*, the regiment had 85 sets of *housses* and *chaperons* in use. The squadron also had 126 pairs of linen *caleçons* in service.

## 13ᵉ *Dragons*

Clothing and equipment in use was as follows:[248]

| | *Habits* | *Vestes* | *Surtouts* | *Culottes de peau* | *Bonnets de police* | *Gilets d'écurie* | Helmets | Black twill gaiters | Gauntlets | Stable trousers | Black stocks | *Manteaux* | *Gibernes* | *Banderolles* |
|---|---|---|---|---|---|---|---|---|---|---|---|---|---|---|
| 4ᵉ Company | 115 | 115 | 6 | 115 | 115 | 109 | 115 | 109 | 115 | 109 | 115 | 115 | 115 | 115 |
| 8ᵉ Company | | | | | | | | | | | | | | |
| Total | 115 | 115 | 6 | 115 | 115 | 109 | 115 | 109 | 115 | 109 | 115 | 1115 | 115 | 115 |

The squadron mustered 115 rank and file – every man was fully equipped. The *sous-officiers* and trumpeters had no *gilets d'écurie* or stable trousers: as these men employed grooms to attend their horses, in lieu they wore *surtouts*. Arguably therefore, as with the 2ᵉ *Dragons*, the trumpeters' *habit* was in reversed colours with white lace decoration, and the *surtout* was perhaps also reversed colours. No plumes or epaulettes existed. The squadron had 115 horses, all fully equipped, and in lieu of the sheepskin *schabraque* had laced broadcloth *chaperons*.[249]

## 17ᵉ *Dragons*

Clothing and equipment in use was as follows:[250]

| | *Habits* | *Vestes* | *Culottes de peau* | *Bonnets de police* | *Gilets d'écurie* | Helmets | Black twill gaiters | Gauntlets | Stable trousers | Black stocks | *Manteaux* | *Gibernes* | *Banderolles* |
|---|---|---|---|---|---|---|---|---|---|---|---|---|---|
| 4ᵉ Company | 50 | 50 | 50 | 50 | 50 | 50 | 22 | 50 | 47 | 50 | 50 | 49 | 49 |
| 8ᵉ Company | 50 | 50 | 50 | 50 | 50 | 50 | 25 | 50 | 47 | 50 | 50 | 50 | 50 |
| Total | 100 | 100 | 100 | 100 | 100 | 100 | 47 | 100 | 94 | 100 | 100 | 99 | 99 |

The squadron had 100 horses allocated to it, and were issued with 100 pairs of *chaperons* and 100 *housses*.

## 19ᵉ *Dragons*

Clothing and equipment in use was as follows:[251]

|  | Habits | Vestes | Culottes de peau | Bonnets de police | Gilets d'écurie | Helmets | Plumes | Black twill gaiters | Gauntlets | Stable trousers | Black stocks | Manteaux | Gibernes | Banderolles |
|---|---|---|---|---|---|---|---|---|---|---|---|---|---|---|
| 4ᵉ Company | 67 | 67 | 67 | 67 | 67 | 67 | 62 | 67 | 67 | 0 | 67 | 67 | 67 | 67 |
| 8ᵉ Company | 61 | 61 | 61 | 61 | 61 | 61 | 0 | 61 | 61 | 61 | 61 | 61 | 61 | 61 |
| Total | 128 | 128 | 128 | 128 | 128 | 128 | 62 | 62 | 62 | 61 | 128 | 128 | 128 | 128 |

The squadron was allocated 124 horses, and were issued 128 *housses* and 128 sheepskin *schabraques*. Of interest, only the 4ᵉ company had plumes and only 8ᵉ company stable trousers.

## 20ᵉ *Dragons*

Clothing and equipment in use was as follows:[252]

|  | Habits | Vestes | Culottes de peau | Bonnets de police | Gilets d'écurie | Helmets | Plumes | Black twill gaiters | Gauntlets | Stable trousers | Black stocks | Manteaux | Gibernes | Banderolles |
|---|---|---|---|---|---|---|---|---|---|---|---|---|---|---|
| 4ᵉ Company | 57 | 57 | 57 | 57 | 57 | 57 | 57 | 57 | 57 | 57 | 57 | 57 | 57 | 57 |
| 8ᵉ Company | 58 | 58 | 58 | 58 | 58 | 58 | 58 | 58 | 58 | 58 | 58 | 58 | 58 | 58 |
| Total | 115 | 115 | 115 | 115 | 115 | 115 | 115 | 115 | 115 | 115 | 115 | 115 | 115 | 115 |

The squadron was allocated 115 horses, and were equipped with 115 saddles, 155 *housses* and 155 sheepskin *schabraques*.

Perhaps befitting a largely dismounted unit, the men had black tricot gaiters rather than boots.

The next document we have concerning the regiment is dated 6 August, and records that it had 34 officers and 956 other ranks and was waiting for the men from 13ᵉ and 14ᵉ to arrive; ultimately the 13ᵉ only sent a single company. These men were literally the last shakings of regimental *dépôt* in France and were far from ideal 'army material', according to General Bourcier.[253]

By January 1813 just 136 horses remained in Hanover, all the others – well over 1,000 – had been allocated to the wreck of the Grande Armée for immediate needs.[254] Despite lacking horses, hundreds of men were still hanging around in the *dépôt:* by May, the regiment mustered 27 officers and 508 other ranks.[255] By July the ad hoc formation had 16 officers and 947 other ranks. To clothe every man, the regiment needed 17 *habits*, 53 pairs of *pantalons*, 94 pairs of *culottes de peau*, 18 helmets, 32 pairs of boots, 25 *manteaux*, 18 *porte-manteaux* and 4 sabres. The major stumbling block to the regiment taking to the field was that it had just 218 horses![256] The regiment now drops out of history. It was ordered to Hanau on 11 July to be mounted.[257] After this we have no trace at all of the regiment's existence.

## Dragons du Roi

Created on 23 April 1814, the regiment was an amalgam of the old 2$^e$ *Dragons*, Royalist volunteers and *émigré* officers, and the few men that remained from the *Compagnie d'Elite du Grande Quartier General*. The regiment was formally constituted on 21 June 1814. During the 100 days the *Dragons du Roi* took the title *Dragons du 1*. As a King's regiment, the men were authorised to wear white *contre-epaulettes* and *aiguilettes* and white *aigrettes* in their helmets, and *fleur-de-lys* to the tails of the *habits*. The elite company wore beards. A total of 14,498fr 54 was spent on clothing the new regiment.

Trooper of the *Dragons du Roi* by Colonel Jolly. (Collection KM)

Printed by Bassett during the Restoration of 1814 is this image of a trooper of the *Dragons du Roi*.

On 8 December, the regiment had the following items in the *dépôt* and in use:[258]

| Item | In *dépôt* 1 September 1815 | Items in service | Total |
| --- | --- | --- | --- |
| *Habits-vestes* | 11 | 432 | 443 |
| *Vestes sans manche* | 1 | 43 | 44 |
| *Gilets d'écurie* | 8 | 366 | 374 |
| Stable trousers | 0 | 0 | 0 |
| *Culottes de peau* | 69 | 378 | 456 |
| *Surculottes* | 1 | 378 | 379 |
| *Manteaux* | 0 | 52 | 52 |
| *Manteaux-capote* | 9 | 288 | 297 |
| *Bonnets de police* | 0 | 387 | 387 |
| Helmets | 130 | 378 | 508 |
| Plumes | 90 | 269 | 359 |
| Scarlet epaulettes | 74 | 0 | 74 |
| White *aiguillettes* | 565 | 0 | 565 |
| White *contre-epaulettes* | 456 | 0 | 456 |
| Sabre waistbelts | 198 | 336 | 534 |
| *Gibernes* | 162 | 504 | 666 |
| *Porte-gibernes* | 143 | 554 | 697 |
| *Banderole-Porte-Mousquetons* | 0 | 96 | 96 |
| Musket slings | 0 | 355 | 355 |
| Sword knots | 90 | 270 | 360 |
| *Porte-manteaux* | 99 | 427 | 526 |
| Pairs of boots | 16 | 458 | 526 |
| Pairs of spurs with straps | 16 | 387 | 403 |
| Pairs of gauntlets | 0 | 269 | 269 |
| Trumpets | 0 | 14 | 14 |
| Saddles complete | 0 | 390 | 390 |
| Curb bridles | 0 | 326 | 326 |
| Snaffle bridles | 0 | 335 | 335 |
| *Housses* | 50 | 295 | 345 |
| *Demi-schabraques* | 0 | 301 | 301 |
| Wool saddle blankets | 0 | 227 | 227 |
| Watering bridles | 0 | 369 | 369 |
| Stirrup irons | 0 | 310 | 310 |
| *Porte-crosses* | 0 | 238 | 238 |
| *Bottes de carabine* | 0 | 102 | 102 |
| Stable head collars | 0 | 201 | 201 |

Regulations in Practice 149

| Item | In dépôt 1 September 1815 | Items in service | Total |
|---|---|---|---|
| Pairs of bosettes | 17 | 0 | 17 |
| Parade head collars | 0 | 341 | 341 |
| *Schabraque* surcingles | 0 | 173 | 173 |
| Dragoon muskets | 0 | 96 | 96 |
| Infantry muskets | 0 | 1 | 1 |
| Light cavalry *mousquetons* | 0 | 133 | 133 |
| Pairs of pistols | 0 | 243 | 243 |
| Sabres | 190 | 454 | 644 |
| Bayonets | 0 | 140 | 140 |
| Bayonet scabbards | 0 | 128 | 128 |

Of interest, two patterns of *manteaux* were in use, the old-style *manteaux* and the new 1813-pattern *manteaux-capote*. The three types of firearms in use is remarkable. One can only imagine how unwieldly an infantry musket would have been on horseback, compared to the dragoon musket or much smaller light cavalry *mousquetons*.

The scarlet epaulettes were either those left over from re-equipping the elite company with these items in the 100 days, or were all those taken from use in 1814 and had never been reissued. The documents also prove that the white *contre-epaulettes* and *aiguillettes* introduced in February 1815 and shown by Genty were indeed made and issued for, it seems, the entire regiment. The plumes were no doubt white, as introduced in February 1815, along with the *aiguillettes* etc.

## Officers' uniform and equipment

Officers provided their own clothing and equipment at their expense. Sub-Lieutenant Fleury Brossette had his horse killed under him on 18 June 1815 and submitted the following claim for expenses to replace his lost effects:

| Item | Quantity | Value | Total expense claim | Circumstances for the loss |
|---|---|---|---|---|
| *Habit* | 1 | 50fr | 50fr | At the affair of Mont St Jean 18 June |
| Waistcoat | 2 | 15fr | 30fr | |
| *Culottes de peau* | 2 | 15fr | 30fr | |
| *Pantalons* | 1 | 17fr | 17fr | |
| Pair of boots | 1 | 30fr | 30fr | |
| Pair of shoes | 1 | 6fr | 6fr | |
| *Chapeaux* | 1 | 12fr | 12fr | |
| Pairs of socks | 2 | 4fr | 8fr | |

| Item | Quantity | Value | Total expense claim | Circumstances for the loss |
|---|---|---|---|---|
| Cravats | 6 | 5fr | 30fr | |
| *Manteaux* | 1 | 70fr | 70fr | |
| *Porte-manteaux* | 2 | 12fr | 12fr | |
| Sabre | 1 | 20fr | 20fr | |
| Pair of Epaulettes | 1 | 15fr | 15fr | |
| Shirts | 4 | 6fr | 24fr | |
| Saddle | 1 | 26fr | 26 | |
| Bridle | 1 | 6fr | 6fr | |
| Total | | | 400fr | |

In the midst of the battle, Brossette was able to draw up a list of lost effects, provide receipts for the items, as well as manage to locate General Lhéritier to sign the document, along with his company commander Suchet, his squadron commander, Rigau, and his colonel, Planzeaux. Quite what these officers made of a junior officer wanting to submit an expense claim during the battle is lost to history. One suspects that Brossette was something of a 'jobsworth', making sure that paperwork was duly submitted to the relevant authorities for his lost equipment during the Battle of Waterloo. Oddly, he does not claim for a horse.

Brossette was a career soldier, enlisting in the regiment 13 August 1803. He made corporal on 22 March 1805, *fourrier* on 12 March 1807, sergeant on 6 May 1808, and sergeant major on 1 February 1809. He was promoted to sub-lieutenant on 6 November 1813, and this was confirmed by the King on 24 June 1814. He had served in the campaigns of Austerlitz, Jena, Eylau, and Spain in 1808, Austria in 1809, and then in Spain from 1809 through to spring 1813.[259]

# Chapter 5

# Dragoon Concluding Remarks

So, what does all this research mean? Well, it shows that the dragoons were rather flexible with the application of some decrees over clothing, but the 1801 regulation that removed the sheepskin *schabraque* from use until the Bardin regulation was enforced rigorously. Despite what some modern authors and artists say, from 1805 into 1813, sheepskins were not in use across all regiments: just the 3$^e$, 9$^e$ and 11$^e$ had these items, neatly demonstrating why research is necessary. Again, the undress *surtout* was entirely green with no distinctive facings, which is exactly as period artwork shows yet not how re-enactors, wargamers and artists understand them to have appeared.

## Habits or habits-vestes?

Bardin regulation, as we have seen earlier, in theory introduced the *habit-veste*. Yet given that the bulk of Dragoon regiments were in Spain, and miles away from their *dépôt*, it is likely that they were never issued these garments. When we look at the inspection returns from summer 1814, we find just the 30$^e$ *Dragons* were universally wearing *habits-vestes*! This means that 99% of all dragoon regiments did not adopt Bardin regulation until 1814 into 1815. Furthermore, we note from the disbandment records that the 13$^e$, 15$^e$ and 18$^e$ regiments had a mix and match approach, the *dépôt* company had *habits-vestes* and the war squadrons *habits*. This left 21 regiments fully decked out in old-pattern clothing. Bardin regulation for the dragoons simply did not exist. It existed in the mind of Bardin, but the reality was remarkably different. The 11$^e$ *Dragons* by 1815 still had old- and new-pattern *habits* in use! Indeed, Inspector of Review Raphael Sabathier reports that 5$^e$, 6$^e$, 7$^e$, 13$^e$, 19$^e$, 22$^e$ and 25$^e$ had not adopted Bardin regulation in July 1814.[1] The Sauerweid manuscript shows the 22$^e$ wearing *habits a revers* in 1813 with grey cloth *pantalons*, with leather reinforcement to the inner leg and a facing colour side stripe. Again, this is not a major surprise as the bulk of the dragoon regiments were in Spain and had no real opportunity to adopt new-regulation clothing.

## Elite company

Formed under the decree of *18 Vendémiaire An X* (10 October 1801), Article 13 of the decree stipulates:

> The first company of the first squadron of each cavalry regiment, dragoons, *chasseurs* and *hussards*, will take the name of Elite Company. This company will be formed of

men chosen in all Corps, conforming to the instructions which will be given by the Minister of War.[2]

Under this decree, the elite company was allowed to wear a bearskin with no front plate as a particular distinction, but nothing was specified as to the colour of plumes and bearskin cords or use of other attributes. In the mind of the Minister of War, these companies were to keep the same dress and the same plume as the centre companies. The bearskin probably had the same composition, shape and dimensions as those in use in the *carabinier* regiments, ostensibly the grenadiers of the line cavalry. These two regiments having red plume and fringed epaulettes of the grenadiers, it is understandable that they became the model for the elite companies of dragoons. In the absence of any precise regulation, the choice was left to the initiative of the colonel, and because of this, a wide array of variations existed that we know in part, thanks to contemporary documents and iconography. Perhaps due to the ambiguity over what was allowed to be worn, a circular of *18 Brumaire An XI* (19 November 1802) tells us that the elite companies of several regiments of dragoons had adopted *aiguillettes* for the elite company in imitation of the *Garde Impériale*: the War Minister took advantage of this circular to point out that the sole distinction accorded to the said companies consisted of the bearskin and epaulettes and that all other distinguishing items were forbidden.[3] No colour was officially prescribed for the plume, bearskin cords and epaulettes, but the understanding was probably to be scarlet. We know from iconography that this assumption by the minister was overlooked by colonels. We assume elite companies were allowed moustaches, although in La Houssaye's division, and that of Grouchy, at the close of July 1806 all dragoons were ordered to shave theirs off. This seems all the more remarkable as in theory moustaches were worn in the summer (1 May to 1 October) rather than the winter. No regulations existed for the men to wear these, yet clearly they did. In theory again, they also wore their hair in a queue.

Nothing more is said officially about elite companies until the Bardin regulations, whereby scarlet-fringed epaulettes were introduced and a red horse hair *aigrette*. In theory, bearskins were abolished. This is of course all 'in theory', as we see below:

### 1ᵉ *Dragons*
91 bearskins in service in October 1807, none in stores.[4]

### 2ᵉ *Dragons*
The 2ᵉ *Dragons* disposed of their bearskins at the close of the 1807 campaign – we do not know if they were ever replaced.[5] *Dépôt* in 1815 held 74 pairs of scarlet epaulettes – clearly the elite company had troopers' helmets but fringed epaulettes.[6]

### 3ᵉ *Dragons*
No bearskins in use in 1807.[7] The 3ᵉ *Dragons*, when disbanded in 1811 to become the 2ᵉ *Lanciers*, handed bearskins over to the 6ᵉ and 11ᵉ *Dragons*' elite companies.[8] Clearly an innovation of 1808 and later.

# Dragoon Concluding Remarks

1ᵉ *Dragons* wearing Bardin regulation by Rousselot. (*Collection KM*)

Trumpeters of the 1ᵉ *Dragons* wearing the first design of Imperial Livery. From April 1813, the troopers' *habit* with lace around the *revers* etc. was replaced by the same *habit* as used by infantry drummers and *cuirassiers* with breast loops to standardise all musicians' uniforms. It is impossible to know which of the two regulations were adhered to, if at all. (*Collection KM*)

### 4ᵉ *Dragons*

We have three points of reference to conform the elite company with bearskins: 100 bearskins are listed in stores in 1815 at time of disbandment, we have eyewitness accounts of the regiment wearing them in the field, and the Sauerweid manuscript shows bearskins with white cords, scarlet plumes and scarlet-fringed epaulettes to the *habit*. He also shows an officer with gilt bearskin cords as opposed to the expected silver. He also shows a *sapeur* carrying an axe, wearing a full-length apron and riding on dragoon harness.[9]

### 5ᵉ *Dragons*

In 1814 the regiment still had bearskins in 1814, some 121 in service and a further 17 in stores along with 54 scarlet feather plumes. Not a single pair of epaulettes existed, but they may have been counted with the *habits*.[10] It had worn white epaulettes and *aiguilettes* at the start of the Empire. The regiment conceivably wore bearskins during the 100 days as 80 were in service when the regiment was disbanded.[11]

### 6ᵉ *Dragons*

In 1804, 56 bearskins were in use.[12] A stores inventory of the unit from August 1814 most interestingly reports 50 *aigrettes* and 3 pairs of trumpeters' epaulettes, all

Dismounted troopers of the 1ᵉ *Dragons* by Rousselot. (*Collection KM*)

7ᵉ *Dragons* wearing Bardin regulation by Rousselot. (*Collection KM*)

brand new and unissued in the regimental *dépôt*. The *aigrettes* and epaulettes were destined for the elite company.[13] These were the only epaulettes in the regiment, so clearly the only distinction for the elite company was the *aigrette*.

### 7ᵉ Dragons

In January 1808 the regiment had 121 bearskins in use, all in good condition.[14] Martinet shows a member of the elite company wearing a bearskin adorned with white cords and a scarlet plume. He wears scarlet-fringed epaulettes.[15]

### 8ᵉ Dragons

56 bearskins in use during 1803,[16] but at the end of 1807 campaign all bearskins were in *dépôt*: 20 needed repairs and 20 were fit only for throwing out. No more were purchased after this date.[17] The paperwork for the 8ᵉ *Dragons* reports in 1811 the following purchases:[18]

> 350 red and white plumes. Total 1,066fr
> 100 red plumes at 4fr 55 each. Total 455fr
> Grenades for *gibernes*, buttons for musket slings, rosettes for helmets, bayonet ferrules, '*fleurones de plaques des gibernes*', buckles for sword slings. Total 650fr

We assume that the red plumes and grenades for the *gibernes* were restricted to the regiment's elite company.

Dragoon Concluding Remarks 155

Officer of dragoons wearing society dress on the left and campaign dress on the right by Rousselot. (*Collection KM*)

Elite company trooper of the 10ᵉ *Dragons* wearing a hybrid of Bardin regulation and the 1802 regulation: the bearskin with the *habits-vestes* looks incredibly smart. (*Collection KM*)

### 9ᵉ *Dragons*
119 bearskins existed in 1804/05.[19] No bearskins in use in 1807.[20] Clearly all had been lost in action in 1805, 1806, and 1807 and never replaced.

### 10ᵉ *Dragons*
127 bearskins in use 1804/05.[21]

### 11ᵉ *Dragons*
107 bearskins in use 1804/05. In 1815, the regiment had 100 pairs of grenadiers' epaulettes and 43 grenadiers' *aigrettes*. None existed in 1814, so were all purchased post-August 1814.[22]

### 12ᵉ *Dragons*
No bearskins recorded in 1804/05 or 1808.[23]

### 13ᵉ *Dragons*
56 bearskins in use 1804/05.[24]

### 14ᵉ *Dragons*
1804/05 107 bearskins in use.[25] The 14ᵉ had both bearskins and fringed epaulettes, 56 pairs of epaulettes were in use, along with 72 bearskins and 136 plumes![26]

### 15ᵉ *Dragons*
107 bearskins and 587 plumes in use 1804/05.[27]

### 16ᵉ *Dragons*
No bearskins in use 1804 or 1808.

### 17ᵉ *Dragons*
51 bearskins in use 1804/05.[28] In use in summer 1814 were 41 bearskins and 24 feather plumes. No epaulettes are listed for the elite company either in store or in use, so we assume the men only had bearskins to mark their status, unless the epaulettes being fixed to the *habit* were counted with the *habits*.[29]

### 18ᵉ *Dragons*
No bearskins in use 1804 or 1808.

### 19ᵉ *Dragons*
At the time of the amalgam in summer 1814 the regiment boasted 184 bearskins and helmets in good condition, 40 needing repairs and 6 needed to be disposed as no longer fit for service. Alas we do not have the number of helmets or bearskins, but it is proof positive that the elite company and them. Not a single *aigrette* or pair of epaulettes existed – presumably the bearskin plume and cords were counted with the bearskin and the epaulettes with the *habits*? Or did the regiment really not have these items?[30] Martinet shows a member of the elite company wearing a bearskin adorned with white cords and a scarlet plume. He wears scarlet-fringed epaulettes.[31]

### 20ᵉ *Dragons*
No bearskins in use 1805 or 1808.

### 21ᵉ *Dragons*
56 bearskins in use 1804/05.[32] The regiment in 1814 had 50 new pairs of grenadiers epaulettes in *dépôt* along 104 *aigrettes* and 32 bearskins.[33]

### 22ᵉ *Dragons*
67 bearskins in use in October 1804.[34] Rousselot cites the Sauerweid manuscript as evidence of the regiment having its elite company in bearskins and fringed epaulettes in 1813.[35] No archive sources support this statement.[36]

### 23ᵉ *Dragons*
No bearskins reported in 1804/05 or 1808. Presumably the regiment never had any.[37] However, Rousselot cites the elite company with bearskins and trumpeters with white bearskins.[38] Therefore these items must have been obtained between 1808 and 1814, if, and it's a big if, they existed.

### 24ᵉ Dragons
61 bearskins in use in 1807.[39] In summer 1814, the standout item in the inspection return is the presence of 92 bearskins, of which 4 were in need of replacement and a further 17 were in the *dépôt*. No plumes or epaulettes are listed.[40]

### 25ᵉ Dragons
7 bearskins in use 1804, presumably with *sous-officiers*, or trumpeters and *sapeurs*? A further 107 were authorised for production.[41] When the 1st and 2nd squadrons were disbanded in summer 1814, they were wearing 155 helmets and bearskins in good condition, 26 needed repairs and 1 was fit for disposal. Alas we don't have the number of bearskins in use, but these were no doubt allocated to trumpeters and perhaps also the elite company. The *dépôt* held for the elite company of the 25ᵉ *Dragons* in 1814, 42 scarlet feather plumes, 42 pairs of red epaulettes and 42 sets of bearskin cords! In addition, the *dépôt* held 16 bearskins that needed repairs. Proof positive of bearskins, with cords and plumes and elite company men with fringed epaulettes.[42]

### 26ᵉ Dragons
20 bearskins with 615 plumes in use in 1808.[43] The standout item in 1814 inspection are the 35 bearskins in use – clearly the elite company and more bearskins were obtained post-1808.[44]

### 27ᵉ Dragons
50 bearskins in use 1808.[45] Twenty-two bearskins in use at disbandment in 1814.[46]

### 28ᵉ Dragons
Martinet shows a member of the elite company wearing a bearskin adorned with white cords and a scarlet plume. He wears scarlet-fringed epaulettes.[47]

### 29ᵉ Dragons
78 bearskins in stores in new July 1808.[48] None had existed in 1805, so clearly these were an innovation of 1808.

### 30ᵉ Dragons
Inspected in August 1805, the regiment had its elite company decked out in 56 *hussard* colpacks – the regiment had been the 12ᵉ *Hussard*. By 1808 106 bearskins were in use.[49]

## Sapeurs

When were the *sapeurs* introduced into the dragoon regiments? What was their strength? It is not easy to provide answers to either question. The circular of *4 Thermidor An X*

(23 July 1802) stated that the men of the newly formed elite companies should be equipped with tools. The *sous-officiers* were provided with billhooks, one third of the force with a hatchett carried in the left pistol holster, one third with picks and one third with spades. A document dated *1 Vendemiaire AnXIII* (24 September 1804) allowed dragoons 8 *sapeurs*, a corporal *sapeur* and a sergeant *sapeur* in the foot companies. On 18 *Vendemiaire* (10 October 1804) allowed *sapeurs* to be the escort to the squadron guidon on parade, in the foot companies only. Clearly these were not mounted. On 30 October 1807 Marshal Berthier ordered that where foot companies had been mounted, 8 *sapeurs* were to be retained in the new organisation. 25 February 1808, confirmed 8 *sapuers*, commanded by a corporal. Yet the new organisation of the cavalry which took place on 30 October 1808 made no allowances for *sapeurs*. The decree of 18 January 1809 once more allowed sapeurs, allowing these 8 men to be commanded by a corporal and a sergeant, to act as escort to the regiments eagle.[50] Archive evidence attests to colonels ignoring such dictates.

*Sapeur* of the 11e *Dragons* reconstructed from a reportedly contemporary image.

We have Otto MS presenting a *sapeur* of the 1e and also the 11e *Dragons*. The 12 November 1808 inspection of the Division of General La Houssaye informs us that the *sapeur*s of the 17e, 19e, and 27e regiments carried small axes, while those of the 18e were armed with muskets.[51] Regimental archive documents inform us that:

### 1e *Dragons*

Otto shows a *sapeur* of the regiment wearing a bearskin with white cords and plume. The bearskin has a brass grenade attached to its front. He wears scarlet-fringed epaulettes and has red cut out crossed axe badges on the upper arms of his *habit*. The axe case and belt is shown as white as is the apron. He has a light cavalry style S-clasped waistbelt in buff leather seemingly holding up the apron. He wears his sabre belt across his right shoulder. He also shows a trooper of the same regiment and a trumpeter.[52]

### 3e *Dragons*

Otto shows a *sapeur*, but the regimental archive is totally silent on *sapeurs*.[53] However, despite the lack of supporting archive papers, we cannot discount the image.

## 4ᵉ Dragons

Sauerweid shows a *sapeur* carrying an axe, wearing a full-length apron and riding on dragoon harness.[54]

## 7ᵉ Dragons

The *dépôt* of the 7ᵉ *Dragons* in April 1808 held 9 sets of *sapeurs*, equipment, all of which was issued to the *sapeurs* in the war squadrons.[55] An iconographic source also presents the uniform of a *sapeur*.

## 11ᵉ Dragons

Otto shows a *sapeur* of the regiment wearing a bearskin with red cords and plume. He wears scarlet-fringed epaulettes and has red cut out crossed axe badges on the upper arms of his *habit*. The axe case and belt is shown as chamois/buff, as is the apron.[56]

## 15ᵉ and 25ᵉ Dragons

The paper archive for the regiment reveals that in the fourth quarter of 1809, 162fr was spent on the purchase of grenadier bearskins. The purchase was authorised by the Colonel of the Provisional Regiment of Dragoons, which comprised the 15ᵉ and 25ᵉ *Dragons*. Between them, a squad of 12 *sapeurs* was to be raised, 6 from each elite company. Also purchased was broadcloth for the *habit*. In addition, 48fr was spent buying epaulettes for the *sapeurs*. The epaulettes must have been fairly extravagant as the War Ministry allowance was 22fr for 6 pairs.[57] Were *sapeurs* unique to the provisional regiment formed from the 3rd and 4th squadrons of each regiment? Or did the parent regiments have *sapeurs*? Given *sapeurs* were drawn from the 1st company of 1st squadron, it is not surprising that the 3rd and 4th squadrons had to supply these items, as in theory both regiments were supplying men to an ad hoc elite company. On balance we assume the parent regiments had *sapeurs*.

## 17ᵉ Dragons

In the painting reproduced in the *Carnet de la Sabretache* of December 1928 the *sapeur* of the 17ᵉ *Dragons* holding Colonel Grouvel's horse is wearing two cross belts joined by a brass button. This is probably the axe belt attached to that to the *giberne* belt. This *sapeur* has neither apron nor distinguishing axes on the arms, his bearskin has a red plume and white cords, and he also wears red epaulettes.[58]

## 20ᵉ Dragons

Disbanded on 24 November 1815, we know beyond any shadow of a doubt that the 20ᵉ *Dragons* had *sapeurs* in 1815 as 180fr was spent on equipping the 9 *sapeurs* of the regiment.[59]

### 27ᵉ Dragons

The *sapeurs* were armed with small axes.[60] Their clothing and equipment in summer 1805 cost 1,842fr and a further 157fr 57 for their horse furniture – which we assume to be black sheepskin *schabraques*.[61]

### 30ᵉ Dragons

Rousselot shows a *sapeur* wearing a *habit-longe*, with scarlet epaulettes at the shoulder and bearskin with scarlet cords. The axe case for the axe is shown as white. He presents a second image of a *sapeur* wearing a *habit* with an apron worn over it.[62]

This is the sum total of our knowledge on the subject. Certainly, *sapeurs* did not exist in every regiment.

## Trumpeters

Traditionally trumpeters had worn reversed colours, yet the 2ᵉ, 5ᵉ, 7ᵉ, 10ᵉ, 12ᵉ, 13ᵉ, 14ᵉ ,15ᵉ and 30ᵉ had worn *bleu de ciel* as part of their uniform, and the 22ᵉ, 23ᵉ, 24ᵉ and 27ᵉ carried over crimson facings from the previous *cavalerie* regiment, the 25ᵉ wore *rose*, so too the 26ᵉ, while the 7ᵉ and 30ᵉ wore scarlet as the *habit* colour. Thus 50% of all regiments did not adopt reversed colours as is popularly believed until the middle years of the Empire. Yet we have to admit that very little is known about trumpeters' uniforms for much of the Empire.

Under Bardin, the trumpeters of dragoons had two different regulations. The first state of Bardin is represented by the plate accompanying the text. This shows a standard dragoon *habit* with lace to the collar, *revers*, cuffs, pockets and sleeves.[63] No text authorising this uniform survives as Bardin himself redacted it sometime between February 1812 and April 1813. In the replacement text Bardin ordered that dragoon trumpeters were to wear the same *habits* as line infantry drummers, i.e., with horizontal breast loops.[64]

Elite company trumpeters had scarlet-fringed epaulettes. The turnback ornaments on the *habit* were cut from white cloth and not green. Just 12 regiments had Imperial Livery. Regiments so adorned in 1814 were:

### 7ᵉ Dragons

The regiment was by inference wearing Imperial Livery in 1814 when it was ordered into Royalist Livery for the trumpeters.[65]

### 13ᵉ Dragons

*Dépôt* held 16m 92 Imperial Livery for trumpeters in 1814.[66]

### 15ᵉ Dragons

Some 31m 14 of Imperial Livery for the trumpeters was in *dépôt* in August 1814.[67]

### 19ᵉ Dragons

Trumpeters were decked out in Imperial Livery as stores held 16m 92 in summer 1814.[68]

## 20ᵉ Dragons

The regiment had Imperial Livery in use in 1814, and was ordered to replace it with Royalist Livery.[69]

## 21ᵉ Dragons

When disbanded in summer 1814, we are sure that the regiment had its trumpeters decked out in Imperial Livery as the *dépôt* held 103m 21 of trumpeters' lace.[70]

## 24ᵉ Dragons

At the time of the amalgamation in 1814 the regiment had its trumpeters in Imperial Livery.[71]

## 25ᵉ Dragons

At the time of the amalgamation in 1814 the regiment had its trumpeters in Imperial Livery. The *dépôt* held 47m 84 of Imperial Livery. The trumpeters of the elite company had bearskins, scarlet plumes and epaulettes, given these items were worn by the elite company as a whole.[72]

## 27ᵉ Dragons

The regiment had had 167m 22 of Imperial Livery in summer 1814.[73]

In 1815 regiments with Imperial Livery during the 100 days were:

## 2ᵉ Dragons

The *dépôt* in December 1815 reported: 'There also exists 120 metres of livery for trumpets marked with "N" and eagles, and also 600 tricolour cockades with have been burnt.'[74]

## 4ᵉ Dragons

When disbanded on 1 December 1815 the *dépôt* had 208m of trumpeters' livery – no lace existed in March 1815, so clearly it was purchased in the 100 days.[75]

## 6ᵉ Dragons

At the time of disbandment in 1815 present in the *dépôt* was 316m 70 of trumpeters' livery, which may have in reality been Royalist Livery.[76]

## 11ᵉ Dragons

In December 1815 the 11ᵉ *Dragons* had the following items marked as 'de modelle': '*habit* for trumpet major, 1 trumpeters' *habit*'.[77] Yet no stocks of Imperial Livery existed in 1814 or 1815. Were these ever made for the trumpeters of the regiment? When do they date from? Were they Royalist sealed patterns rather than Imperial? The regiment only returned to France in July 1813 on its way to join 5th Cavalry

Corps and would fight at Leipzig and Hanau – hardly an auspicious time to reclothe trumpeters. The regiment had been in Spain since 1809, so no doubt it continued to wear pre-Bardin clothing.

### 19e *Dragons*
Looking at the regiment in 1815, *dépôt* held 23m of blue broadcloth that been used to make Royalist Livery *habits*, along with 590m of livery for trumpeters – clearly the regiment had started to make Imperial Livery trumpeters' coats but never applied the lace to them.[78]

### 20e *Dragons*
Disbanded on 24 November 1815, we know beyond any shadow of a doubt that the regiment's trumpeters had Imperial Livery. The inspecting general ordered all 306m of trumpeters' livery to be burnt on 2 December 1815.[79]

Just 12 regiments out of 24 regiments wore Imperial Livery, so 50% of dragoon regiments dressed their trumpeters in something else.

The decree of 22 April 1814 retained the decree of 19 January and 7 February 1812 for the dress of the army and made the following amendments:

> On the retroussis of the *habits* the crowned N will be removed and replaced by a *fleur-de-leys*, 70mm tall (2 pouces ½ or thereabouts) and of proportionate width.
>
> The crowned N will be removed from the *schako* plates.
> The crowned N will be removed from the *gibernes*.
> The crowned N will be removed from sabretaches.
> The crowned N will be removed from the buttons of the gendarme
> The drummers, trumpeters and musicians will abandon the colour green and will use *bleu de roi* in its place for *habits* and will use the Livery of the Royal Household.
> All other aspects will be in strict conformity to the two decrees.[80]

We know from the review of the archive documents that numerous regiments did indeed re-dress their trumpeters in blue:

### *Dragons du Roi*
At disbandment *dépôt* held 4m 40 blue broadcloth for trumpeters' *habits*.[81]

### 4e *Dragons*
Stores held *bleu de ciel* broadcloth, which we assume was used to make trumpeters *habits* adorned with Royalist Livery.[82]

### 5e *Dragons*
The *dépôt* held blue broadcloth, which was clearly used to make trumpeters *habits* adorned with Royalist Livery.[83]

## 6ᵉ *Dragons*
Stores held *bleu de ciel* broadcloth in 1814, arguably used for making Royalist Livery *habits*, along with the crimson cloth held in stores.⁸⁴

## 7ᵉ *Dragons*
The trumpeters were ordered into Royalist Livery in 1814.⁸⁵

## 11ᵉ *Dragons*
The *dépôt* in 1815 held a small quantity of blue broadcloth, clearly left over from making Royalist Livery.⁸⁶

## 13ᵉ *Dragons*
The regiment was ordered in 1814 to adopt blue *habits* faced in crimson with Royalist Livery.⁸⁷

## 15ᵉ *Dragons*
Cloth in the *dépôt* included 22m 54 of blue broadcloth suggesting that trumpeters were in blue, accompanied by Royalist Livery.⁸⁸

## 16ᵉ *Dragons*
The regiment adopted Royalist Livery in the first Restoration.⁸⁹

## 19ᵉ *Dragons*
In 1815, *dépôt* held 23m of blue destined for trumpeters: clearly the regiment had started to make blue Royalist Livery trumpeters' *habits*.⁹⁰

## 20ᵉ *Dragons*
The inspector in August 1814 ordered the trumpeters into blue *habits* and Royalist Livery.⁹¹

It is very likely that all dragoon regiments were so equipped during the restoration, and a small percentage changed to Imperial Livery in the 100 days. The regiments ordered into blue, but where no archive document confirms the change, we assume obeyed the order, but this is assumption and not fact.

# Chapter 6

# The Lancers

In 1811, the composition of the French cavalry was changed with the radical transformation of six dragoon units into lancers. The 1$^e$ *Lanciers* were formed from 1$^e$ *Dragons*, the 2$^e$ *Lanciers* were formed from the 3$^e$ *Dragons*, the 3$^e$ *Lanciers* were formed from the 8$^e$ *Dragons*, the 4$^e$ *Lanciers* from the 9$^e$ *Dragons*, the 10$^e$ *Dragons* became the 5$^e$ *Lanciers* and the 29$^e$ *Dragons* became the 6$^e$ *Lanciers*. The process of forming the new regiments took time.

The decree of 15 July 1811 reported:

> The clothing will comprise a short *habit* in green broadcloth for the first six regiments and in blue for the 7$^e$, 8$^e$ and 9$^e$ regiments, with white lining to the collar, the cuffs and *revers* in distinctive colour. The *revers* will be cut long and descend to the waist and will be closed by hooks and eyes in all their length and will be capable of being buttoned over one another; a round cut *gilet* made from white broadcloth with no sleeves, the buttons of the *habit* and *gilet* being flat, round, in yellow metal with the number of the regiment; a *gilet d'écurie* cut from green broadcloth with buttons made from the same cloth with no piping and distinctive colour, a pair of *culottes hongroise* in green broadcloth, a pair of *surculottes* cut from green broadcloth garnished with black leather and a piping in the regiment's distinctive colour; a pair of linen *caleçons*, a *bonnets de police* cut from green broadcloth, hussar-style boots with iron spurs at the heel. The distinctive colours for the *revers* and cuffs of the first six regiments will be scarlet, aurore, rose, crimson, *bleu celeste* and madder red. The light horse will wear an eagle cut from green broadcloth on the *retroussis*. The first six regiments will have a helmet like that of the dragoons, and the 7$^e$, 8$^e$ and 9$^e$ in the Polish manner. The *giberne* and *porte-giberne* will be the same as of the *chasseurs*. The waistbelt, worn over the *habit*, is 64mm wide, and will have a plate in copper garnished with an Imperial eagle. The sabre will be the *chasseur* model.[1]

So, rather than the lancer-style helmet with a *chenille*, the lancers were to keep their dragoon helmets! This made perfect sense, as they were costly items and the men all had them.

Yet when did the famous lancer helmet appear?

In a letter from *Duc de Feltre* General Clarke, the Minister for War, to the Emperor, dated 30 August 1811 he proposed a new helmet design, 'a black *chenille* to replace the *marmouset* and the floating *criniere* … another major innovation to be a neck guard in the same form as on the recently adopted helmets for the *carabiniers*'.[2] Yet when we look at

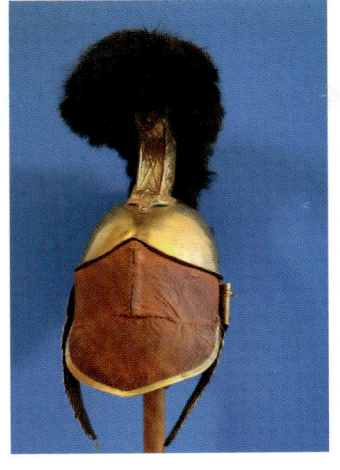

Sumptuous officers' helmet. The leopard fur turban has disintegrated, but overall, this helmet is a fantastic example of quality and elegance of officers' apparel. (*Private Collection, Belgium*)

extant helmets, the neck guard for troopers was literally a half circle of black leather sewn to the back of the helmet and has only a passing resemblance to a *carabinier* helmet neck guard. After handling a dozen or so original helmets, it shows that only officers, *sous-officiers* and trumpeters ever wore the highly elegant lancer helmet of popular imagination with a neck guard in the same form as the *carabiniers*. The trooper's helmet was literally a dragoon helmet with a *chenille* and a very basic neck guard, confirmed under Bardin where the body of the lancer helmet and dragoon helmet was identical.

Another change took place on 11 September 1811 when the lancers gained a sleeve cloak (*manteaux-capote*), made from green broadcloth to facilitate the use of the lance. The *porte-manteaux* was likewise, under this decree, to be made from green broadcloth with yellow lace, the

## 166  Napoleon's Dragoons and Lancers

Incredibly well preserved example of the Bardin regulation lancer pattern helmet. (*Private Collection, Switzerland*)

Trumpeters' helmet, reportedly of the 5ᵉ *Lanciers*. (*Musee de l'Armée*)

Hungarian breeches, *gilet d'écurie* and *pantalons à cheval* were to be all made from green broadcloth.[3] Change occurred again on 30 September 1811 when the War Ministry decreed that the sabre belt was to be of the *chasseur* model, fastened with a hook clasp rather than the much wider *cuirassier*-style belt.[4]

The lancers were formed with a specific object in mind. In order to preserve the combat effectiveness of the heavy cavalry in battle, the tasks of courier duty, screening, reconnaissance, and pursuit typically fell to lighter cavalry units so that the heavy cavalry

These boots are of the type used by the 10 regiments of lancers. (*Private Collection*)

could be employed with maximum effectiveness at the critical time in battle. Napoléon noted that:

> under no consideration shall cuirassiers be detailed as orderlies. This duty shall be done by lancers; even generals shall use lancers for this purpose. The service of communications, escort, sharpshooters, shall be done by lancers.[5]

The lancers also acted in line of battle: with the front rank of each squadron armed with lances, the second rank armed with sabres and carbines, they were highly versatile units.

## Bardin regulation

The Bardin regulations laid out the following for the dress of the lancers. As with other chapters, it was heavily edited on 30 April 1813, making many parts of the original text from 1812 virtually impossible to read:[6]

> ### Section 5 French Light Horse
> ### Art 1. Clothing
> ~~1415~~1429. The clothing of the light horse will be that of the 1$^e$, 2$^e$, 3$^e$, 4$^e$, 5$^e$, 6$^e$ regiments currently wear. The clothing will be in the French manner. The 7$^e$, 8$^e$ and 9$^e$ regiments will wear the habit, headdress and boots of the polish manner.
>
> ~~1416 The six French regiments of light horse will wear a habits-vestes with the collar, revers, lining, piping and cuffs in the distinctive colour Viz the table of uniforms No, 1562.~~
>
> ~~1417. The clothing of the sous-officiers and the light horse will comprise a habit, a gilet with no sleeves, a gilet d'écurie, a pair of Culotte Hongroise, a pair of linen caleçon, a pair of stable trousers, a bonnet de police and a sleeved cloak.~~

The only known example of a Bardin regulation Pokalem. This example clearly belonged to an officer of the 1$^e$ Lanciers. (*Musee de l'Armée*)

# The Lancers

1430. The clothing of the French light horse will be the general disposition.

1431. The habit will be of the same proportions as those of the light infantry, except that the sleeves will be cut larger, as will the cuffs. The pockets will not be figured on their outside edge, however there will be placed in the pleat below the centre back a patch of cloth the same form as for the Chasseurs à Cheval Viz. No. 1368. The collar, the cuffs, the revers, the lining and piping will conform to the general dispositions, Viz. Table No. 1562

1432. The gilet is made from white broadcloth and conform to model No, 301 ~~will be the same as the Chasseurs à Cheval Viz. No. 1365.~~

1433. The gilet d'écurie is made from green tricot and will conform to the ~~general~~ model Viz. No. 302.

1434. The buttons which will be of one and the same proportions for all the items of dress, of the middle size, and will be of copper. The back has two crossed armes, the outer edge is decorated with holes and bears the regiment's number. The placing and number of buttons on each habit will be the same as for the Chasseurs à Cheval.

1435. The Culotte Hongroise are in green broadcloth and will conform to the general model Viz. No. 306.

1436. The caleçon are identical to those of the infantry Viz. No. 302.

1437. The pantalons à cheval are in dark green tricot ~~and will be the same as for the hussars~~ will conform to the general model Viz. No, 308

1438. The stable trousers ~~will be the same as for the carabiniers~~ will conform to the general model Viz. No. 311

1439. The braces will be the same as for the infantry.

Complete uniform to the Bardin regulation, issued to Pierre Cornion of the 4e *Lanciers* in 1813. This is the sole known example of this uniform in existence. It reflects the April 1813 regulation.

1440. The manteau-capote will be cut from white broadcloth. At the front it will be 1m 190mm to 1m 245mm tall. At the back it will measure 1m 30. The diameter at the [illegible] will be 650mm, at the chest it will be 700mm at the base 4 meters 44. Four buttonholes are on the back of the manteau and are set 70mm below the edge of the collar.

1441. The collar is 95mm tall at the back and is 10mm lower at the front. There is also a collar adopted as a rotonde which measures 450mm at the back to 460mm tall at the front and is 1m 95 in circumference. The leading edge is turned back. The rotonde has three buttons and buttonholes placed equally. A strong hook and eye are placed at the top to fasten the manteau.

1442. There will be an opening 215mm deep set at vertically the height of the small of the back at a distance of 190mm. The opening is covered with a patch 40mm wide the same height as the opening. From the middle of the small of the back will be an opening and it will descend 490mm. There will be a strip of broadcloth 25mm wide, sewn on each side of the opening to support the buttons, which will be closed in the middle by four buttons, equally placed along the opening, the last one to be 160mm from the bottom edge.

1443. The sleeves will be lined in linen and will be 230mm wide at the opening, 200mm at the middle and 190mm at the cuff; they will be 600mm long and have cuffs, cut square, 130mm tall.

1444. The manteau is lined in milled serge of the facing colour, from 215 to 240mm wide and will descend until 160mm from the bottom edge of the manteau.

## Art 2. Headdress

1445. There will be supplied from the clothing fund for the sous-officiers and light horsemen a helmet of the dimensions given below, and they will also be furnished with a bonnet de police, the same as the infantry, No. 45.

1446. The helmet comprises a calotte or bombe in copper, the cimier, the criniere and the turban: see engraved design No. 1446.

1455. The bonnet de police are made in green broadcloth recovered from the old clothing and will conform to that of the Infantry, Viz. No. 45.

## Art 3. Distinctive Marks

1456. The distinctive marks of the sergeants and fourriers is in gold, and of the corporals in yellow wool. They will conform to the general dispositions No. 335 and 337 and be placed as for the light infantry Viz. No. 58, 59, and 63. The distinctions of the veterinarians and the farriers will conform to No. 326 and 340.

1457. The distinctions of the trumpeters will conform to the general dispositions No. 338 and 339. Their habit will be the same as detailed in No. 83 except that there will be no figuring on the pocket flap. The cuffs will be in the form of the light cavalry.

1458. The Elite company will be distinguished by their epaulettes and aigrette.

### Art 4. Weapons and Equipment
1459. The weapons of the corporals and light horse will comprise a lance, a sabre, a mousqueton and a pistol. An axe or sycle will be carried in the left pistol holster, and there will also be too lance boots, attachment strap fixed to the ring the ring between the pistol holsters. In order for the lancer to mount and dismount and to fight on foot, the mousqueton will be attached to the porte-mousqueton, and the lance will be placed on the left side, placed in the boot fixed to the stirrup. The pistol will be carried in the right-hand side holster.

The sergeants, fourriers, trumpeters and farriers will not be armed with a lance or carbine. Instead, they will be armed with two pistols.

1440. The equipment ~~is the same as for the hussars,~~ is the same as for the chasseurs. The lance pennant is comprised of two different pieces of milled serge. The pennant is cut with two points. The top and bottom are cut straight and it measures 670mm in length. In the middle where the two colours meet, from the origin to the start of the points is 335mm. The opposite end is reinforced with a strip of leather 20mm wide and covered in lien and pierced with three eyelets. The pennant is attached to the lance shaft by iron eyelets that are fixed to the middle of the wood below the lance head. The band measures 245mm top to bottom. The top piece of the pennant is the same colour as the body of the habit, the lower band is the colour of the regiment's facings.

1441. ~~The lance strap is made from white cuir de hongre it is~~ [illegible] ~~will conform to engraved design 1390~~ The lance strap.

### Art 5. Petit Equipement, Linen and Footwear
1442. The petit équipement of the light horse will comprise and conform to that prescribed in general disposition Viz. No. 373.

### Art 6. Harness
1443. The harness of the sous-officiers and light horse will comprise a saddle in a particular form, a schabraque, a surcingle, a curb bridle, a snaffle bridle and head collar.

The decree has a number of surprises: green and facing colour lance pennants for a start! The original text for the trumpeters states the *revers* were edged in Imperial Livery, altered in April 1813 to horizontal Brandenburgs like the rest of the cavalry and preserved on the *habit* of trumpeter Pierre Cornion of the 4ᵉ *Lanciers*! Bardin regulation resulted in minor changes – the front plate of the helmet no longer bore crossed lances. What follows is a review of the extant archive for each of the six regiments. It is interesting also that the body of the sleeved cloak – *manteau-capote* – was not fastened by buttons as artists and re-enactors like to suggest.

### *Bardin changes*

Created in August 1814, a committee was established to assess the uniform and equipment of the army as it then stood and to recommend changes. The first issue raised by the committee was quality control and standard of workmanship and materials used. The committee agreed that the use of private contractors to clothe and equip the army was a total failure: low-grade workmanship using 'cheap substandard materials' was harmful to the army, and the contractors had been able to inflate prices to maximise their profit, and had put many regiments into debt. Hence forward, everything would be made in the regimental workshops using regulated materials. In order to ensure standards were met, inspectors of review would inspect the materials and quality of workmanship rather than colonels. Instead of being issued both *culottes hongroise* and *pantalons à cheval* they were to be replaced by *pantalons en drap*, i.e., broadcloth. The General *Comte* de Saint Germain proposed that the *lanciers* were to adopt grey *pantalons* with the inner leg reinforced with black leather, worn over boots. The bottom of the leg was to be reinforced with a leather cuff. Rather than *hussard* boots, low-ankle boots – *bottines* – were to be used. Removing the costly *culottes hongroise* was a logical and cost-saving exercise. Next up the committee ordered 'pockets to be made in the sheepskins to access the pistols': this is a very common-sense idea, as it is on practical experience almost totally impossible to get to the pistols under the sheepskin! Lastly, a new broad waistbelt was introduced, the same as used by the *cuirassiers*, replacing the *chasseur*-style sabre belt.

The committee's recommendations were signed off on 12 January 1815 by *Comte* Victor Latour-Maubourg. Trumpeters were to be dressed in *bleu de roi* with new livery, and *régiment du roi* was allowed yellow *contre-epaulettes* and *aiguilettes*.[7] How far the new regulations were rolled out before Waterloo is hard to say: yet the official abandonment of *culottes hongroise* in favour of *pantalons* was merely reflecting current practice, but made from green rather than grey broadcloth.

# Chapter 7

# Regulations in Practice

The six regiments of lancers have left very little in terms of a paper archive. What follows is a discussion of all the extant archive material that can be located.

## 1ᵉ *Lanciers*

The regiment's paperwork says little about the uniform. For 105 dismounted men taken into the regiment in March 1812, the *dépôt* held 67 *habits-vestes*, 121 pairs of boots, 61 *porte-carbine*s and 104 sabres. The men had no other arms, equipment of uniform available to them.[1] We do know that on 18 March 1813 431fr 87 was spent on broadcloth, 8fr 66 on linen, 135fr 12 on basane leather hides, 96fr with the regimental tailor to make 32 *habits* and 54 pairs of *pantalons à cheval*, and 60 pairs of ankle boots were purchased for 793fr 95. In theory lancers wore hussar boots over the *culottes hongroise*: clearly with the use of *pantalons à cheval* in lieu of *culottes hongroise* cheaper ankle boots were used.[2]

We know nothing about the dress of the regiment until 11 August 1814. On that day the men were wearing the following items:[3]

| Item | In service, but due to expire in the next year | In need of repair | To be replaced in the next year | To be replaced | Items short |
|---|---|---|---|---|---|
| *Habits* | 102 | 69 | 65 | 53 | 41 |
| *Gilets* | 16 | | 24 | 248 | 42 |
| *Gilets d'écurie* | 51 | 35 | 27 | 97 | 120 |
| *Culottes hongroise* | 81 | 30 | 63 | 96 | 60 |
| *Pantalons à cheval* | 57 | 35 | 43 | 84 | 111 |
| Stable trousers | 37 | 36 | 62 | 99 | 96 |
| Garricks | 17 | 50 | 15 | 35 | 213 |
| Bonnets de police | 103 | | 43 | 132 | 52 |
| Helmets | 112 | 33 | 5 | 59 | 121 |
| Braces | 68 | | 30 | 227 | 5 |
| Waistbelts | 188 | 19 | | | 123 |
| Gibernes | 151 | 74 | | | 105 |
| Porte-gibernes | 208 | 17 | | | 105 |
| Banderole-porte-carabines | 160 | 5 | | | 165 |
| Sword knots | 195 | | | | 135 |
| Pairs of boots | 60 | 21 | 32 | 32 | 185 |

| Item | In service, but due to expire in the next year | In need of repair | To be replaced in the next year | To be replaced | Items short |
|---|---|---|---|---|---|
| Pairs of gloves | 84 | | | | 246 |
| Lance pennants | 59 | | | | 271 |
| Lance straps | 60 | | | 9 | 261 |
| Trumpets with cords | 6 | | | | |

The regiment was armed with 30 carbines: thus 130 men had the *banderole-porte-carbine* with no corresponding firearm! Some 188 sabres were in good condition and 14 needed repairs, 29 pistols were in good condition and 3 needed repairs. Just 56 lances were in use! Items of *petit équipement* included 714 shirts, 266 black stocks – one for nearly every man, 226 pairs of shoes, and 238 pairs of knee-length grey linen gaiters. Materials in the *dépôt* were just 838m 35 white broadcloth and 460m 88 white serge. Clothing and equipment in the *dépôt* included stocks of brand-new items waiting to be issued: 123 *gilets*, 240 garricks – this is the English name for a greatcoat with a shoulder cape – 186 helmets, 167 *gibernes*, 69 *porte-gibernes*, 252 *banderole-porte-carabines*, 68 waistbelts, 129 sword knots and 204 pairs of boots.[4]

On 4 November 1814, the Administrative Council of the regiment agreed to the production of 95 new *habits*, as well as to make arrangements for the purchase of

Portrait of an officer of the 1ᵉ *Lanciers*. (*Musee de l'Armée*)

Officer of the 1ᵉ *Lanciers* depicted by Martinet.

# Regulations in Practice 175

Trooper of the 1ᵉ *Lanciers* by Martinet.    Trooper of the 1ᵉ *Lanciers* in a print published in early 1815 by Chez Bassett of Paris.

additional materials to make 90 *habits* as replacements for 1815 and to set in motion the repair of those *habits* and other items of clothing needing to be repaired.[5]

The clothing of the regiment was still very much ad hoc. For the 745 men only 381 *habits* were in use. For the 12 new trumpeters' *habits*, 104m of trumpeters' livery was purchased for 26fr, and each *habit* cost 7fr 65 to make. We also note, 154 pairs of *pantalons à cheval* were made from 208m 40 white broadcloth, which had cost 521fr to purchase and due to local shortages of green broadcloth had been dyed green. On 1 March 1815 the Administrative Council authorised the purchase of 395 *habits*, sleeveless waistcoats, *gilets d'écurie*, cloaks, *culottes hongroise* and *bonnets de police*. The lace and clothing were delivered to the regiment on 2 May 1815. Regimental records also show that 375 pairs of yellow-fringed epaulettes accompanied by yellow *aiguillettes* were also delivered to the regiment on the same day.[6]

Clothing in use at the time of disbandment was as follows, which the men took away with them upon discharge:[7]

216 *habits*
258 *gilets en drap blanc*

129 *gilets d'écurie*
247 *bonnets de police*
243 pairs *pantalons à cheval*
33 pairs of stable trousers
102 pairs of underwear
221 helmets
126 pairs of gloves
22 *manteaux-capote*
12 trumpeters' *habits*
132 pairs of yellow epaulettes and *aiguillettes*.

Given the men were wearing the yellow *aiguilettes* and epaulettes at disbandment, we assume they were worn during the 100 days along with the blue trumpeters' *habits*. Not a single pair of *culottes hongroise* existed – clearly, they were never taken back into use in 1814 or 1815 as the clothing committee had ordered. Rather than being side opening, we must imagine the *pantalons à cheval* were as regulation, and were literally *pantalons*. The *dépôt* held:[8]

| Item | New | Good condition | To be repaired | To be replaced |
|---|---|---|---|---|
| *Habits* | 6 | | | |
| *Gilets* | 160 | 10 | 34 | 4 |
| *Gilets d'écurie* | 1 | | | |
| *Bonnets de police* | 1 | | | |
| *Manteaux* | | 140 | 38 | |
| *Porte-manteaux* | NIL | | | |
| *Pantalons à cheval* | 2 | | | |
| *Culottes hongroise* | 1 | | | |
| *Caleçons* | 1 | | | |
| Stable trousers | 1 | | | |
| Helmets | | | 33 | |
| Pairs of boots | 1 | | | 23 |
| Waistbelts | | 169 | 75 | |
| *Gibernes* | 171 | 265 | 180 | 5 |
| *Porte-gibernes* | 71 | 284 | 200 | 1 |
| *Porte-carabines* | 171 | 290 | 134 | |
| Trumpets | | 8 | 2 | 1 |
| Sword knots | | 142 | 1 | |
| Lance pennants | | 124 | 56 | 19 |
| Lance straps | | 200 | | 74 |
| Waistbelts in lace | 78 | | | |

The waistbelts in lace we are assume are the girdles used by the three Polish lancer regiments of the Line. Some 157 of these in good repair were taken into the regiment in August 1814 from the 9ᵉ *Lanciers*, with an additional 83 being taken into the stores from men who were wearing them, making some 240 examples in total. Clearly, some 165 of these had been issued and used, and some were retained in the *dépôt*. Were these issued to the elite company of the new *Lanciers du Roi* or even of the new model described in the 1815 regulations?[9]

## 2ᵉ *Lanciers*

We know nothing about the dress of the regiment between 1811 and 1814. At the close of the 1814 campaign the 2ᵉ *Lanciers* were wearing:[10]

| Item | In service, but due to expire in the next year | In need of repair | To be replaced in the next year | To be replaced | Items short |
|---|---|---|---|---|---|
| *Habits-vestes* | 212 | | 17 | | |
| *Gilets sans manches* | 115 | 37 | 6 | | |
| *Gilets d'écurie* | 111 | 55 | 15 | | |
| *Pantalons hongroise* | 112 | 20 | 5 | | |
| *Pantalons* à *cheval* | 73 | 51 | 56 | | |
| *Bonnets de police* | 145 | 29 | 21 | | |
| Underwear | 36 | 7 | | | |
| *Manteaux* | 175 | 40 | 3 | | |
| Stable trousers | 108 | 12 | 3 | | |
| *Porte-manteaux* | 158 | 47 | 10 | | |
| Helmets | 185 | 40 | | | |
| Waistbelts | 187 | 55 | | | |
| *Gibernes* | 209 | 31 | | | |
| *Porte-gibernes* | 209 | 31 | | | |
| *Porte-carabines* | 202 | 6 | | | |
| Pairs of boots with spurs | 57 | 39 | 33 | | |
| Pairs of wrist gloves | 78 | | | | |
| Lance pennants | 59 | 10 | 13 | | |
| Lance straps | 63 | 2 | 2 | | |
| Sword knots | 149 | | 1 | | |
| Braces | 155 | | 36 | | |
| Trumpets | 17 | | | | |
| *Boutons d'assemblage* | 206 | | | | |
| Pistol lanyards | 13 | | | | |
| Trumpet cords | 10 | | | | |

Officer of the 2ᵉ *Lanciers* by Martinet.　　Trooper of the 2ᵉ *Lanciers* by Martinet.

Weapons in use were 43 carbines in good condition and 5 needing repairs – did well over 100 men really carry the *porte-carabine* with no carbine hooked or were pistols carried off the belt? Yet we note just 30 pistols were in use! For the carbines just 10 bayonets existed, along with 208 sabres and 107 lances. Clearly not every lance had a pennant! Items of *petit équipement* included 741 shirts, 247 black stocks, 247 *habit* brushes, 159 tubs of grease, 247 copper buttons for fixing *giberne* belts to the *banderole-porte-carabines*, 247 shoe brushes, 201 brushes for cleaning copper and 211 sets of braces, among other items. Materials in the *dépôt* were minimal: 3,089m 83 *treillis*, 49m yellow worsted lace for corporals' stripes, 494m 9 yellow lace for *porte-manteaux* and 118m 15 of linen. Clothing in *dépôt* was again minimal: 95 brand-new pairs of underwear, 38 brand-new *manteaux*, 86 pairs of *pantalons à cheval*, 65 brand-new helmets and 155 needing repairs, as well as 115 shirts and 46 pairs of linen overalls.

On 18 August 1814 the regiment was ordered to harmonise its clothing i.e., remove from use the dress of the men taken into the new 2ᵉ *Lanciers* from the 20ᵉ *Chasseurs* and the 2ᵉ *Lanciers de la Garde Impériale*, ensuring that the new clothing matched the recent regulation.[11] A report of 10 September 1814 notes that 'the officers neglected their duties, spent too much time at the cafes and billiard tables' and more damningly 'most officers and *sous-officiers* have no understanding of drill, their duties or theory'.

A print by Chez Basset shows an officer of the 2ᵉ *Lanciers* in early 1815.

Trooper of the 2ᵉ *Lanciers* by Bassett.

The colonel was ordered to keep the officers and *sous-officiers* confined to barracks until they were thoroughly conversant with their duties. The colonel was ordered to be stricter with his officers about their mode of dress, as 'many wore civilian clothing off duty, which is imitated by the *sous-officiers*'. Henceforward officers off duty were to wear *habits* with green *revers* piped aurore and *culottes hongroise* with no lace. On the march or in the *menage* officers were to use *pantalons* made from grey broadcloth, which were to be tight fitting and worn over the boots. On parade the *habit* was to have aurore *revers* and the *culottes hongroise* were authorised to be laced 'as for the regulations'. The inspector also reprimanded the colonel about other extravagances in the regiment. The inspector upbraided the colonel stating that the officers' epaulettes 'were too large and extravagant, and the rank stripes too flamboyant … the adjutants and *sous-officiers* are forbidden from imitating the officers with such stripes made from silver lace and showy epaulettes'.[12] Clearly, the officers had adorned their kit with as much gold lace as they 'could possibly cram on', and the *sous-officiers* had followed, both groups of men, when off duty, wearing civilians! Clearly, Colonel Sourde had a lot to do in order to make his regiment as efficient as possible.

Following the 100 days campaign the regiment was disbanded on 30 November, the magazine of the regiment contained:[13]

68 new helmets and 223 helmets in good condition
167 *manteaux-capote*
3 *vestes*
1 pair of *culottes hongroise de modèle*
1 pair of *pantalons à cheval de modèle*
5 *bonnets de police*
261 new model waistbelt with belt plate
24 brand-new old-model waistbelt
464 old-model waistbelts in good condition.

The new-model waistbelts are surely the pattern introduced in February 1815, which were much wider than the type issued under Bardin, and were 65mm wide with a large copper plate to the front bearing – we assume – crossed lances or a *fleur-de-lys*. Talking about Bardin regulation we find several '*effets de modèle*' in the *dépôt*: 1 *habit de trompete-major*, 1 *habit de trompette*, 1 *habit de Lancier*: these were burned on the basis that the

Weiland gives this trooper of the 2ᵉ *Lanciers*. Note the epaulettes have copper fish scale boards.

The Freybourg MS gives this trooper of the 1ᵉ or 2ᵉ regiment in summer 1813. (*Collection KM*)

trumpeters' items were adorned with Imperial Livery and had been issued in October 1812, or possibly at the start of the 100 days.

The men at the time of disbandment were allowed to carry away with them the following items:[14]

67 helmets
250 *habits*
186 white *gilets*
28 pairs of *culottes hongroise*
205 pairs of *pantalons à cheval*
144 *vestes d'écurie*
299 *bonnets de police*
214 pairs of *caleçons*
149 pairs of boots
222 *porte-manteaux*
479 pairs of spurs

The *culottes hongroise* were worn only by *sous-officiers*. Rather than being side opening, we must imagine the *pantalons à cheval* were as regulation, and were literally *pantalons*. The regiment's magazine contained the following stocks of material:[15]

239m green broadcloth
70m aurore broadcloth
17m *blanc picque de bleu* broadcloth for *manteaux*
645m aurore serge
226m green tricot for *gilets d'écurie*
154m aurore braid for *culottes hongroise*
42 leather hides for *pantalons à cheval*
428 *gibernes*
676 *porte-gibernes*
610 *banderole-porte-carabines*
108 sword knots
22 lance pennants
477 lance straps
387 lanyards [?]
12 trumpets with cords
185 lances
30 carbines
236 pistols
285 sabres
365 lance heads.

We assume, therefore, that the regiment was dressed as prescribed in the formation decree of 1811. However, the braid on the *culotte hongroise* appears to have been aurore rather than the decreed yellow: pragmatic use of materials inherited from the 20ᵉ *Chasseurs* were suppose? Also, in the *dépôt* were 2 pack horses for the regiment's *cantiniere* complete with harness.

## 3ᵉ *Lanciers*

We have no detail on the uniform of the regiment until 26 August 1814, when clothing in use that day was:[16]

| Item | In service, but due to expire in the next year | In need of repair | To be replaced in the next year | To be replaced | Items short | Observations |
|---|---|---|---|---|---|---|
| *Habits* | 142 | 88 | | 48 | 54 | The effective strength is 266 men. |
| *Vestes* | 170 | 73 | | 30 | 39 | |
| *Gilets d'écurie* | 100 | 90 | | 56 | 66 | |
| *Culottes hongroise* | 200 | 57 | | 30 | 25 | |
| *Bonnets de police* | 119 | 50 | | 50 | 93 | |
| *Manteaux* | 104 | 58 | | 58 | 92 | |
| *Pantalons* à *cheval* | 110 | 80 | | 43 | 79 | |
| Stable trousers | 130 | | 65 | 5 | 112 | |
| Underwear | 169 | | 95 | | 48 | |
| Helmets | 208 | 81 | | | 23 | |
| *Gibernes* | 202 | 43 | | | 27 | |
| *Porte-gibernes* | 285 | | | | 27 | |
| *Banderole-porte-carabines* | 200 | 43 | | | 69 | |
| Gloves | | | | | | |
| Pair of boots | 112 | 116 | | 24 | 60 | |
| Trumpets | 10 | 6 | | | | |
| Sword knots | 278 | | | | 34 | |

In terms of *petit équipement*, the 266 men had between them 702 shirts, 110 pairs of linen *pantalons*, 250 black stocks, 310 white stocks, 60 pairs of linen socks, and 52 pairs of woollen stockings. Stocks of material in the *dépôt* was almost nil, just 276m 96 of white serge and 154m 70 of *treillis*. Of interest, in 1814 the *dépôt* held 278 helmets, of which 248 were new and 30 needed repairs. These are listed alongside *crinieres*, which suggests that these helmets were dragoon pattern, and had been held in the *dépôt* since 1811. Other brand-new items waiting to be issued were 73 white *vestes*, 309 *manteaux-capotes*, 78 pairs of *culottes hongroise*, 128 *gibernes*, 161 *giberne* belts, 212 *banderole-porte-carabines*, 83 sabre belts, 187 sword knots, 56 pairs of boots and 177 *porte-manteaux*. Needing repair were 6 *habits*.[17]

## Regulations in Practice

In December 1815 the regiment had the following amounts of cloth in the magazine:[18]

0m 83 green broadcloth
0m *rose* broadcloth
0m *blanc picque de bleu*
143m 43 *rose* serge
0m 26 green tricot
180m 44 linen for linings
52m 80 linen for *caleçons*
159m 82 *treillis*

These amounts are clearly what was left over from the production of new items, but sadly we are ignorant of the number

Portrait of an officer of the 3[e] *Lanciers*. (*Musée de l'Armée*)

Martinet presents this image of an officer of the 3[e] *Lanciers*.

Trooper of the 3[e] *Lanciers* by Martinet.

Published in early 1815 by Chez Bassett is this trooper of the 3ᵉ *Lanciers*.

This copy of the Markholsheim manuscript by Rousselot, purportedly shows a trumpeter of the 3ᵉ *Lanciers* in 1812. (*Collection KM*)

of items made during the first restoration and the 100 days. The regiment's *manteaux-capotes* were seemingly *blanc picque de bleu*. Items of clothing in the magazine included:[19]

103 new *porte-manteaux*
32 pairs of new *culotte hongroise*
56 pairs new stable trousers
41 new *caleçons*
7 *bonnets de police*
166 *manteaux*
93 new helmets and 298 in good repair
330 waistbelts
168 new *gibernes* and 469 in good condition
156 new *porte-gibernes* and 526 in good repair
135 new sword knots and 384 in good repair
48 brand-new pairs of boots

133 shirts
125 white stocks
146 black stocks

Also in *dépôt* were '*effets de modèle*', notably 1 *habit de trompette major*, 1 *habit de trompette*, 2 waistbelts of the old model, 1 waistbelt of the new model. Oddly no lancers' *habit* is mentioned: presumably these are all Royalist issue items as they did not exist a year earlier, and are not recorded as being burned. Not a single pair of *pantalons à cheval* existed – clearly, they were never taken back into use in 1814 or 1815 as the clothing committee had ordered. We must imagine the *culottes hongroise* were as regulation, and were worn over the boots and reinforced with leather. We also note the regiment had 302 lances in stores: were they carried on campaign? The regiment had at disbandment 391 sabres – for 330 sabre belts – 58 carbines for the elite company – yet 365 *banderole-porte-carabines* existed – and the same number of pistols. Clearly just the elite company had these. We find no mention of epaulettes or *aigrettes*.

## 4e *Lanciers*

We know very little about the dress of the regiment. One of the few documents to tell us about the subject is an account that lists on 4 March 1812 745m of *blanc pique de bleu* broadcloth costing 7,784fr 25 was obtained to make 498 *manteaux*, which cost 2,614fr. A further 167m 55 was delivered on 24 March along with 96m of green broadcloth.[20] The major reported on 9 July 1812 that he had used all the cloth and materials in the *dépôt* to equip 120 men, and funds would be needed to obtain more cloth and materials.[21]

Following the Russian campaign, the regiment was reformed around the 4e squadron (bis) of the 14e *Cuirassiers*![22] An idea of what the 4e *Lanciers* wore at the close of the campaign of France can be obtained from the following inspection return of August 1814:[23]

| Item | In good repair | In need of repair | To be replaced in the next year | To be replaced | Items missing |
|---|---|---|---|---|---|
| *Habits* | 273 | | | 103 | |
| *Vestes* | 273 | | | | |
| *Gilets* | 93 | | 35 | 145 | 180 |
| *Bonnets de police* | 149 | | 29 | 95 | 124 |
| *Manteaux-capote* | 273 | | | | |
| *Culottes hongroise* | 273 | | | | |
| *Pantalons* à *cheval* | 273 | 29 | | | |
| Stable trousers | 301 | 15 | | | |
| Helmets | 273 | | | | |

Martinet presents an officer of the 4ᵉ *Lanciers*. However, a portrait of Colonel Bro in the Royal Collection, UK, shows the use of dragoon-style *housse* and bear fur *chaperons* by the regiment.

Trooper of the 4ᵉ *Lanciers* by Martinet.

| Item | In good repair | In need of repair | To be replaced in the next year | To be replaced | Items missing |
|---|---|---|---|---|---|
| *Giberne*s | 271 | | | | |
| *Porte-gibernes* | 271 | | | | |
| *Porte-carabines* | 262 | | | | |
| Waistbelts | 273 | | | | |
| Sword knots | 273 | | | | |
| Gauntlets | 273 | | | | |
| Pairs of boots | 177 | | 31 | 65 | 96 |
| Trumpets | 11 | | | | |
| Sabres | 273 | | | | |
| Pistols | | | Nil | | |
| Carbines | 73 | | | | |
| Lances | 175 | | | | |
| Lance pennants | 175 | | | | |
| Lance straps | 175 | | | | |

Bassett gives us this trooper of the 4ᵉ *Lanciers* from early 1815.

This copy of the Markholsheim manuscript by Rousselot, purportedly shows a trumpeter of the 4ᵉ *Lanciers* in 1812. (*Collection KM*)

From the table, it seems that in 1814 only the elite company were armed with carbines, as insufficient were held for equip more than a company, despite there being sufficient number of carbine belts for all the other ranks. Items of *petit équipement* in use by the 273 men included 546 shirts, 234 black stocks, and 234 pairs of ankle boots. The *dépôt* was empty of cloth and materials bar 474m of linen. In the *dépôt* were the following items:[24]

| Item | New | In need of repair | Need replacing as not serviceable |
|---|---|---|---|
| *Habits* | 10 | 14 | |
| White waistcoats | 26 | 10 | |
| *Gilets d'écurie* | 0 | 0 | |
| *Bonnets de police* | 0 | 0 | |
| *Manteaux-capote* | 108 | 8 | |

| Item | New | In need of repair | Need replacing as not serviceable |
|---|---|---|---|
| *Culottes hongroise* | 14 | | |
| *Pantalons à cheval* | 4 | 10 | |
| Stable trousers | 194 | | |
| *Caleçons* | 368 | | |
| Helmets | 82 | | |
| *Crinieres* | 82 | | |
| *Gibernes* | 95 | | |
| *Porte-gibernes* | 95 | | |
| *Porte-carabines* | 159 | | |
| Waistbelts | 165 | | |
| Sword knots | 221 | | |
| Gauntlets | 374 | | |
| Pairs of boots | 0 | | |
| Trumpets | 5 | | |
| Lance straps | 169 | | |
| Lance pennants | 168 | | |

The *crinieres* in *dépôt* strongly suggests that in 1811 the regiment's dragoon helmets were converted to the lancer type by removing the *criniere* and fitting a *chenille*. The stocks of new items in the *dépôt* are at odds to the regiment being short of a great deal of equipment – all the items listed as worn out needed to be replaced. Very little of the clothing was listed as repairable. Presumably these items in the *dépôt* were issued during the first restoration. *Petit équipement* in store included 101 shirts, and 48 pairs of boots. The inspector made no comment about clothing or equipment.[25] No further archive sources can be located for the dress of the regiment.

## 5ᵉ *Lanciers*

With the ministerial decree of 28 May 1814, the 5ᵉ *Lanciers* became the *Lanciers d'Angouleme*. The new regiment was to be an amalgam of the 5ᵉ, the Jérôme Napoléon Hussars, which provided 44 officers and 159 men, and 19ᵉ and 20ᵉ company of the 2ᵉ *Lanciers de la Garde Impériale*, who provided 6 officers and 70 men. The men of the 5ᵉ *Lanciers* were wearing on 11 August 1814 the following items:[26]

Officer of the 5ᵉ *Lanciers* by Martinet.

Trooper of the 5ᵉ *Lanciers* by Martinet.

| Item | In service, but due to expire in the next year | In need of repair | To be replaced in the next year | To be replaced | Items short | Observations |
|---|---|---|---|---|---|---|
| *Habits* | 172 | 8 | 1 | 14 | 25 | The effective strength is 220 men, including 19 men that have been given their discharge, two men who had been sent to the Guard, two on leave. |
| *Gilets en drap blanc* | 149 | 6 | 1 | 13 | 51 | |
| *Gilet d'écurie* | 107 | 20 | 9 | 9 | 81 | |
| *Culottes hongroise* | 80 | 4 | 0 | 4 | 134 | |
| Stable trousers | 75 | 6 | 4 | 6 | 121 | |
| *Caleçons* | 82 | 2 | 4 | | 131 | |
| *Manteaux* | 85 | 9 | | | 126 | |
| *Bonnets de police* | 178 | 1 | 1 | 6 | 34 | |
| Helmets | 185 | 4 | | | 31 | |
| *Pantalons à cheval* | 103 | 27 | | 36 | 54 | |
| Trumpets | 11 | | | | | |

Thus, we see that in 1814 the regiment wore a mix of *culottes hongroise* and *pantalons à cheval* not enough of each existed for a man to have a pair of both.

Elite company trooper of the 5ᵉ *Lanciers* by Colonel Jolly. (*Collection KM*)

Centre company trooper of the 5ᵉ *Lanciers* depicted by Bassett.

The following items of equipment were in use at the date of disbandment:[27]

| Item | In service, but due to expire in the next year | In need of repair | To be replaced in the next year | To be replaced | Items short | Observations |
|---|---|---|---|---|---|---|
| Waistbelts | 189 | | | | 31 | The effective strength is 230 men. |
| *Gibernes* | 186 | 3 | | | 31 | |
| *Porte-gibernes* | 189 | | | | 31 | |
| Sabre slings | 179 | | | | 41 | |
| *Porte-manteaux* | 184 | 9 | | | 27 | |
| Boots | 43 | 26 | 2 | 8 | 141 | |
| Lance shafts | 99 | 2 | | | 119 | |
| Lance straps | 101 | | | | 119 | |
| Gloves | 10 | | | | 210 | |
| *Banderole-porte-carabines* | 187 | | | | 33 | |

For the 187 *banderole-porte-carabines*, just 51 carbines with 49 bayonets were issued – presumably to the elite company. Also in use were 187 sabres, 87 pistols and 101 lances.

Farrier of the 5ᵉ *Lanciers* in a drawing made by an eyewitness in 1814. (*Collection KM*)

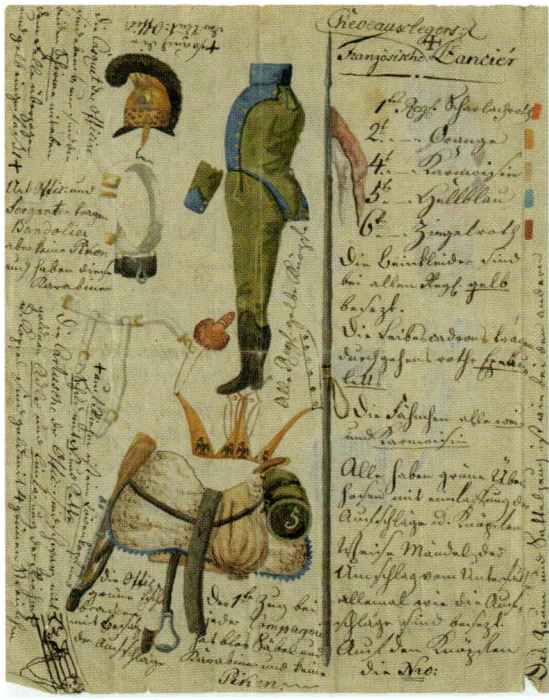

Depicted by Wurttemberg Artillery Officer Breitenbach are these details of the uniform of the 5ᵉ and other lancer regiments. For some reason the 3ᵉ are missing.

The men furthermore had 501 shirts, 171 black stocks, 142 white stocks, 82 pairs of linen socks, 9 pairs of woollen stockings, 168 pairs of shoes and 103 *sacs a distribution*.

Of interest is the fact the *manteaux* were made from beige cloth as opposed to the regulation white ascribed with the Bardin regulations of 1812. In the regiment's magazine were the following items:[28]

| Item | New | In good condition | To be repaired | To be replaced | Items short | Observations [Total] |
|---|---|---|---|---|---|---|
| *Habits* | 164 | | 49 | 23 | | 236 |
| *Gilets* | 173 | | 41 | | | 214 |
| *Pantalons* à *cheval* | 1 | | 15 | | | 16 |
| *Culottes hongroise* | 7 | | 13 | | | 20 |
| *Bonnets de police* | 48 | | | | | 48 |
| Helmets | 248 | | 174 | | | 422 |
| *Manteaux* | 261 | | 123 | | | 384 |
| Stable trousers | 1 | | 3 | | | 4 |
| *Caleçons* | 406 | | | | | 406 |
| Carbine slings | 282 | | 27 | | | 309 |

Officer of the 5ᵉ from Freybourg manuscript, created in summer 1813. (*Collection KM*)

This copy of the Markholsheim manuscript by Rousselot, purportedly shows a trumpeter of the 5ᵉ *Lanciers* in 1812. (*Collection KM*)

| Item | New | In good condition | To be repaired | To be replaced | Items short | Observations [Total] |
|---|---|---|---|---|---|---|
| Lance pennants | 436 | | | | | 36 |
| Lance straps | 490 | | | | | 490 |
| *Porte-manteaux* | 127 | | 132 | | | 259 |
| Pairs of boots | | | 16 | | | 16 |
| *Gibernes* | 210 | | 75 | | | 285 |
| *Porte-gibernes* | 224 | | 50 | | | 274 |
| Waistbelts | 166 | | 54 | | | 220 |
| Sabre slings | 47 | | | | | 47 |
| Sabres | 168 | | | | | |
| Carbines | 69 [+ 22 *mousqueton*s] | | | | | |
| Pistols | | 16 | | | | |
| Lances | 26 | | | | | |
| Bayonets | 72 | | | | | |

Clearly two types of carbines were in use: presumably the Light Cavalry model and the Hussar model.

Small equipment in the regiment's magazine comprised 4 shirts, 1 black stock, 106 pairs of shoes, 72 pairs of *manchettes du botte* and 132 pairs of wrist gloves. The *manchettes* were clearly in store since the regiment converted from dragoons to lancers in 1811, and had lain it seems on a shelf in the *dépôt* for over four years. The regiment inherited a stock of material from the disbanded Jérôme-Napoléon Hussars, notably a large stock of 223m 64 of *bleu de roi* broadcloth and 317m of *bleu de roi* serge. Given the lack of *bleu celeste* broadcloth in the 5e *Lanciers* at the time of the review, it is tempting to suggest that this much richer and deeper cloth was used to make new *habits* for the regiment. Furthermore, the regiment inherited a further 909m of yellow lace, originally intended to lace *dolmans* and *pelisses* of the Jérôme-Napoléon Hussars, and was no doubt used to lace the *culottes hongroise* of the 5e *Lanciers*, and possibly trumpeters' *habits*. General Tilly ordered on 12 August 1814 that new *habits* were to be made for the regiment. Those in service were described as being too small, too tight and that the officers of the regiment had changed the dimensions of the *habit* without authorisation, no doubt, he commented, as a matter of economy. He insisted that the new regiment was to be dressed according to the regulation of 7 February 1812 and that the new *habits* were to be made strictly according to the regulation. General Tilly also authorised that all ranks were to wear red *fleur-de-lys* on the tails of the *habits* and the trumpeters were to have new coats in *bleu de roi* (i.e., a mid-blue) broadcloth ornamented with new livery.

Alas, no further archive paperwork exists for the regiment, so we cannot say how it was dressed at Waterloo.

## 6e *Lanciers*

Archive documents for the dress of the regiment as the 6e *Lanciers* are scarce. On 4 March 1812, General Bourcier reviewed 131 men who had recently arrived with the *dépôt*. Due to acute shortages, the men only had their stable clothing.[29] A month later, Bourcier noted the men still only their stable coats, but had been issued 131 pairs of *pantalons à cheval*, 125 *gibernes*, 123 *porte-carabines* for 117 carbines, and 131 pistols. Bourcier ranted to the War Ministry that he had 'insufficient language' to convey

Centre company trooper in a print by Bassett from spring 1815.

Officer of the 6ᵉ *Lanciers* by Martinet.   Trooper of the 6ᵉ *Lanciers* by Martinet.

to the minister and regimental colonel his anger at how bad the clothing, saddles and harness were in terms of quality. He ordered it all had to be replaced.[30] Despite Bourcier's misgivings, the men marched to war on 11 April.[31] One assumes they were issued their trademark brass helmet with *chenille*.

We know nothing more until the ministerial decree of 28 May 1814, which ordered that the 6ᵉ *Lanciers* were to became the *Lanciers de Berry*. The new regiment was to be an amalgam of the 6ᵉ, which mustered 23 officers and 184 with 159 horses; and the 12ᵉ *Hussard*, which provided 65 officers and 520 men, of which there were 325 men with 309 horses. The colonel of the 12ᵉ *Galbois* became the new colonel of the *Lanciers de Berry*. In essence, the new regiment was formed around the nucleus of the 12ᵉ *Hussard*. The men of the 6ᵉ *Lanciers* were wearing on 11 August 1814 the following items:[32]

# Regulations in Practice

Elite company trooper of the 6ᵉ *Lanciers*. This image correctly shows the *garance* crest to the helmet and legwear mentioned in the regimental standing orders.

This copy of the Markholsheim manuscript by Rousselot, purportedly shows a trumpeter of the 6ᵉ *Lanciers* in 1812. An image by Jolly in the collection of JN and published in *Soldats Napoléonienne* gives the dress of the trumpeters and *sapeurs* during the first Restoration. This article is essential reading. (*Collection KM*)

| Item | In service, but due to expire in the next year | In need of repair | To be replaced in the next year | To be replaced | Items short | Observations |
|---|---|---|---|---|---|---|
| *Habits* | 79 | 32 | | 43 | 30 | The effective strength is 184 men. |
| *Gilets sans manche* | | | | | 184 | |
| *Gilets d'écurie* | | | | | 184 | |
| *Culottes hongroise* | 83 | | | | 101 | |
| *Pantalons à cheval* | 61 | 41 | | 42 | 40 | |
| Stable trousers | 70 | | | | 114 | |
| *Caleçons* | 49 | 35 | | 36 | 64 | |
| *Manteaux* | 125 | 21 | 1 | 7 | 30 | |
| *Bonnets de police* | 158 | | | | 26 | |
| Helmets | 143 | 16 | | | 25 | |
| Pairs of boots | 9 | 10 | | 10 | 175 | |

Excellent example of a trooper's helmet made to the Bardin regulation. (*Private collection, UK*)

Thus, we see that in 1814 the regiment wore a mix of *culottes hongroise* and *pantalons à cheval*. No *gilets d'écurie* or waistcoats were in service, plus we assume in stable duties the men wore their *habits* and whatever legwear they had due to the huge deficiency in stable trousers.

The following items of equipment were in use at the date of disbandment:[33]

| Item | In service, but due to expire in the next year | In need of repair | To be replaced in the next year | To be replaced | Items short | Observations |
|---|---|---|---|---|---|---|
| *Gibernes* complete | 140 | | | | 44 | The effective strength is 184 men. |
| *Banderole-porte-carabines* | 122 | | | | 62 | |
| Waistbelts | 158 | | | | 26 | |
| *Porte-manteaux* | 134 | 18 | | 4 | 29 | |
| Sword knots | 149 | | | | 35 | |
| Pairs of gloves | 25 | | | | 159 | |

| Item | In service, but due to expire in the next year | In need of repair | To be replaced in the next year | To be replaced | Items short | Observations |
|---|---|---|---|---|---|---|
| Lance pennants | 138 | | | | 46 | |
| Lance straps | 129 | | | | 55 | |
| Trumpets and cords | 15 | | | | | |
| Carbines | The regiment has none | | | | | |
| Sabres | 131 | 22 | | | | |
| Pistols | 67 | 27 | 5 | | | |
| Lances | 138 | | | | | |

Clearly it seems in 1814 all the troops were armed with lances with no differentiation between front- and second-rank men. The *sous-officiers* were not lance armed. Neither were any men designated as *carabiniers* as the regiment had not firearms beyond the pistols. Yet 122 carbine belts were issued! The regiment also lacked bayonets, a fact noted in a painting of the regiment by Major Jolly, discussed below. The men were issued 552 shirts, 184 black stocks and 100 pairs of ankle boots, which were worn over bare feet as not a single pair of socks were in use. Of interest is the fact the *manteaux* were made from grey cloth as opposed to the regulation white ascribed with the Bardin regulations of 1812, some 27m grey broadcloth for *manteaux* being in stores. In the regiment's magazine were the following items:[34]

| Item | New | In good condition | To be repaired | Total |
|---|---|---|---|---|
| *Habits* | 3 | | | 3 |
| *Gilets* | | | | |
| *Pantalons à cheval* | 12 | | | 12 |
| Stable trousers | | | | |
| *Culottes hongroise* | 4 | | | 4 |
| *Caleçons* | | | | |
| *Manteaux* | 40 | 40 | | 80 |
| *Bonnets de police* | 5 | | | 5 |
| Helmets | 60 | 48 | | 108 |
| Boots | | | | |
| *Gibernes* | 158 | | | 158 |
| *Banderole-porte-carabines* | 205 | | | 205 |
| Waistbelts | 101 | | | 101 |
| Sword knots | 62 | | | 62 |
| *Porte-manteaux* | 30 | 20 | | 50 |
| Lance pennants | 180 | | | 180 |
| Lance straps | 85 | | | 85 |
| Trumpets and cords | 2 | | | 2 |

Once the review was completed, in order to 'knock the regiment into shape', on 24 August, the regiment's colonel, Galbois, ordered that the men who had joined the new regiment from the 12ᵉ *Hussard* were to place into the regimental stores, their *pelisses*, *dolmans*, barrel sash and sabretaches, and draw from stores '*habits a polonaise*', i.e., kurtkas. This was naïve thinking as just three garments existed in store! Galbois further ordered that *sous-officiers* were to wear *garance* (deep red) *pantalons*, the stable coats were to be fastened by a single row of buttons and have *garance* collars in the elite company.[35] An officer's kurtka exists in a private collection in France, and an image of the regiment executed by its major, Louis-Claude Jolly, shows the use of kurtkas by other ranks.[36] On 25 August Galbois ordered the production of 485 sets of harness and saddlery, ordered damaged helmets repaired, new *chenilles* were to be made and new helmets ordered for men from the 12ᵉ *Hussard*. He also ordered 200 pairs of *pantalons* were to be made.[37]

On 24 November 1814 Galbois issued instructions on the dress of his regiment in barracks. Each trooper was to obtain a pair of clogs and a pair of shoes for stable duties and wearing in barracks. His boots with spurs were to be always polished and worn only on mounted duties. In stables a trooper was allowed a black linen cravat, which was to be worn so as to totally conceal the collar of the shirt. The stable coat was to be buttoned fully and the trooper was not allowed to keep anything in the pockets bar the comb. The *bonnet de police* was to be worn, placed obliquely on the head, the tassel to be over the left eye. The grooming kit was to be carried in the horse's nose bag, the *musette*, and the snaffle bridle over their left arm when walking to and from stables. Once the trooper had mucked out and swept the barrack yard, the officers were to ensure no trace of straw or dirt remained on the men's clothing. Once back in barracks, the men were allowed to unfasten the collars to their stable coats.

About the general appearance of his men, Galbois ordered that the *sous-officiers* were to ensure the men fastened all the buttons of their *gilet*s and had nothing in the pockets before wearing the *habit* over the *gilet*. The *habit* was to be only worn for parades to preserve it from damage and wear. Officers were instructed to wear before 10 a.m. a green *redingote* over their white *gilet*, along with green knee breeches, and stockings in winter and white breeches and stockings in summer, with their buckled shoes, epee, waistbelt and *bonnet de police*. In the afternoon officers were to wear their *frac* and *chapeau* with the same legwear. On 1 December, Major Jolly ordered that the elite company were to receive red *chenilles*, which were to be ready for the parade on 10 December 1814, and the *sous-officiers* were to wear their *rouge-garance pantalons* on this occasion. New lance pennants were to be issued and the men were ordered to polish their boots and brasses every day. All ranks it seems wore plumes. In the winter, Galbois ordered clogs to be worn in barracks and not shoes, to preserve the shoes 'from damp and dirt'. In new year 1815 Galbois instructed his officers to ensure that their *habits* had seven buttons on each *revers*, and that one side of the *revers* was to be green, and the other *rouge-garance*, the red side to be shown only on parade. Here Galbois seems to be talking about a removable plastron, with the *régiment du roi* certainly used judging by an extant garment. Galbois furthermore ordered that other ranks' *habits* were to follow the same model.³⁸ We know nothing else about the dress of the regiment as no disbandment records have survived.

## *Régiment de Royal Chevau-Leger-Lanciers*

Created during the 100 days, the regiment was raised from Royalist volunteers and officers who refused to serve Napoléon. The regiment was mobilised on 5 July and was reviewed by the Come de Bourmont – he who defected to the Royalist cause on 14/15 June! – on 16 August. De Bourmont noted that by 30 June, over 6,400 volunteers had flocked to the Royalist cause in the Pas-de-Calais alone. The *dépôt* by August 1815 was in Amiens; present under arms on 16 August 1815 were 2 *sous-officiers* on the *petit état-major*, a corporal trumpeter and veterinarian. The single squadron comprised 2 sergeant majors, 16 sergeants, 2 *fourriers*, 20 corporals, 179 lancers, 10 trumpeters and *1 enfant de troupe*; 236 all ranks.³⁹ The regiment was commanded by the Colonel *Comte* d'Astorg, former colonel of the 5ᵉ *Hussard*. The regiment was disbanded into the National Guard on 8 September 1815. The men had been dressed as lancers and were wearing green *habits-veste*s with white facings and piping.

## Conclusion

The lack of archive documents means we can say nothing meaningful about the dress of the elite company or trumpeters of these six regiments, or indeed anything definite about the evolution of the regiments' dress. Such are the perils of archive research. On paper no regiment received Imperial Livery: however, the extant garments for trumpeter Cornion of the 4ᵉ regiment suggests, that this unit at least did adopt the livery. It is impossible to say which other regiments adopted Imperial Livery. Assuming because one regiment did that the other five followed may be wrong.

# Chapter 8

# Polish Lancers

The Poles had been allies of France since the Revolution, and the Vistula Legion had cut a swathe through Europe fighting alongside the French. The 1ᵉ and 2ᵉ *Regiment de Vistula Lanciers* had been formed at Sedan on 27 May 1811. The decree of 8 June 1811 transformed the Vistula Legion Lancers into the 7ᵉ and 8ᵉ regiments of Light Horse, and the 30ᵉ *Chasseurs* became the 9ᵉ regiment. Armed with lancers and wearing Polish *Czapka*, they were every inch Polish Lancers. The 8ᵉ regiment was disbanded on 19 January 1814 into the 7ᵉ. Neither regiment were 100% Polish: in the 7ᵉ the colonel, the 4 squadron commanders, the quarter-master, both pay officers and 2 sous-lieutenants were French, 1 squadron commander, 1 captain, 1 lieutenant and 1 sous-lieutenant were Italian and 1 squadron commander, 6 captains, 9 lieutenants and 17 sous-lieutenants were Croatian.[1]

Both units were wound up in May 1814 and marched to join the Tsar of Russia's Army on 13 May.[2] The 7ᵉ was hastily re-raised in April 1815 and charged to glory on 2 July 1815 in defence of Paris. Not a single piece of paper exists that details the dress of the 7ᵉ and 8ᵉ regiment. We include the 9ᵉ in this section as from 1813 they were dressed – in theory – identically to the 7ᵉ and 8ᵉ. Bardin made, it seems, no changes to the dress of these two regiments.

## Bardin

For the other ranks of the three regiments, Bardin states as follows:

> **Section 5: Polish Light Horse**
> **Art 1. Clothing**
> 1526. The clothing of the Polish Light Horse will comprise a habit dit Kurtka, a waist sash, a white broadcloth gilet with no sleeves, a veste d'écurie, a pair of culottes hongroise, a pair of pantalons à cheval, a pair of pantalon de treillis and a manteau-capote.
>
> 1527. The Kurtka on the back from the waist to the bottom of the tails falls to be 400mm from the ground when the man is on bended knee. The seams on back, cuffs and the sea to the back of the sleeves are garnished with a piping in the distinctive colour. The Kurtka is lined in linen to a depth at the back of 100mm below the revers a sloping line. The length of the facings on the back are proportional to the length of the tails and height of the man, the tails at the

# Polish Lancers 201

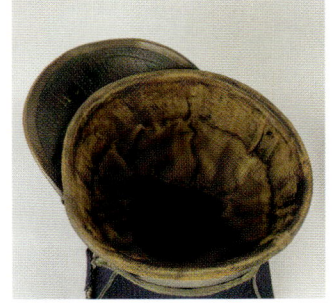

Troopers *czapka*, thought to be of the 9e *Lanciers*, dating to 1813. (*Private Collection, UK*)

bottom measure 230, 245 or 260mm. The width of the tails from one button to the other is 35mm.

The back of the Kurtka does not have a seam [illegible] the seams at the bottom edge of the back are piped along the body where it joins the pleat [illegible]

1528. The epaulettes of the Kurtka are in blue broadcloth garnished with a piping in the distinctive colour, and carry a button hole placed in the points close to the opening of the sleeve. Each epaulette is 35mm wide where it emerges from the collar, piping included and measures 55mm across the points at the end; their length depends on the size of the man and will conform to the engraved design 1528 and are the same as those of the habits of the infantry.

1529. The revers at the base measure 70mm wide. Viz No. 8.

Officers of the 7ᵉ and 8ᵉ *Lanciers* in summer 1813 from the Freburg manuscript. (*Collection KM*)

Officer of the 7ᵉ or 8ᵉ *Lanciers* by Martinet.

1530. The sleeves are cut in the same manner as the light infantry Viz. No. 647 with the exception that the rear seam of the sleeve is garnished with a piping in the distinctive colour.

1531. It is necessary to mention no pockets exist on the lining of the kurtkas, it is simulated externally with a flap measuring 215mm long. This flap is 15mm wide and level with the buttons in the small of the back; the pocket arrives 25mm from the bottom edge of the habit. [illegible]

1532. The waist sash is unique to the uniform of the Polish Light Horse and is supported by a flap set vertically on the side of the Kurtka; this flap is 120mm long, the top edge being cut into the shape of an escutcheon, with a uniform button 20mm diameter passing through the corresponding button hole. The buttonhole is placed 20mm below, the piping included, of the central point of the escutcheon and is 40mm long. Viz. See engraved design No. 1532.

1533. The sash is worn over the habit and is made from strong linen lace and fastens with buckles. It is 90mm tall and 1metre 890mm long. It is striped with four white lines and three blue lines passing along the length of the sash. The blue lines are in

Württemberg Artillery officer Breitenbach gives us these notes on the dress of the 8ᵉ Lanciers. (*Collection KM*)

Trooper of the 8ᵉ *Lanciers* depicted by an eyewitness, an officer in the French army, in 1814. (*Collection KM*)

wool. It is lined in waxed linen. It is interlined with leather [illegible] it is garnished at the ends with three copper buckles and slides in buff leather [illegible] at the opposite ends are three buff leather tabs equally spaced 25mm wide used to fasten the sash.

1534. The <sub>gilet is made from white broadcloth and will conform to the general model No [illegible]</sub> ~~will be the same as those of the carabiniers except that the buttons will be round and made from white metal~~

1535. The veste d'écurie is made from blue tricot and will be no different to the general model No. 392; except that at the bottom of the back will be two pockets surmounted by a button and will be 95mm deep.

1536. The buttons are in white metal and domed like those of the Hussards. The Kurtka is garnished with 25 large buttons and 8 small; each revers has 7 large buttons, each pocket 3, two are placed at the head of the pleats, one supports the waist sash; three small buttons fasten each cuff and one small button appears at each shoulder.

Portrait of an officer of the 9ᵉ *Lanciers*. (*Private Collection*)   Trooper of the 9ᵉ *Lanciers* by Martinet.

1537. The culotte hongroise are made from blue broadcloth and are made to the general model Viz. No. 306 with the exception of the garnishing which is white and are fastened about the leg with laces surmounted by a small button.

1538. The underwear are the same as the infantry Viz. No. 21.

1539. The pantalon a cheval are made from blue tricot and are of the general model ~~and are garnished according to the regiment Viz. No. 1423.~~ Viz No. 3 [illegible]

1540. The pantalon de treillis are the same as the general dispositions No. 311.

~~1540. The braces are the same as those of the infantry.~~

1541. The manteau-capote is in white broadcloth and is cut to the same dimensions as the French Light Horse Viz. No. 1140.

### Art 2. Headdress
1542. The headdress of the sous-officiers and men comprise a czapka and bonnet de police.

1543. The czapka is 220mm tall, and measures across the top which is square 245mm. The turban is made from strong cow leather and is 75mm tall. The top is covered

# Polish Lancers

Centre company trooper of the 8ᵉ *Lanciers* by Martinet. The plume is black tipped red.

Officer of the 9ᵉ *Lanciers* by Martinet. The plume is blacked tipped light blue.

in blue broadcloth, stitched in place. The junction of the leather and broadcloth is covered with a piece of white linen lace 35mm wide, its mid-point being placed at the junction of the two parts of the czapka. The former corners of the czapka are garnished with white braid dit soutache and crosses at angles over the top; at each corner are tin nails. The right-hand nail is fitted with a hook destined to support the chinstrap. The interior of the czapka is made from cardboard and is covered in oiled cloth, all four sides are supported by a folded stick of willow.

1544. On each side of the turban of the czapka are lions' heads; one is garnished with a white metal chain which is destined to form the chinstrap and is 40mm wide. The chinstrap is lined with blue broadcloth and comprised 32 rings; on the other side is attached a hook into the mouth of the lion Viz. the general engraving No. 1544.

1545. The czapka is garnished on the exterior with a visor made from varnished leather and is lightly concave and is bordered with a white metal edge in the shape of the horse shoe and is 7mm wide.

Centre company trooper of the 7ᵉ *Lanciers*. Of note is the black cross belt, and the black plume has a yellow tip.

Elite company trooper of the 8ᵉ *Lanciers*. The plume is black with a yellow tip.

~~1544. The interior is made from cardboard which is covered in oiled fabric, each face is reinforced with a folded stick of willow.~~

1546. The neck cover is adapted to cover the czapka [illegible]. There is placed a cockade in wool on the left side of the czapka. It is surmounted by a pompom in the company colour, the same as used by the cavalry No. 326.

### Art 3. Distinctive Marks

1547. The sous-officiers have the same distinctive marks as the light infantry and are placed the same. The distinctions of the veterinarians and farriers conform to No. 328 and 340. The elite company is distinguished by their epaulettes and aigrette of the grenadier.

1548. The trumpeters of the Polish Light Horse will follow the general dispositions 338 and 339 except for the form of the habit. The Kurtka, as for all trumpeters, will be green, cut as for the regiment but with no revers. The lace will be placed along the top of the collar, on the cuffs, on the back and facings, and will conform to that of the drummers. Each sleeve will be decorated with 7 inverted chevrons. The small

of the back will be garnished with lace in the form of two points, the points being upper most. The pockets will be garnished with three Brandenburgs ending with points. The height of the points on the back will be 70mm and will stop where it touches the piping on the pockets. The buttons on the back are placed 80mm apart.
The Kurtka is lined in green.

### Art 4. Weapons and Equipment
1549. The weapons and equipment are exactly the same as for the French Light Horse, except the boots which are Polish style.

1550. The boots will conform to the regulation; the boot is cut short and round; they rise 190mm and are cut so that the top edge is perfectly flat.

1551. The spurs are of the general model and fit to the heels of the boots.

### Art 5. Petit Equipement, Linen and Footwear
1552. The petit équipement of the Polish Light Horse will be as for the general dispositions Viz. No. 372 to 386. ~~Will comprise one musette, one trousse, three shirts, two stocks with three rabats, two handkerchiefs, a night cap and a pair of manchettes du botte.~~

### Art. 6 Harness
1553. The harness of the Polish Light Horse is the same as for the French Light Horse Viz. No. 1464 to 1517.[3]

*Regulations in practice*
No archive paperwork exists that comments on the dress of the 7e and 8e regiments.

## 9e *Lanciers*

Formed from the 30e *Chasseurs* on 18 June 1811, we know nothing about the regiment's dress and equipment until October 1814, when the remaining 175 men of the regiment were taken into the *Lanciers du Roi*. The inspecting general reports that the clothing was either in good condition or missing:[4]

| Item | In service, but due to expire in the next year | In need of repair | To be replaced in the next year | To be replaced | Items short | Observations |
|---|---|---|---|---|---|---|
| *Habits* | 166 | | | 8 | 8 | The effective strength is 175 men. |
| *Gilets en drap blanc* | 136 | | | 1 | 38 | |
| *Gilets d'écurie* | 145 | | | 2 | 39 | |
| *Culottes hongroise* | 170 | | | | 5 | |
| Underwear | 159 | | | 5 | 14 | |
| *Manteaux* | 155 | | | | 20 | |
| *Pantalons à cheval* | 166 | | | 1 | 8 | |
| *Pantalons de toile* | 103 | | | 13 | 56 | |
| *Bonnets de police* | 162 | | | | 13 | |
| *Czapka* | 172 | | | | 3 | |
| Waistbelts | 156 | | | | 19 | |
| *Gibernes* | 161 | | | | 14 | |
| *Porte-gibernes* | 161 | | | | 14 | |
| Sword knots | 148 | | | | 26 | |
| Pairs of boots | 128 | 24 | | 8 | 15 | |
| Lance pennants | 57 | | | | 118 | |
| Lancers | 56 | | | | 119 | |
| Waist sashes | 157 | | | | 18 | |

Despite being a lancer regiment, 119 men had no lance, just 56 were in service with a further 63 brand-new unissued lances in *dépôt*, 53 men were 'carabiniers' and were armed with An XI light cavalry carbine, while 165 sabres were in use. The regiment's remaining 100 horses had 98 *schabraques*. The men had 168 *porte-manteaux* in good condition, and 6 men were missing this most essential piece of equipment, but we note 168 brand-new *schabraques* and 50 *porte-manteaux* were in stores ready to be issued! The 175 men were furthermore issued with 348 shirts and 175 black stocks: not a single pair of socks were in use. The *dépôt* held no cloth whatsoever but did hold brand-new clothing ready to be issued, which included 60 white *gilets*, 180 pairs of *culottes hongroise*, 8 *gilets d'écurie*, 15 *bonnets de police*, 24 *manteaux* – marked out as such in contract to garricks, i.e., *manteaux-capote!* – 50 *czapka*, 160 *gibernes*, 82 *porte-gibernes*, 82 *porte-carabines*, 60 waistbelts, 30 sword knots and 82 waist sashes. The *dépôt* also held 30 *habits* needing repairs, and 22 pairs of *pantalons à cheval* in similar condition. In addition there were 100 *czapka* awaiting disposal. We have no details of the dress of the elite company. The lack of cloth in stores means it impossible to say if the regiment wore blue or indeed green as some contemporary iconography depicts, or how the trumpeters were dressed.[5] Among Rousselot's papers we find an engraving by Martinet showing the regiment with blue kurtka faced in yellow, and red *pantalons à cheval*, with black side stripes in lieu of buttons and with the inner seat reinforced with black leather. The latter garments Rousselot cites as existing from General Bordessoulle's correspondence, who also reports grey stable coats. Rousselot's papers also hold several other prints by Martinet, who shows black leather work for the 7ᵉ, 8ᵉ and 9ᵉ in a plate dated to 1813, by which time the 9ᵉ had blue legwear. Officially, the lancers were exempt from the adoption of blackened cow hide leather work: if Martinet is correct, then the use of such items was one of pragmatism rather than regulation.[6]

## Conclusion

The lack of archive documents means we can say nothing meaningful about the dress of the elite company or trumpeters of these three regiments, or indeed anything definite about the evolution of the regiments' dress. Such are the perils of archive research. Fanciful reconstructions abound of the trumpeters of the 9ᵉ, but in reality, they have no basis in hard fact but have become so embedded in popular imagination that it is almost impossible to correct the historical narrative.

# Notes

### Introduction
1. Service Historique de la Armée du Terre (hereafter SHDDT) Xc 263.
2. Paul Lindsay Dawson, *Crippled Splendour: The French Cavalry from Valmy to Toulouse*. Black Tent: Stockton-on-Tees, 2016.

### Chapter 1
1. SHDDT Xs 525 PROJET D'ARRÊTÉ Relatif à l'Habillement des troupes pour l'an X.
2. SHDDT Xs 525 PROJET D'ARRÊTÉ Portant établissement d'une Masse générale destinée à l'Habillement et à l'Entretien des Troupes. 1er vendémiaire an 11.
3. Bibliotheque Musée de l'Armée, Manuscripts and printed books, Volume 1 du projet de règlement sur l'habillement du major Bardin. pp.27–31.
4. SHDDT Xc 145 8$^e$ *Dragons*. Dossier 1815, Rapport 1 Janvier 1817.
5. SHDDT Xc 145 8$^e$ *Dragons*. Dossier 1815.
6. Etienne Alexandre Bardin (1808), *Manuel d'infanterie, ou Résumé de tous les règlements, décrets, usages, renseignements concernant l'infanterie, dans lequel se trouve renfermé tout ce que doivent savoir les sergents et caporaux*. Paris: Chez Magimel, p.335.
7. SHDDT Xc 150 5$^e$ *Dragons*. Dossier 1813. Rapport 5$^e$ Compagnie 1$^e$ Trimestre 1813 Etat des réparations.
8. SHDDT Xc 150 5$^e$ *Dragons*. Dossier 1813. Récit 9 Mars 1813.
9. SHDDT Xc 150 5$^e$ *Dragons*. Dossier 1813. Récit 1$^e$ Trim 1813 pour ferrage.
10. SHDDT Xc 150 5$^e$ *Dragons*. Dossier 1813. Récit 4$^e$ Trim 1813.
11. Bibliotheque Musée de l'Armée. Fonds Rousselot. Fiche Dragons 1$^e$ Empire.

### Chapter 2
1. SHDDT GR 2C 201 Correspondance de la grande armée du 16 fructidor an 13 au 7 nivôse an 14 (3 Septembre–28 Décembre 1805).
2. SHDDT Xab 4.
3. SHDDT Xb 344 2$^e$ Ligne. Dossier 1807. Rapport 4 Janvier 1807.
4. SHDDT C2 275 Habillement, Rapport 8 Avril 1807 sur les Dragons a Pied.
5. SHDDT Xc 134 2$^e$ *Dragons*, Dossier An 10. Rapport 10 Floréal An 10.
6. SHDDT Xc 134 2$^e$ *Dragons*. Dossier An 13. Rapport 1 Vendémiaire An 13.
7. SHDDT Xc 143 7$^e$ *Dragons*. Dossier An 11. Rapport 18 Thermidor An 11.
8. SHDDT Xc 143 7$^e$ *Dragons*. Dossier An 13. Rapport 20 Nivoise An 13.
9. SHDDT Xc 147 10$^e$ *Dragons*. Dossier An 11. Rapport 30 Messidor An 11.
10. SHDDT Xc 147 10$^e$ *Dragons*. Dossier An 13. Rapport 27 Vend An 13.
11. SHDDT Xc 151 12$^e$ *Dragons*. Dossier An 13. Rapport 5 Fructidor An 13.
12. SHDDT Xc 153 13$^e$ *Dragons*. Dossier An 10. Rapport 26 Floréal An 11.
13. SHDDT Xc 154 13$^e$ *Dragons*. Dossier An 13. Rapport 29 Vend An 13.
14. SHDDT Xc 153 13$^e$ *Dragons*. Dossier An 13. Rapport 6 Thermidor An 13.
15. SHDDT Xc 155 14$^e$ *Dragons*. Dossier An 13. Rapport 22 Vend An 13.
16. SHDDT Xc 155 14$^e$ *Dragons*. Dossier An 13. Rapport 1 Fructidor An 13.
17. SHDDT Xc 155 14$^e$ *Dragons*. Dossier An 13. Rapport 26 Décembre 1807.
18. SHDDT Xc 157 15$^e$ *Dragons*. Dossier An 1. Rapport 25 Messidor An 11.

19. Archives Nationales [hereafter AN] AF/IV/1116 Baraguay de Hilliers au Napoleon.
20. AN AF/IV/1116 Baraguay de Hilliers au Napoleon 110 Nivôse An 13. See also Ibid. Napoléon au Baraguay de Hilliers 8 Ventôse An 13, Baraguay de Hilliers au Napoléon 16 Fructidor An 13.
21. SHDDT GR 1M 247 bis Habillement. Résumé 8 Avril 1808.
22. SHDDT GR 1M 247 bis Habillement, Résume de reveux 27 Juillet 1807.
23. SHDDT Xc 164 18$^e$ Dragon. Dossier 1808. Rapport 4 Janvier 1808.
24. SHDDT GR C2 261 Registre d'ordres General Houssaye 1806 a 1808.
25. Ibid.
26. Ibid.
27. Ibid.
28. Les Gupil (1812) No. 32 Devis de dragons.
29. AN, AF/IV/1179. Rapports et Projet de Décret Relatifs à une nouvelle Fixation de la Masse générale d'Habillement. 21 février 1811.
30. AN, AF/IV/1179. Rapports et Projet de Décret Relatifs à une nouvelle Fixation de la Masse générale d'Habillement. 11 Mars 1811.
31. AN, AF/IV/1179. Bourcier to Berthier 30 Avril 1811.
32. Archives Nationales de France (hereafter AN) AF/IV/1179.
33. Etienne Alexandre Bardin (1813), *Mémorial de l'officier d'infanterie*. Chez Magimel Paris. 2 Volumes. Volume 2, p.695.
34. Les Gupil, p.219.
35. Bardin, tome 2, p.703.
36. AN AF/IV/1119.

## Chapter 3

1. Bibliotheque Musée de l'Armée, Manuscripts and printed books, Volume 1 du projet de règlement sur l'habillement du major Bardin, pp.222–223.
2. Ibid., p.70.
3. Ibid., pp.222–223.
4. Les Gupil (1812) No. 32 Devis de dragons.
5. Bibliotheque Musée de l'Armée, Manuscripts and printed books, Volume 1 du projet de règlement sur l'habillement du major Bardin, pp.90–110.
6. Ibid., p.234.
7. Journal Militaire 2$^e$ tremestre 1812, p.111.
8. Journal Militaire 1$^e$ tremestre 1813, pp.148–149.
9. Journal Militaire 2$^e$ tremestre 1813, p.81.
10. Journal Militaire 2$^e$ semester 1814, p.28.
11. Journal Militaire 2$^e$ semester 1814, p.28.
12. SHDDT Xc 23 pièce 10 Rapport 10 Janvier 1815.
13. SHDDT C15 39 Decrets 1815.
14. SHDDT C15 39 Decrets 1815.
15. SHDDT Xc 23 Décret 23 Avril 1814.
16. SHDDT Xc 23 Décret 1 Mai 1815.

## Chapter 4

1. SHDDT Xc 132 1$^e$ *Dragons* 1792 a An 10. Rapport 10 Nivôse An 10.
2. SHDDT Xc 132 1$^e$ *Dragons* 1792 a An 10. Dossier An 10. Proces verbal de la formation de la compagnie d'elite.
3. SHDDT Xc 133 1$^e$ *Dragons* An 12 a 1811. Dossier An 13. Rapport 13 Vend An 13.
4. SHDDT Xc 133 1$^e$ *Dragons* An 12 a 1811. Dossier An 13. Rapport 19 Thermidor An 13.
5. SHDDT Xc 133 1$^e$ *Dragons* An 12 a 1811. Dossier 1808. Rapport 30 8bre 1808.
6. SHDDT Xc 134 2$^e$ *Dragons*. Dossier An 10. Rapport 10 Floréal An 10.

7. SHDDT Xc 134 2ᵉ *Dragons*. Dossier An 13. Rapport 1 Vendémiaire An 13.
8. SHDDT Xc 134 2ᵉ *Dragons*. Dossier An 13. Rapport 2 Fructidor An 13.
9. SHDDT Xc 135 2ᵉ *Dragons*. Dossier 1808. Rapport 22 Décembre 1807.
10. SHDDT Xc 135 2ᵉ *Dragons*. Dossier 1808.
11. SHDDT Xc 135 2ᵉ *Dragons*. Dossier 1808.
12. SHDDT Xc 135 2ᵉ *Dragons*. Dossier 1808.
13. SHDDT Xc 135. 2ᵉ *Dragons*. Dossier 1808. Rapport 22Xbre 1807.
14. SHDDT Xc 135. 2ᵉ *Dragons*. Dossier 1814. Rapport 21 Juin 1814.
15. Carnet de la Sabretache 1893, pp.208–215.
16. Carnet de la Sabretache 1930, p.133.
17. SHDDT Xc 136 3ᵉ *Dragons*. Dossier An 13. Rapport 13 Thermidor An 13.
18. SHDDT Xc 136 3ᵉ *Dragons*. Dossier 1808. Rapport 308bre 1807.
19. SHDDT Xc 181 2ᵉ *Lanciers*.
20. SHDDT Xc 181 2ᵉ *Lanciers*.
21. SHDDT Xc 181 2ᵉ *Lanciers*.
22. SHDDT Xc 181 2ᵉ *Lanciers*.
23. SHDDT Xc137 4ᵉ *Dragons*. Dossier An 10. Rapport 10 Pluvoise An 10.
24. SHDDT Xc 137 4ᵉ *Dragons*. Dossier An 13. Rapport 1 Thermidor An 13.
25. SHDDT Xc 138 4ᵉ *Dragons*. Dossier 1808. Rapport 27 9bre 1807.
26. Bibliotheque Musée de l'Armée. Fonds Rousselot. Fiche Dragons 1ᵉ Empire.
27. Lemaitre, *Histoire de 4ᵉ regiment de dragons, 1672–1895* (Paris: 1894), pp.261–265.
28. Lemaitre, pp.261–265.
29. SHDDT Xc 138 4ᵉ *Dragons*. Dossier 1814. Rapport 18 Juin 1814.
30. SHDDT Xc 138 4ᵉ *Dragons*. Dossier 1814. Rapport 30 Mars 1815.
31. SHDDT Xc 138 4ᵉ *Dragons*. Dossier 1814. Rapport 30 Mars 1815.
32. SHDDT Xc 138 8ᵉ *Dragons*. Dossier 1814. Rapport 25 Décembre 1815.
33. SHDDT Xc 140 5ᵉ *Dragons*. Dossier An 13. Rapport 16 Vend An 13.
34. SHDDT Xc 140 5ᵉ *Dragons*. Dossier An 14. Rapport 19 Brumaire An 14.
35. SHDDT Xc 140 5ᵉ *Dragons*. Dossier 1808. Rapport 28 8bre 1807.
36. Bibliotheque Musée de l'Armée. Fonds Rousselot. Fiche Dragons 1ᵉ Empire.
37. SHDDT Xc 140 5ᵉ *Dragons*. Dossier 1814. Lettre 14 Juillet 1814.
38. SHDDT Xc 140 5ᵉ *Dragons*. Dossier 1814. Lettre 15 Juillet 1814.
39. SHDDT Xc 140 5ᵉ *Dragons*. Dossier 1814. Etat des habits refait en nouveau model.
40. SHDDT Xc 140 5ᵉ *Dragons*. Dossier 1814. Lettre 28 Juillet 1814.
41. SHDDT Xc 140 5ᵉ *Dragons*. Dossier 1814. Lettre 30 Juillet 1814.
42. SHDDT Xc 136 3ᵉ *Dragons*. Dossier 1814. Rapport 3 Octobre 1814. The 5ᵉ *Dragons* became the 3ᵉ *Dragons* in April 1814.
43. SHDDT Xc 136 3ᵉ *Dragons*. Dossier 1814. Rapport 3 Octobre 1814.
44. SHDDT Xc 140 5ᵉ *Dragons*. Dossier 1815. Rapport 1 Décembre 1815.
45. SHDDT Xc 140 5ᵉ *Dragons*. Dossier 1815. Rapport 1 Décembre 1815.
46. S SHDDT Xc 136 3ᵉ *Dragons*. Dossier 1814. Rapport 3 Octobre 1814.
47. SHDDT Xc 140 5ᵉ *Dragons*. Dossier 1814. Lettre concernant M. Galeaux.
48. SHDDT Xc 141 6ᵉ *Dragons*. Dossier An 11. Rapport 27 Prairial An 11.
49. SHDDT Xc 142 6ᵉ *Dragons*. Dossier 1807. Rapport 7 Xbre 807.
50. SHDDT Xc 142 6ᵉ *Dragons*. Dossier 1814. Rapport 25 août 1814.
51. SHDDT Xc 142 6ᵉ *Dragons*. Dossier 1814. Rapport 25 août 1814.
52. SHDDT Xc 138 4ᵉ *Dragons*. Dossier 1814. Rapport 30 Mars 1815.
53. SHDDT Xc 138 4ᵉ *Dragons*. Dossier 1814. Rapport 30 Mars 1815.
54. SHDDT Xc 142 6ᵉ *Dragons*. Dossier 1814. See Also Dossier 1815. Rapport 1 Novembre 1815.
55. SHDDT Xc 143 7ᵉ *Dragons*. Dossier An 11. Rapport 18 Thermidor An 11.
56. SHDDT Xc 143 7ᵉ *Dragons*. Dossier An 13. Rapport 20 Nivoise An 13.

57. SHDDT Xc 143 7ᵉ *Dragons*. Dossier An 13. Rapport 23 Fructidor An 13.
58. SHDDT Xc 144 7ᵉ *Dragons*. Dossier 1815. Historique du Corps a 1820.
59. Ibid.
60. SHDDT Xc 144 7ᵉ *Dragons*. Dossier 1808.
61. SHDDT Xc 144 7ᵉ *Dragons*. Dossier 1808.
62. SHDDT Xc 144 7ᵉ *Dragons*. Dossier 1808.
63. SHDDT Xc 35 2ᵉ *Dragons*. Dossier 1808. Rapport 21 Avril 1808.
64. SHDDT Xc 35 2ᵉ *Dragons*. Dossier 1808.
65. SHDDT Xc 144 7ᵉ *Dragons*. Dossier 1814. Rapport 15 7bre 1814.
66. SHDDT Xc 144 7ᵉ *Dragons*. Dossier 1814. Rapport 15 7bre 1814.
67. SHDDT Xc 144 7ᵉ *Dragons*. Dossier 1815. Proces Verbal.
68. SHDDT Xc 145 8ᵉ *Dragons*. Dossier An 13. Rapport 8 Vendémiaire An 13.
69. SHDDT Xc 145 8ᵉ *Dragons*. Dossier An 13. Rapport 20 Thermidor An 13.
70. SHDDT Xc 145 8ᵉ *Dragons*. Dossier 1808. Rapport 10 Mars 1808.
71. SHDDT Xc 149 9ᵉ *régiment de Dragons* 1792 a 1811. Dossier An 10. Rapport 11 ventôse An 10.
72. SHDDT Xc 149 9ᵉ *régiment de Dragons* 1792 a 1811. Dossier An 11. Rapport 15 Messidor An 11.
73. SHDDT Xc 149 9ᵉ *régiment de Dragons* 1792 a 1811. Dossier An 11. Lettre fait au ministre 19 Fructidor an 11.
74. SHDDT Xc 149 9ᵉ *régiment de Dragons* 1792 a 1811. Dossier An 13. Rapport 15 Vend. An 13.
75. SHDDT Xc 149 9ᵉ *régiment de Dragons* 1792 a 1811. Dossier An 13. Rapport 10 Thermidor An 13.
76. SHDDT Xc 149 9ᵉ *régiment de Dragons* 1792 a 1811. Dossier An 13. Rapport 10 Thermidor An 13.
77. SHDDT Xc 146 9ᵉ *régiment de Dragons* 1792 a 1811. Dossier 1807. Rapport 9 9bre 1807.
78. SHDDT Xc 146 9ᵉ *régiment de Dragons* 1792 a 1811. Dossier 1807. Rapport 9 9bre 1807.
79. SHDDT Xc 146 9ᵉ *régiment de Dragons* 1792 a 1811. Dossier 1807. Lettre General Grouchy au Ministre de Guerre 17 9bre.
80. SHDDT Xc 147 10ᵉ *Dragons*. Dossier An 11. Rapport 30 Messidor An 11.
81. SHDDT Xc 147 10ᵉ *Dragons*. Dossier An 13. Rapport 27 Vend An 13.
82. SHDDT Xc 147 10ᵉ *Dragons*. Dossier An 13. Rapport 9 Thermidor An 13.
83. SHDDT Xc 148 10ᵉ *Dragons*. Dossier 1808. Rapport 16 9bre 1807.
84. SHDDT Xc 149 11ᵉ *régiment de Dragons* 1791 a An 12. Dossier An 10. Rapport 12 Pluvoise An 10.
85. SHDDT Xc 149 11ᵉ *régiment de Dragons* 1791 a An 12. Dossier An 11. Rapport 9 Thermidor An 11.
86. SHDDT Xc 149 11ᵉ *régiment de Dragons* 1791 a An 12. Dossier An 13. Rapport 23 Vend An 13.
87. SHDDT Xc 149 11ᵉ *régiment de Dragons* 1791 a An 12. Dossier An 13. Rapport 30 Thermidor An 13.
88. SHDDT Xc 142 6ᵉ *Dragons* 1791–1815. Dossier 1814. Rapport 2 Aout 1814.
89. SHDDT Xc 150. 11ᵉ *Dragons*. Dossier 1815. Rapport 14 Novembre 1815 A.
90. SHDDT Xc 15 11ᵉ *Dragons*. Dossier 1815. Rapport 14 Novembre 1815 B.
91. SHDDT Xc 151 12ᵉ *Dragons*. Dossier An 10. Rapport 13 Germinal An 10.
92. SHDDT Xc 151 12ᵉ *Dragons*. Dossier An 11. Rapport 11 Messidor An 11.
93. SHDDT Xc 151 12ᵉ *Dragons*. Dossier An 13. Rapport 18 Vend An 13.
94. SHDDT Xc 151 12ᵉ *Dragons*. Dossier An 13. Rapport 5 Fructidor An 13.
95. SHDDT Xc 152 12ᵉ *Dragons*.
96. SHDDT Xc 158 15ᵉ *Dragons*. Dossier 1814. Rapport 1 Aout 1814.
97. SHDDT Xc 153 13ᵉ *Dragons*. Dossier An 10. Rapport 26 Floréal An 11.
98. SHDDT Xc 153 13ᵉ *Dragons*. Dossier An 10. Rapport 10 Nivôse An 10.
99. SHDDT Xc 154 13ᵉ *Dragons*. Dossier An 13. Rapport 29 Vend An 13.

100. SHDDT Xc 153 13ᵉ *Dragons*. Dossier An 13. Rapport 6 Thermidor An 13.
101. SHDDT Xc 154 13ᵉ *Dragons*. Dossier 1807. Rapport 12 Xbre 1807.
102. SHDDT Xc 154 13ᵉ *Dragons*. Dossier 1814. Rapport 26 Juillet 1814.
103. SHDDT Xc 154 13ᵉ *Dragons*. Dossier 1814. Rapport 26 Juillet 1814.
104. SHDDT Xc 154 13ᵉ *Dragons*. Dossier 1814. Rapport 26 Juillet 1814.
105. SHDDT Xc 154 13ᵉ *Dragons*. Dossier 1814. Rapport 26 Juillet 1814.
106. SHDDT Xc 155 14ᵉ *Dragons*. Dossier An 10. Rapport 12 Germinal An 10.
107. SHDDT Xc 155 14ᵉ *Dragons*. Dossier An 11. Rapport 20 Prairial An 11.
108. SHDDT Xc 155 14ᵉ *Dragons*. Dossier An 13. Rapport 22 Vend An 13.
109. SHDDT Xc 155 14ᵉ *Dragons*. Dossier An 13. Rapport 1 Fructidor An 13.
110. SHDDT Xc 155 14ᵉ *Dragons*. Dossier An 13. Rapport 26 Décembre 1807.
111. SHDDT Xc 156 14ᵉ *Dragons*. Dossier 1814. Rapport 3 Octobre 1814.
112. SHDDT Xc 156 14ᵉ *Dragons*. Dossier 1814. Rapport 3 Octobre 1814.
113. SHDDT Xc 157 15ᵉ *Dragons*. Dossier An 1. Rapport 25 Messidor An 11.
114. SHDDT Xc 157 15ᵉ *Dragons*. Dossier An 12. Rapport 18 Brumaire An 12.
115. SHDDT Xc 157 15ᵉ *Dragons*. Dossier An 13. Rapport 15 Vendémiaire Year XIII.
116. SHDDT Xc 157 15ᵉ *Dragons*. Dossier An 13. Rapport 20 Thermidor An 13.
117. SHDDT Xc 158 15ᵉ *Dragons*. Dossier 1808. Rapport 30 8bre 1807.
118. SHDDT Xc 158 15ᵉ Dragons. Dossier 1815. Rapport 3 Avril 1821.
119. SHDDT Xc 158 15ᵉ *Dragons*. Dossier 1813. Rapport 16 Mars 1813.
120. SHDDT Xc 158 15ᵉ *Dragons*. Dossier 1815. Rapport 3 Avril 1821.
121. SHDDT Xc 158 15ᵉ *Dragons*. Dossier 1815. Rapport 1 Aout 1814.
122. Ibid.
123. SHDDT Xc 158 15ᵉ *Dragons*. Dossier 1815. Rapport 3 Avril 1821.
124. SHDDT Xc 158 15ᵉ *Dragons*. Dossier 1815. Rapport 2 Fevrier 1821.
125. SHDDT Xc 160 16ᵉ *Dragons*. Dossier An 12. Rapport 5 jour complémentaire An 12.
126. SHDDT Xc 160 16ᵉ *Dragons*. Dossier An 13. Rapport 13 Thermidor An 13.
127. SHDDT Xc 160 16ᵉ *Dragons*. Dossier 1804. Rapport 16 Xbre 1807.
128. SHDDT Xc 160 16ᵉ *Dragons*. Dossier 1815. Rapport 22 Mars 1819.
129. SHDDT Xc 160 16ᵉ *Dragons*. Dossier 1814. Rapport 3 Octobre 1814.
130. SHDDT Xc 160 16ᵉ Dragons. Dossier 1814. Rapport 3 Octobre 1814.
131. Bibliotheque Musée de l'Armée. Fonds Rousselot. Fiche Dragons 1ᵉ Empire.
132. SHDDT Xc 161 17ᵉ *Dragons*. Dossier An 12. Rapport 6 jour complémentaire An 12.
133. SHDDT Xc 161 17ᵉ *Dragons*. Dossier An 13. Rapport 20 Thermidor An 13.
134. SHDDT Xc 162 17ᵉ *Dragons*. Dossier 1808. Rapport 8 Janvier 1808.
135. SHDDT Xc 162 17ᵉ *Dragons*. Dossier 1815. Rapport 29 Aout 1820.
136. SHDDT Xc 162 17ᵉ *Dragons*. Dossier 1813. Rapport 23 Fevrier 1813.
137. SHDDT C2 187. Rapport 13 Mars 1813.
138. SHDDT C2 187. Rapport 12 Avril 1813.
139. SHDDT Xc 162 17ᵉ *Dragons*. Dossier 1813. Rapport 30 Avril 1813.
140. SHDDT Xc 162 17ᵉ *Dragons*. Dossier 1813. Rapport 1 Novembre 1813.
141. SHDDT Xc 162 17ᵉ *Dragons*. Dossier 1815. Rapport 29 Aout 1820.
142. SHDDT Xc 162 17ᵉ *Dragons*. Dossier 1814. Rapport 3 Octobre 1814.
143. SHDDT Xc 162 17ᵉ *Dragons*. Dossier 1814.
144. SHDDT Xc 162 17ᵉ *Dragons*, Dossier 1815. Rapport 16 Novembre 1815.
145. SHDDT Xc 164 18ᵉ *Dragons*. Dossier An 13. Rapport 4 Vend An 13.
146. SHDDT Xc 164 18ᵉ *Dragons*. Dossier An 13. Rapport 17 Thermidor An 13.
147. SHDDT Xc 164 18ᵉ *Dragons*. Dossier 1808. Rapport 4 Janvier 1808
148. SHDDT Xc 164 18ᵉ *Dragons*. Dossier 1813. Rapport 20 Mars 1813.
149. SHDDT Xc 154 13ᵉ *Dragons*. Dossier 1814. Rapport 3 Octobre 1814..
150. SHDDT Xc 154 13ᵉ *Dragons*. Dossier 1814. Rapport 3 Octobre 1814.

151. SHDDT Xc 164 18ᵉ *Dragons*. Dossier 1815. Rapport 1 Juin 1819.
152. SHDDT Xc 166 19ᵉ *Dragons*. Dossier An 13. Rapport 26 Vend An 13.
153. SHDDT Xc 166 19ᵉ *Dragons*. Dossier An 13. Rapport 25 Therm An 13.
154. SHDDT Xc 166 19ᵉ *Dragons*. Dossier 1808. Rapport 17 Xbre 1807.
155. SHDDT Xc 166 19ᵉ *Dragons*. Dossier 1810. Rapport 14 Mars 1810.
156. SHDDT Xc 166 19ᵉ *Dragons*. Dossier 1814. Rapport 3 Octobre 1814.
157. SHDDT Xc 166 19ᵉ *Dragons*. Dossier 1814. Rapport 3 Octobre 1814.
158. SHDDT Xc 166 19ᵉ *Dragons*. Dossier 1815. Rapport 30 Aout 1815.
159. SHDDT Xc 166 19ᵉ *Dragons*. Dossier 1815. Rapport 30 Aout 1815.
160. SHDDT Xc 166 19ᵉ *Dragons*. Dossier 1815. Rapport 30 Aout 1815.
161. SHDDT Xc 167 20ᵉ *Dragons*. Dossier An 13. Rapport 8 Thermidor An 13.
162. SHDDT Xc 168 20ᵉ *Dragons*. Dossier 1808. Rapport 28 Xbre 1807.
163. SHDDT Xc 158 15ᵉ *Dragons*. Dossier 1814. Rapport 1 Juillet 1814.
164. SHDDT Xc 158 15ᵉ *Dragons*. Dossier 1814. Rapport 1 Juillet 1814.
165. SHDDT Xc 158 15ᵉ *Dragons*. Dossier 1814. Rapport 1 Juillet 1814.
166. SHDDT Xc 168 20ᵉ *Dragons*. Dossier 1815. Rapport 24 Novembre 1815.
167. SHDDT Xc 168 20ᵉ *Dragons*. Dossier 1815. Rapport 3 Avril 1821.
168. SHDDT Xc 168 20ᵉ *Dragons*. Dossier 1815. Rapport 3 Avril 1821.
169. SHDDT Xc 169 21ᵉ *Dragons* An 14 a 1814. Dossier An 11. Rapport 1 Nivôse An 10.
170. SHDDT Xc 169 21ᵉ *Dragons* An 14 a 1814. Dossier An 11. Rapport 25 Nivôse An 10.
171. SHDDT Xc 169 21ᵉ *Dragons* An 14 a 1814. Dossier An 11. Rapport 9 Messidor An 11.
172. SHDDT Xc 169 21ᵉ *Dragons* An 14 a 1814. Dossier An 11. Rapport 9 Messidor An 11.
173. SHDDT Xc 169 21ᵉ *Dragons* An 14 a 1814. Dossier An 11. Rapport 20 Pluviôse An 11.
174. SHDDT Xc 170 21ᵉ *Dragons*. Dossier An 13. Rapport 1 Vend An 13.
175. SHDDT Xc 170 21ᵉ *Dragons*. Dossier An 13. Rapport 12 Thermidor An 13.
176. SHDDT Xc 170 21ᵉ *Dragons*. Dossier 1808. Rapport 5 Fevrier 1808.
177 SHDDT Xc 142 6ᵉ *Dragons* 1791–1815. Dossier 1814.
178 SHDDT Xc 142 6ᵉ Dragons 1791–1815. Dossier 1814. Rapport 2 Aout 1814.
179. SHDDT Xc 171 22ᵉ *Dragons* An 13 a 1814. Dossier An 2. Rapport 1 Vend An 12.
180. SHDDT Xc 171 22ᵉ *Dragons* An 13 a 1814. Dossier An 2. Rapport 1 Vend An 12.
181. SHDDT Xc 171 22ᵉ *Dragons* An 13 a 1814. Dossier An 13. Lettre General Bourcier a Ministre de Guerre 5 Vend. An 13.
182. SHDDT Xc 171 22ᵉ *Dragons* An 13 a 1814. Dossier An 13. Rapport 16 vendémiaire An 13.
183. SHDDT Xc 171 22ᵉ *Dragons* An 13 a 1814. Dossier An 13. Rapport 2 Thermidor An 13.
184. SHDDT Xc 171 22ᵉ *Dragons* An 13 a 1814. Dossier An 13. Rapport 2 Thermidor An 13.
185. SHDDT Xc 171 22ᵉ *Dragons*. An 13 a 1814. Dossier An 13. Rapport 2 Thermidor An 13.
186. SHDDT Xc 136 3ᵉ *Dragons*. Dossier 1814. Rapport 3 Octobre 1814.
187. SHDDT Xc 171 22ᵉ *Dragons*. Dossier 1814. Rapport 12 Décembre 1820.
188. SHDDT Xc 154 13ᵉ *Dragons*. Dossier 1814.
189. SHDDT Xc 171 22ᵉ *Dragons* An 11 a 1815. Dossier 1815. Rapport 12 Xbre 1820.
190. SHDDT Xc 172 23ᵉ *Dragons*. Dossier An 13. Rapport 15 Vend An 13.
191. SHDDT Xc 172 23ᵉ *Dragons*. Dossier An 14. Rapport 2 Frimaire An 14.
192. SHDDT Xc 172 23ᵉ *Dragons*. Dossier 1808. Rapport 15 Juillet 1808.
193. SHDDT Xc 158 15ᵉ *Dragons*. Dossier 1815. Rapport 1 Aout 1814.
194. SHDDT Xc 158 15ᵉ *Dragons*. Dossier 1815. Rapport 1 Aout 1814.
195. SHDDT Xc 173 24ᵉ *Dragons*. Dossier An 14. Rapport 29 Vend An 14.
196. SHDDT Xc 173 24ᵉ Dragons. Dossier 1808. Rapport 26 Novembre 1807.
197. SHDDT Xc 136 3ᵉ *Dragons*. Dossier 1814. Rapport 3 Octobre 1814.
198. SHDDT Xc 160 16ᵉ *Dragons*. Dossier 1814. Rapport 3 Octobre 1814.
199. SHDDT Xc 162 17ᵉ *Dragons*. Dossier 1814. Rapport 3 Octobre 1814.
200. SHDDT Xc 174 25ᵉ *Dragons*. Dossier An 13. Rapport 24 Vend An 13.

201. SHDDT Xc 174 25ᵉ *Dragons*. Dossier An 13. Rapport 21 Thermidor An 13.
202. SHDDT Xc 173 24ᵉ *Dragons*. Proces Verbal 25ᵉ Dragons 26 Septembre 1811.
203. SHDDT Xc 166 19ᵉ *Dragons*. Dossier 1814.
204. SHDDT Xc 166 19ᵉ *Dragons*. Dossier 1814.
205. SHDDT Xc 158 15ᵉ *Dragons*. Dossier 1814.
206. SHDDT Xc 175 26ᵉ *Dragons*. Dossier An 12. Lettre 6 Brumaire An 12.
207. SHDDT Xc 175 26ᵉ *Dragons*. Dossier An 13. Rapport 12 Vend An 13.
208. SHDDT Xc 175 26ᵉ *Dragons*. Dossier An 13. Rapport 12 Vend An 13.
209. SHDDT Xc 175 26ᵉ *Dragons*. Dossier An 12. Rapport 10 thermidor An 13 a.
210. SHDDT Xc 175 26ᵉ *Dragons*. Dossier An 12. Rapport 10 thermidor An 13 b.
211. SHDDT Xc 175 26ᵉ *Dragons*. Dossier 1808. Rapport 28 Janvier 1808.
212. SHDDT Xc 175 26ᵉ *Dragons*. Dossier 1814. Rapport 24 Juillet 1820.
213. SHDDT Xc 162 17ᵉ *Dragons*. Dossier 1814. Rapport 3 October 1814.
214. SHDDT Xc 162 17ᵉ *Dragons*. Dossier 1814. Rapport 3 Octobre 1814.
215. SHDDT Xc 176 27ᵉ *Dragons*. Dossier An 13. Rapport 1 sansculottides An 12.
216. Archives Nationales AFIV 1116 Baraguay de Hilliers au Napoléon 110 Nivoise An 13. See also Ibid., Napoleon au Baraguay de Hilliers 8 Ventose An 13, Baraguay de Hilliers au Napoléon 16 Fructidor An 13.
217. SHDDT Xc 176 27ᵉ *Dragons*. Dossier An 13. Rapport 5 Thermidor An 13.
218. SHDDT Xc 176 27ᵉ *Dragons*. Dossier An 13. Rapport 5 Thermidor An 13.
219. SHDDT Xc 176 27ᵉ *Dragons*. Dossier 1808. Rapport 6 Janvier 1808.
220. SHDDT Xc 176 27ᵉ *Dragons*. Dossier An 13. Rapport 5 thermidor An 13.
221. SHDDT Xc 160 16ᵉ *Dragons*. Dossier 1814. Rapport 3 Octobre 1814.
222. SHDDT Xc 142 6ᵉ *Dragons* 1791–1815. Dossier 1814. Rapport 25 Aout 1814.
223. SHDDT Xc 142 6ᵉ *Dragons* 1791–1815. Dossier 1814. Rapport 25 Aout 1814.
224. SHJDDT Xc 177 28ᵉ *Dragons*. Dossier An 13. Rapport 14 Germinal An 13.
225. SHJDDT Xc 177 28ᵉ *Dragons*. Dossier An 13. Rapport 4 Thermidor An 3.
226. SHJDDT Xc 177 28ᵉ *Dragons*. Dossier 1814. Rapport 15 Novembre 1820.
227. SHDDT Xc 142 6ᵉ *Dragons* 1791–1815. Dossier 1814. Rapport 2 Aout 1814.
228. SHDDT Xc 144 7ᵉ *Dragons*. Dossier 1814.
229. SHDDT Xc 144 7ᵉ *Dragons*. Dossier 1814. Rapport 15 8bre 1814.
230. SHDDT Xc 144 7ᵉ *Dragons*. Dossier 1814.
231. SHDDT Xc 178 29ᵉ *Dragons*. Dossier An 12. Rapport 30 Fructidor An 12.
232. SHDDT Xc 178 29ᵉ *Dragons*. Dossier An 14. Rapport 7 Vend An 14.
233. SHDDT Xc 178 29ᵉ *Dragons*. Dossier 1808. Rapport 8 Janvier 1808.
234. SHDDT Xc 178 29ᵉ *Dragons*. Dossier 1808. Rapport 9 Fevrier 1808.
235. SHDDT Xc 178 29ᵉ *Dragons*. Dossier 1808. Rapport 15 Juillet 1808.
236. SHDDT Xc 179 30ᵉ *Dragons*. Dossier An 12 Rapport 2 Sansculottides An 12.
237. Bibliotheque Musée de l'Armée. Fonds Rousselot. Fiche Dragons 1ᵉ Empire.
238. SHDDT Xc 179 30ᵉ *Dragons*. Dossier An 13 Rapport 1 Thermidor An 13.
239. SHDDT Xc 179 30ᵉ *Dragons*. Dossier 1808. Rapport 8 Janvier 1808.
240. SHDDT Xc 179 30ᵉ *Dragons*. Dossier 1814. Rapport 1 8bre 1821.
241. SHDDT Xc 158 15ᵉ *Dragons*. Dossier 1814.
242. SHDDT Xc 166 19ᵉ *Dragons*. Dossier 1814.
243. SHDDT Xc 166 19ᵉ *Dragons*. Dossier 1814.
244. SHDDT Xc 158 15ᵉ *Dragons*. Dossier 1814. Rapport 1 Juillet 1814.
245. SHDDT Xc 263 1ᵉ *régiment provisoire de dragon* rapport 26 Juillet 1812.
246. Ibid., Dossier 5ᵉ *Dragons*.
247. Ibid., 12ᵉ *Dragons*.
248. Ibid., 13ᵉ *Dragons*.
249. Ibid.

250. Ibid., 17ᵉ *Dragons*.
251. Ibid., 19ᵉ *Dragons*.
252. Ibid., 20ᵉ *Dragons*.
253. SHDDT Xc 263 1ᵉ régiment provisoire de dragon rapport 6 Aout 1812.
254. SHDDT 2C 545 fol. 301, Bourcier to Clarke, 26 Janvier 1813.
255. SHDDT 2C 545 fol. 301, Bourcier to Clarke, 1 Mai 1813.
256. SHDDT 2C 545 fol. 301, Bourcier to Clarke, 11 Juillet 1813.
257. SHDDT 2C 545 fol. 301, Bourcier to Clarke, 11 Juillet 1813.
258. SHDDT Xc 135 2ᵉ *Dragons*. Dossier 1815. Rapport 8 12bre 1815.
259. SHDDT Xc 135 2ᵉ *Dragons*. Dosser 1815 Fleury Brossette.

**Chapter 5**
1. SHDDT Xc 154 13ᵉ *Dragons*. Dossier 1814. Rapport 26 Juillet 1814.
2. Bibliotheque Musée de l'Armée. Fonds Rousselot. Fiche Dragons 1ᵉ Empire.
3. Ibid.
4. SHDDT Xc 133 1ᵉ *Dragons*. Dossier 1808. Rapport 30 8bre 1807.
5. SHDDT Xc 135 2ᵉ *Dragons*. Dossier 1808.
6. SHDDT Xc 135 2ᵉ *Dragons*. Dossier 1815.
7. SHDDT Xc 136 3ᵉ *Dragons*. Dossier 1807. Rapport 30 8bre 1807.
8. SHDDT Xc 181 2ᵉ *Lanciers*.
9. Bibliotheque Musée de l'Armée. Fonds Rousselot. Fiche Dragons 1ᵉ Empire.
10. SHDDT Xc 136 3ᵉ *Dragons*. Dossier 1814. Rapport 3 Octobre 1814.
11. SHDDT Xc 136 3ᵉ *Dragons*. Dossier 1814. Rapport 3 Octobre 1814.
12. SHDDT Xc 141 6ᵉ *Dragons*. Dossier An 13.
13. SHDDT Xc 142 6ᵉ *Dragons*. Dossier 1814.
14. SHDDT Xc 144 7ᵉ *Dragons*. Dossier 1808.
15. Bibliotheque Musée de l'Armée. Fonds Rousselot. Fiche *Dragons* 1ᵉ Empire.
16. SHDDT Xc 145 8ᵉ *Dragons*. Dossier An 11. Rapport 10 Fructidor An 11.
17. SHDDT Xc 145 8ᵉ *Dragons*. Dossier 1808. Rapport 12 Mars 1808.
18. SHDDT Xc 145 8ᵉ *Dragons*. Dossier 1815.
19. SHDDT Xc 146 9ᵉ *Dragons*. Dossier An 13. Rapport 10 Thermidor An 13.
20. SHDDT Xc 146 9ᵉ *Dragons*. Dossier 1808. Rapport 9 9bre 1807.
21. SHDDT Xc 147 10ᵉ *Dragons*. Dossier An 13. Rapport 9 Thermidor An 13.
22. SHDDT Xc 150 11ᵉ *Dragons*. Dossier 1815. Rapport 14 Novembre 1815 A.
23. SHDDT Xc 151 12ᵉ *Dragons*.
24. SHDDT X153 13ᵉ *Dragons*. Dossier An 13.
25. SHDDT Xc 155 14ᵉ *Dragons*. Dossier An 13. Rapport 1 Fructidor An 13.
26. SHDDT Xc 156 14ᵉ *Dragons*. Dossier 1814. Rapport 3 Octobre 1814.
27. SHDDT Xc 157 15ᵉ *Dragons*. Dossier An 13. Rapport 20 Thermidor An 13.
28. SHDDT Xc 161 17ᵉ *Dragons*. Dossier An 13. Rapport 20 Thermidor An 13.
29. SHDDT Xc 162 17ᵉ *Dragons*. Dossier 1814.
30. SHDDT Xc 166 19ᵉ *Dragons*. Dossier 1814. Rapport 1 Aout 1814.
31. Bibliotheque Musée de l'Armée. Fonds Rousselot. Fiche Dragons 1ᵉ Empire.
32. SHDDT Xc 169 21ᵉ *Dragons*. Dossier An 13.
33. SHDDT Xc 142 6ᵉ *Dragons* 1791–1815. Dossier 1814
34. SHDDT Xc 171 22ᵉ *Dragons* An 13 a 1814. Dossier An 13. Rapport 16 vendémiaire An 13.
35. Bibliotheque Musée de l'Armée. Fonds Rousselot. Fiche *Dragons* 1ᵉ Empire.
36. SHDDT Xc 171 22ᵉ *Dragons*.
37. SHDDT Xc 172 23ᵉ *Dragons*.
38. Bibliotheque Musée de l'Armée. Fonds Rousselot. Fiche *Dragons* 1ᵉ Empire.
39. SHDDT Xc 173 24ᵉ *Dragons*. Dossier 1808. Rapport 26 Novembre 1807.

40. SHDDT Xc 136 3ᵉ *Dragons*. Dossier 1814. Rapport 3 Octobre 1814.
41. SHDDT Xc174 25ᵉ *Dragons*. Dossier An 13.
42. SHDDT Xc 166 19ᵉ *Dragons*. Dossier 1814.
43. SHDDT Xc 175 26ᵉ *Dragons*. Dossier 1808. Rapport 28 Janvier 1808.
44. SHDDT Xc 162 17ᵉ *Dragons*. Dossier 1814. Rapport 3 Octobre 1814
45. SHDDT Xc 176 27ᵉ *Dragons*. Dossier 1808. Rapport 6 Janvier 1808.
46. SHDDT Xc 160 16ᵉ *Dragons*. Dossier 1814. Rapport 3 Octobre 1814.
47. Bibliotheque Musée de l'Armée. Fonds Rousselot. Fiche *Dragons* 1ᵉ Empire.
48. SHDDT Xc 178 29ᵉ *Dragons*. Dossier 1807. Rapport 15 Juillet 1808.
49. Bibliotheque Musée de l'Armée. Fonds Rousselot. Fiche *Dragons* 1ᵉ Empire.
50. Bibliotheque Musée de l'Armée. Fonds Rousselot. Fiche *Dragons* 1ᵉ Empire.
51. SHDDT GR C2 261 Registre General Houssaye 1806 a 1808.
52. Bibliotheque Musée de l'Armée. Fonds Rousselot. Fiche *Dragons* 1ᵉ Empire.
53. SHDDT Xc 136 3ᵉ *Dragons* 1791 a 1811.
54. Bibliotheque Musée de l'Armée. Fonds Rousselot. Fiche *Dragons* 1ᵉ Empire.
55. SHDDT Xc 35 2ᵉ *Dragons*. Dossier 1808.
56. Bibliotheque Musée de l'Armée. Fonds Rousselot. Fiche Dragons 1ᵉ Empire.
57. SHDDT Xc 158 15ᵉ *Dragons*. Dossier 1815. Rapport 3 Avril 1821.
58. Bibliotheque Musée de l'Armée. Fonds Rousselot. Fiche Dragons 1ᵉ Empire.
59. SHDDT Xc 168 20ᵉ *Dragons*. Dossier 1815. Rapport 3 Avril 1821.
60. Bibliotheque Musée de l'Armée. Fonds Rousselot. Fiche Dragons 1ᵉ Empire.
61. SHDDT Xc 176 27ᵉ *Dragons*. Dossier An 13. Rapport 5 Thermidor An 12.
62. Bibliotheque Musée de l'Armée. Fonds Rousselot. Fiche Dragons 1ᵉ Empire.
63. Bibliotheque Musée de l'Armée, Manuscripts and printed books. Planche 88 du volume IV du projet de règlement sur l'habillement du major Bardin. Dragons. Trompette 1ᵉ Régiment.
64. Bibliotheque Musée de l'Armée, Manuscripts and printed books, Volume 1 du projet de règlement sur l'habillement du major Bardin. p.78.
65. SHDDT Xc 144 7ᵉ *Dragons*. Dossier 1814.
66. SHDDT Xc 154 13ᵉ *Dragons*. Dossier 1814.
67. SHDDT Xc 160 16ᵉ *Dragons*. Dossier 1814. Rapport 3 Octobre 1814.
68. SHDDT Xc 166 19ᵉ *Dragons*. Dossier 1814. Rapport 3 Octobre 1814.
69. SHDDT Xc 168 20ᵉ *Dragons*. Dossier 1815. Rapport 3 Avril 1821.
70. SHDDT Xc 142 6ᵉ *Dragons* 1791–1815. Dossier 1814.
71. SHDDT Xc 158 15ᵉ *Dragons*. Dossier 1814.
72. SHDDT Xc 158 15ᵉ *Dragons*. Dossier 1814.
73. SHDDT Xc 142 6ᵉ *Dragons*. Dossier 1814. See Also Dossier 1815.
74. SHDDT Xc 135 2ᵉ *Dragons*. Dossier 1815.
75. SHDDT Xc 138 4ᵉ *Dragons*. Dossier 1814. Rapport 1 Xbre 1815.
76. SHDDT Xc 142 6ᵉ *Dragons*. Dossier 1814. See Also Dossier 1815.
77. SHDDT Xc 150 11ᵉ *Dragons*. Dossier 1815. Rapport 14 Novembre 1815.
78. SHDDT Xc 166 19ᵉ *Dragons*. Dossier 1815.
79. SHDDT Xc 168 20ᵉ *Dragons*. Dossier 1815. Rapport 3 Avril 1821.
80. SHDDT Xs 528 Décret 22 Avril 1814.
81. SHDDT Xc 135 2ᵉ *Dragons*. Dossier 1815.
82. SHDDT Xc 138 4ᵉ *Dragons*. Dossier 1814. Rapport 1 Xbre 1815.
83. S SHDDT Xc 136 3ᵉ *Dragons*. Dossier 1814. Rapport 3 Octobre 1814.
84. SHDDT Xc 142 6ᵉ *Dragons*. Dossier 1814. See Also Dossier 1815.
85. SHDDT Xc 144 7ᵉ *Dragons*. Dossier 1814.
86. SHDDT Xc 150 11ᵉ *Dragons*. Dossier 1815. Rapport 14 Novembre 1815 A.
87. SHDDT Xc 154 13ᵉ *Dragons*. Dossier 1814. Rapport 26 Juillet 1814.
88. Ibid.

89. SHDDT Xc 160 16ᵉ *Dragons*. Dossier 1814. Rapport 3 Octobre 1814.
90. SHDDT Xc 166 19ᵉ *Dragons*. Dossier 1815.
91. SHDDT Xc 168 20ᵉ *Dragons*. Dossier 1815. Rapport 3 Avril 1821.

## Chapter 6
1. Fonds Rousselot Journal Militaire 2ᵉ Trimestre 1811. Décret 15 Juillet 1811.
2. SHDDT Xs 526 Clarke to Napoleon 30 Aout 1811.
3. Journal Militaire 2ᵉ Trimestre 1811. Décret 11 Septembre 1811.
4. Journal Militaire 2ᵉ Trimestre 1811. Décret 30 Septembre 1811.
5. Fonds Rousselot.
6. Bibliotheque Musée de l'Armée, Manuscripts and printed books, Volume 1 du projet de règlement sur l'habillement du major Bardin, pp.319–353.
7. SHDDT Xc 23 pièce 10 Rapport 10 Janvier 1815.

## Chapter 7
1. SHDDT 2C 400 fol. 405 Bourcier to Napoleon 19 Mars 1812.
2. SHDDT Xc 180 5 1ᵉ *Lanciers* 1811–1814. Dossier 1815. Rapport 5 Décembre 1820.
3. SHDDT Xc 180 5 1ᵉ *Lanciers* 1811–1814. Dossier 1814. Rapport 11 Aout 1814.
4. SHDDT Xc 180 5 1ᵉ *Lanciers* 1811–1814. Dossier 1814. Rapport 16 Xbre 1814.
5. SHDDT Xc 180 5 1ᵉ *Lanciers* 1811–1814. Dossier 1815. Rapport 5 Décembre 1820a.
6. SHDDT Xc 180 5 1ᵉ *Lanciers* 1811–1814. Dossier 1815. Rapport 5 Décembre 1820b.
7. SHDDT Xc 180 5 1ᵉ *Lanciers* 1811–1814. Dossier 1815. Rapport 25 Décembre 1815.
8. SHDDT Xc 180 1ᵉ *Lanciers* 1811–1814.
9. SHDDT Xc 180 5 1ᵉ *Lanciers* 1811–1814. Dossier 1815. Rapport 25 Décembre 1815.
10. SHDDT Xc 181 2ᵉ *Lanciers* 1811–1814. Dossier 1814. Rapport 14 Aout 1814.
11. SHDDT Xc 181 2ᵉ *Lanciers* 1811–1814. Dossier 1814. Rapport 18 Aout 1814.
12. SHDDT Xc 181 2ᵉ *Lanciers* 1811–1814. Dossier 1815. Rapport 10 7bre 1814.
13. SHDDT Xc 181 2ᵉ *Lanciers* 1811–1814. Dossier 1815. Rapport 2 Xbre 1815.
14. SHDDT Xc 181 2ᵉ *Lanciers* 1811–1814. Dossier 1815.
15. SHDDT Xc 181 2ᵉ *Lanciers* 1811–1814. Dossier 1815.
16. SHDDT Xc 182 3ᵉ et 4ᵉ *Lanciers* 1811–1814. Dossier 3ᵉ *Lanciers* 1814. Rapport 26 Aout 1814.
17. SHDDT Xc 182 3ᵉ et 4ᵉ *Lanciers* 1811–1814. Dossier 3ᵉ *Lanciers* 1814. Rapport 26 Aout 1814.
18. SHDDT Xc 182 3ᵉ et 4ᵉ *Lanciers* 1811–1814.
19. SHDDT Xc 182 3ᵉ et 4ᵉ *Lanciers* 1811–1814. Dossier 3ᵉ *Lanciers*. Rapport 1 8bre 1815.
20. SHDDT Xc 182 3ᵉ et 4ᵉ *Lanciers* 1811–1814. Dossier 4ᵉ Lanciers 1814. Rapport 27 Avril 1819.
21. SHDDT Xc 182 3ᵉ et 4ᵉ *Lanciers* 1811–1814. Dossier 4ᵉ Lanciers 1814. Rapport 9 Juillet 1812.
22. SHDDT Xc 182 3ᵉ et 4ᵉ *Lanciers* 1811–1814. Dossier 4ᵉ Lanciers 1814. Lettre 28 Janvier 1813.
23. SHDDT Xc 182 3ᵉ et 4ᵉ *Lanciers* 1811–1814. Dossier 4ᵉ *Lanciers* 1814. Rapport 24 7bre 1814.
24. SHDDT, Xc 182 3ᵉ et 4ᵉ *Lanciers* 1811–1814. Dossier 4ᵉ *Lanciers* 1814. Rapport 24 7bre 1814.
25. SHDDT Xc 182 3ᵉ et 4ᵉ *Lanciers* 1811–1814. Dossier 4ᵉ *Lanciers* 1814. Rapport 24 7bre 1814 .
26. SHDDT Xc 183 5ᵉ et 6ᵉ *Lanciers* 1811–1814. Dossier 5ᵉ *Lanciers*. Rapport 11 Aout 1814.
27. SHDDT Xc 183 5ᵉ et 6ᵉ *Lanciers* 1811–1814. Dossier 5ᵉ *Lanciers*. Rapport 11 Aout 1814.
28. SHDDT Xc 183 5ᵉ et 6ᵉ Lanciers 1811–1814. Dossier 5ᵉ Lanciers. Rapport 11 Aout 1814.
29. SHDDT 2C 400 fol. 405 Bourcier to Napoleon 19 March 1812.
30. SHDDT 2C 400 fol. 405 Bourcier to Napoleon 19 March 1812.
31. SHDDT 2C 400 fol. 406 Bourcier to Napoleon 10 April 1812. See also SHDDT 2C 400 fol. 406 Lauriston to Napoleon 11 April 1812.
32. SHDDT Xc 183 5ᵉ et 6ᵉ *Lanciers* 1811–1814. Dossier 6ᵉ *Lanciers*. Rapport 11 Aout 1814.
33. Ibid.
34. SHDDT Xc 183 5ᵉ et 6ᵉ *Lanciers* 1811–1814.
35. SHDDT GR 1M 2252 Papiers Galbois, Ordre du Regiment des Lancers de Berry, No. 6 p.4.

36. Bourgeot Vincent Analyse d'une aquarelle execute par le colonel Jolly in *Soldats Napoléoni*ennes No. 5. Mars 2005, pp.43–46.
37. SHDDT GR 1M 2252 Papiers Galbois, Ordre du Regiment des Lancers de Berry, No. 6, p.5.
38. SHDDT GR 1M 2252 Papiers Galbois, Ordre du Régiment des Lancers de Berry, No. 6.
39. SHDDT Xc 184. Dossier Régiment Royal des Chevau-Leger-Lanciers. Rapport 16 Aout 1815.

**Chapter 8**
1. SHDDT Xc 184 7ᵉ, 8ᵉ, 9ᵉ Chevau-Léger. Dossier 7ᵉ Régiment. Rapport 30 Décembre 1813.
2. SHDDT Xc 184 7ᵉ, 8ᵉ, 9ᵉ Chevau-Léger. Dossier 7ᵉ Régiment. Ordre du Jour 13 Mai 1814.
3. Bibliotheque Musée de l'Armée, Manuscripts and printed books, Volume 1 du projet de règlement sur l'habillement du major Bardin, pp.343–350.
4. SHDDT Xc 180 1ᵉ *Lanciers* 1811–1814. Dossier 1814. Rapport 8 8bre 1814.
5. SHDDT Xc 180 1ᵉ *Lanciers* 1811–1814. Dossier 1814. Rapport 8 8bre 1814.
6. SHDDT Xs 525 Décret 19 Aout 1813.

# Bibliography

**Printed Works**
Etienne Alexandre Bardin (1813), *Mémorial de l'officier d'infanterie.* Chez Magimel Paris
Journal Militaire
Les Goupil (1812), *Administration du Masses*, Chez Magimel, Paris
Archives Nationales de France
AF/IV/1116
AF/IV/1179

Bibliotheque Musée de l'Armée
Fonds Rousselot
Volume 1 du projet de règlement sur l'habillement du major Bardin

Service Historique de Défence Armée du Térre
GR C2 187
GR 2C 201 Correspondance de la grande armée du 16 fructidor an XIII au 7 nivôse an XIV (3 septembre-28 décembre 1805)
GR C2 247
GR C2 247 Bis Habillement
GR C2 261 Correspondence Houssaye 1806 a 1808
Xab 4 Garde Imperiale generalities
Xc 132 1ᵉ *Dragons* 1791 à An XI
Xc 133 1ᵉ *Dragons* An XII à 1811
Xc 134 2ᵉ *Dragons* 1792 à AXI
Xc 135 2ᵉ *Dragons* An XI à 1815
Xc 136 3ᵉ *Dragons*
Xc 137 4ᵉ *Dragons* 1791 à An XI
Xc 138 4ᵉ *Dragons*
Xc 139 5ᵉ *Dragons*
Xc 140 5ᵉ *Dragons*
Xc 141 6ᵉ *Dragons*
Xc 142 6ᵉ *Dragons*
Xc 143 7ᵉ *Dragons*
Xc 144 7ᵉ *Dragons*
Xc 145 8ᵉ *Dragons* 1791 à 1811
Xc 146 9ᵉ *Dragons* 1791 à 1811
Xc 147 10ᵉ *Dragons* 1791 à An XI
Xc 148 10ᵉ *Dragons*
Xc 149 11ᵉ *Dragons*
Xc 150 11ᵉ *Dragons* An XII à 1815

Xc 151 12ᵉ *Dragons* 1791 à An XI
Xc 152 12ᵉ *Dragons*
Xc 153 13ᵉ *Dragons* 17891 à An XI
Xc 154 13ᵉ *Dragons*
Xc 155 14ᵉ *Dragons* 1791 à An XI
Xc 156 14ᵉ *Dragons*
Xc 157 15ᵉ *Dragons* 1791 à An XI
Xc 158 15ᵉ *Dragons* An XII à 1815
Xc 159 16ᵉ *Dragons* 1791 à An XI
Xc 160 16ᵉ *Dragons*
Xc 161 17ᵉ *Dragons* 17914 à An XI
Xc 162 17ᵉ *Dragons*
Xc 163 18ᵉ *Dragons* 1791 à An XI
Xc 164 18ᵉ *Dragons*
Xc 165 19ᵉ *Dragons* 1791 à An XII
Xc 166 19ᵉ *Dragons* An XII à 1815
Xc 167 20ᵉ *Dragons* 1791 à An XI
Xc 168 20ᵉ *Dragons*
Xc 169 21ᵉ *Dragons* An IV à 1814
Xc 170 21ᵉ *Dragons*
Xc 171 22ᵉ *Dragons* An XII à 1814
Xc 172 23ᵉ *Dragons* An XI à 1814
Xc 173 24ᵉ *Dragons* An XI à 1814
Xc 174 25ᵉ *Dragons* An XII à 1814
Xc 175 26ᵉ *Dragons* An XII à 1814
Xc 176 27ᵉ *Dragons* An XII à 1814
Xc 177 28ᵉ *Dragons* An XII à 1814
Xc 178 29ᵉ *Dragons* An XII à 1814
Xc 179 30ᵉ *Dragons* An XII à 1814
Xc 180 1ᵉ *Lanciers*
Xc 181 2ᵉ *Lanciers*
Xc 182 3ᵉ et 4ᵉ *Chevau-légère-lanciers*
Xc 183 5ᵉ et 6ᵉ *Chevau-légère-lanciers*
Xc 184 7ᵉ, 8ᵉ et 9ᵉ *Chevau-légère-lanciers*
Xc 263 *régiments provisoires des dragons*
Xs 526 *Habillement*

Dear Reader,

We hope you have enjoyed this book, but why not share your views on social media? You can also follow our pages to see more about our other products: facebook.com/penandswordbooks or follow us on X @penswordbooks

You can also view our products at www.pen-and-sword.co.uk (UK and ROW) or www.penandswordbooks.com (North America).

To keep up to date with our latest releases and online catalogues, please sign up to our newsletter at: www.pen-and-sword.co.uk/newsletter

If you would like a printed catalogue with our latest books, then please email: enquiries@pen-and-sword.co.uk or telephone: 01226 734555 (UK and ROW) or email: uspen-and-sword@casematepublishers.com or telephone: (610) 853-9131 (North America).

We respect your privacy and we will only use personal information to send you information about our products.

Thank you!